ECONOMIC ISSUES, PROBLEMS AND PERSPECTIVES SERIES

T0291340

GLOBAL MODEL SIMULATION: A FRONTIER OF ECONOMIC SCIENCE

ECONOMIC ISSUES, PROBLEMS AND PERSPECTIVES SERIES

Trust, Globalisation and Market Expansion
*Jacques-Marie Aurifeille,
Christopher Medlin,
and Clem Tisdell*
2009. ISBN: 978-1-60741-812-2

TARP in the Crosshairs: Accountability in the Troubled Asset Relief Program
Paul W. O'Byrne (Editor)
2009. ISBN: 978-1-60741-807-8

TARP in the Crosshairs: Accountability in the Troubled Asset Relief Program
Paul W. O'Byrne (Editor)
2009. ISBN: 978-1-60876-705-2
(Online Book)

Government Interventions in Economic Emergencies
Pablo Sastre (Editor)
2010. ISBN: 978-1-60741-356-1

NAFTA Stock Markets: Dynamic Return and Volatility Linkages
*Giorgio Canarella, Stephen M. Miller
and Stephen K. Pollard*
2010. ISBN: 978-1-60876-498-3

Economic Forecasting
Alan T. Molnar (Editor)
2010. ISBN: 978-1-60741-068-3

Lectures and Thoughts on Mineral Economics
K.K. Chatterjee
2010. ISBN: 978-1-60741-589-3

Minerals Price Increases and Volatility
Petro Martinovich (Editor)
2010. ISBN: 978-1-60741-653-1

Global Model Simulation: A Frontier of Economic Science
Akira Onishi
2010. ISBN: 978-1-60876-843-1

ECONOMIC ISSUES, PROBLEMS AND PERSPECTIVES SERIES

GLOBAL MODEL SIMULATION: A FRONTIER OF ECONOMIC SCIENCE

AKIRA ONISHI

Nova Science Publishers, Inc.
New York

For permission to use material from this book please contact us:
Telephone 631-231-7269; Fax 631-231-8175
Web Site: http://www.novapublishers.com

NOTICE TO THE READER

The Publisher has taken reasonable care in the preparation of this book, but makes no expressed or implied warranty of any kind and assumes no responsibility for any errors or omissions. No liability is assumed for incidental or consequential damages in connection with or arising out of information contained in this book. The Publisher shall not be liable for any special, consequential, or exemplary damages resulting, in whole or in part, from the readers' use of, or reliance upon, this material.

Independent verification should be sought for any data, advice or recommendations contained in this book. In addition, no responsibility is assumed by the publisher for any injury and/or damage to persons or property arising from any methods, products, instructions, ideas or otherwise contained in this publication.

This publication is designed to provide accurate and authoritative information with regard to the subject matter covered herein. It is sold with the clear understanding that the Publisher is not engaged in rendering legal or any other professional services. If legal or any other expert assistance is required, the services of a competent person should be sought. FROM A DECLARATION OF PARTICIPANTS JOINTLY ADOPTED BY A COMMITTEE OF THE AMERICAN BAR ASSOCIATION AND A COMMITTEE OF PUBLISHERS.

LIBRARY OF CONGRESS CATALOGING-IN-PUBLICATION DATA

Available upon Request.

ISBN: 978-1-60876-843-1

Published by Nova Science Publishers, Inc. † New York

CONTENTS

PREFACE

The FUGI (*Fu*tures of *G*lobal *I*nterdependence) global modeling system has been developed as a scientific policy modeling and future simulation tool of providing global information to the human society and finding out possibilities of policy coordination among countries in order to achieve sustainable development of the global economy co-existing on the planet Earth in the ever changing universe. The FUGI global model M200 classifies the world into 200 countries/regions where each national/regional model is globally interdependent. Each national/regional model has nine subsystems as population, foods, energy, environment, economic development, peace & security, human right, healthcare and quality of life (IT revolution). This is a super complex dynamic system model using *integrated multidisciplinary systems analysis* where number of structural equations is over 170.000. Economic model as a core includes major economic variables such as production of GDP, employment, expenditures of GDP, income distribution, prices, money, interest rates & financial assets, government finance, international balance of payments, international finance, foreign exchange rates and development indicators.

The purpose of this book is twofold, namely to provide information on *a new frontier of economic science: global model simulation* as well as appropriate policy exercise for sustainable development of the interdependent global economy. The world economy is facing "green" energy revolution to change from fossil to create alternative energy and energy saving technology against sky rocketing higher oil prices. Japan not only closely involved in the Asian community but also in the global community should take a lead in this field of technology innovation. Under such circumstances, Japan should take an initiative to create a new peaceful world as a sole nation suffered from nuclear weapons during the World War II. Through not only harmonized adjustments of the Japanese economic policy but also wise cosmic mind to promote human solidarity with the ever changing nature will be desirable to adjust orbit of the fluctuated global economy. Japan should challenge to a new strategy for accelerating economic growth rates by *"CO_2 reducing environment investment"* based on technology innovations.

Keywords: A new frontier of economic science; global model simulation; FUGI global modeling system; integrated multidisciplinary systems analysis; global syndromes; global CO_2 emissions; global interdependence; Global Interdependence Table; alternative futures of global economy; global coordination of polices

Note: Onishi would like to offer this book to Prof. Tobin who came to talk with me to join Yale but could not perform the promise, because of my official duty as vice-president of Soka University.

Chapter 1

INTRODUCTION

In the 21st century it is expected that *"global syndromes"* will be appeared in the human society. The global issues seem likely to confront with every country around the world co-existing on the planet Earth. As a matter of fact, development policy in the globalizing world should be modified in coping with such historical trends toward sustainable global economy. It is worth noting that, in the 21st century, integrated progress of science & technology and human mind will be desirable in the human society where consists of a globally interdependent complex system.

In the globalizing world, globally interdependent system structures are getting more and more complex so that nobody might easily percept cause and effect relationships at a first glance. Unfortunately, human brain intuitions are not so efficient enough to analyze impacts of synergy effects on complex policy mixtures. Therefore, policy makers should largely depend on scientific computer simulations of policy exercises in the globalizing world.

The FUGI (Futures of Global Interdependence) global modeling system has been developed as a scientific policy modeling and simulation tool of providing global information to the human society and finding out possibilities of policy coordination among countries in order to achieve sustainable development of the global economy under the constraints of rapidly changing global environment.

The FUGI global model (FGMS 200) classifies the world into 200 countries/regions. Each country/regional model is globally interdependent through direct linkages of the world trade matrices, export/import prices, primary commodities prices, foreign exchange rates, official development assistance, private foreign direct investment, external debt, interest rates and etc. It is also globally interdependent through indirect linkages such as population changes, economic development policies, energy policies, environmental policies, etc.

Each national/regional model consists of integrated nine major sub-systems: (I) population, (II) foods, (III) energy, (IV) environment, (V) economic development, (VI) peace and security, (VII) human rights, (VIII) health care and (IX) digital divide. Economic development system as a major core of the model has eleven economic sub-blocs. It includes (1) labor and production at constant prices, (2) expenditure on GDP at constant prices, (3) income distribution: profit-wage, (4) prices, (5) expenditure on GDP at current prices, (6) money, interest rate & financial assets, (7) government finance, (8) international balance of payments, (9) international finance, (10) foreign exchange rate and (11) development indicators. The FUGI global model 9.0 M200 is one of the most complex global models around the world. The number of equations is more than 170,000. See *Appendix A: The FUGI global modeling system (FGMS 200).*

The purpose of this book is twofold, namely to provide information on *a new frontier of economics: global model simulation* as well as appropriate policy exercise for sustainable development of the interdependent global economy. The world economy is facing "green" energy revolution to change from fossil energy to create alternative clean energy and energy saving technology against sky rocketing higher oil prices induced by speculations. Japan should take a lead in this field of technology innovation. Under such circumstances, Japan should not only closely involve in the "Asian community" but also "Global human community". Under such circumstances, Japan should take an initiative to create a new peaceful world as a sole nation suffered from nuclear weapons during the Second World War. Through not only harmonized adjustments of Japanese economic policy but also wise cosmic mind to promote human solidarity with the ever changing nature will be desirable to adjust orbit of the fluctuated global economy. Japan should challenge to a new strategy for accelerating economic growth rates by CO_2 reducing environment investment based on technology innovations in the new frontiers of fusion of science and technology. It is worth noting that progress in both wheels of technology and human mind would be desirable in the futures of global human community. Without technological progress we could not cope with poverty and IPCID (international per-capita income disparity). Without education, healthcare and social welfare, we could not improve QOL (quality of life) in every country around the world.

Chapter 2

OUTLINE OF FUGI GLOBAL
MODELING SYSTEM

2.1. REGIONAL CLASSIFICATION

The FUGI global model 9.0 M200 divides the world into 200 countries and regions. For three major groupings there are (1) developed economies or advanced market economies (AME), (2) developing countries or developing economies (DME) and (3) economies in transition (EIT). The AME grouping contains the following sub-groupings; these are Developed Asia-Pacific, North America and Western Europe (including 15 member countries of the EU and EURO area). The DME grouping contains the following sub-groupings as Asia-Pacific (subdivided into East Asia, Southeast Asia, Southwest Asia and Pacific Islands); Middle East; Africa (subdivided into North Africa and Sub-Saharan Africa); Latin America & Caribbean; and Mediterranean. The EIT grouping includes two sub-groupings: (a) Eastern Europe and (b) CIS. Ultimately, this global model divides the world as a whole into 200 countries/regions. Because all most of all developed market economies, developing economies and economies in transition are treated as country units, the model has the advantage of being able to analyze precise country-specific relationships within the framework of global interdependence. We have designed seven global table formats such as CGM (above-mentioned regional classification), EU (for the European Commission), IMF (for IMF classification), UN (for the United Nations classification), UNCTAD (for UNCTAD classification), UNESCAP (for the United Nations ESCAP classification) and WB (for the World Bank classification). It is worth noting that a user of FGMS200 can easily make his own format, namely, G20 (G-20 countries groups) and CEPAL (UN Committee for Latin America). Such format classifications can be easily made within a few minutes in the *FUGI global modeling system (FGMS200).*

Table 1. Regional classification of FUGI global modeling system (FGMS200)

Regions	No	Co de	Country name	Regions	No	Code	Country name
Developed Economies					55	PNG	Papua New Guinea
					56	SLB	Solomon Islands
Asia-Pacific	1	JPN	Japan		57	TON	Tonga
	2	AUS	Australia		58	TUV	Tuvalu
	3	NZL	New Zealand		59	WSM	Western Samoa
North America	4	CAN	Canada		60	VUT	Vanuatu
	5	USA	United States	Middle East Asia	61	BHR	Bahrain
Western Europe	6	BEL	Belgium		62	IRN	Iran, I.R. of
	7	DNK	Denmark		63	IRQ	Iraq
	8	FRA	France		64	ISR	Israel
	9	DEU	Germany		65	JOR	Jordan
	10	GRC	Greece		66	KWT	Kuwait
	11	IRL	Ireland		67	LBN	Lebanon
	12	ITA	Italy		68	OMN	Oman
	13	LUX	Luxembourg		69	QAT	Qatar
	14	NLD	Netherlands		70	SAU	Saudi Arabia
	15	PRT	Portugal		71	SYR	Syrian Arab Rep
	16	ESP	Spain		72	ARE	United Arab Emirates
	17	GBR	United Kingdom		73	YEM	Yemen Rep
	18	AUT	Austria	North Africa	74	DZA	Algeria
	19	FIN	Finland		75	EGY	Egypt
	20	ISL	Iceland		76	LBY	Libya
	21	NOR	Norway		77	MAR	Morocco
	22	SWE	Sweden		78	TUN	Tunisia
	23	CHE	Switzerland	Sub-Saharan Africa	79	AGO	Angola
Developing Countries					80	BEN	Benin
Far East Asia	24	CHN	China: mainland		81	BWA	Botswana

Table 1. Continued

Regions	No...	Co de	Country name	Regions	No	Code	Country name
	25	HKG	China: Hong Kong		82	HVO	Burkina Faso
	26	MAC	China: Macau		83	BDI	Burundi
	27	TWN	Taiwan		84	CMR	Cameroon
	28	KOR	Korea, Republic of		85	CPV	Cape Verde
	29	PRK	Korea, North		86	CAF	Central African Rep.
Southeast Asia	30	BRN	Brunei		87	TCD	Chad
	31	IDN	Indonesia		88	COM	Comoros
	32	MYS	Malaysia		89	COG	Congo
	33	PHL	Philippines		90	DJI	Djibouti
	34	SGP	Singapore		91	ERI	Eritrea
	35	THA	Thailand		92	GNQ	Equatorial Guinea
	36	KHM	Kampuchea Dem		93	ETH	Ethiopia
	37	LAO	Lao P. D. Rep		94	GAB	Gabon
	38	BUR	Myanmar (Burma)		95	GMB	Gambia, The
	39	VNM	Viet Nam		96	GHA	Ghana
South West Asia	40	AFG	Afghanistan		97	GIN	Guinea
	41	BGD	Bangladesh		98	GNB	Guinea Bissau
	42	BTN	Bhutan		99	CIV	Ivory Coast
	43	IND	India		100	KEN	Kenya
	44	MNG	Mongolia		101	LSO	Lesotho
	45	NPL	Nepal		102	LBR	Liberia
	46	PAK	Pakistan		103	MDG	Madagascar
	47	LKA	Sri Lanka		104	MWI	Malawi
Pacific Islands	48	FJI	Fiji		105	MLI	Mali
	49	PYF	French Polynesia		106	MRT	Mauritania
	50	GUM	Guam		107	MUS	Mauritius
	51	KIR	Kiribati, Rep. of		108	MOZ	Mozambique
	52	MDV	Maldives		109	NAM	Namibia
	53	NRU	Nauru		110	NER	Niger
	54	NCL	New Caledonia		111	NGA	Nigeria

Table 1. Continued

Regions	No...	Co de	Country name	Regions	No	Code	Country name
	112	REU	Reunion		158.	NIC	Nicaragua
	113	RWA	Rwanda		159	PAN	Panama
	114	SHN	St. Helena		160	PRY	Paraguay
	115	STP	Sao Tome & Principe		161	PER	Peru
	116	SEN	Senegal		162	PRI	Puerto Rico
	117	SYC	Seychelles		163	KNA	St. Kitts Nevis
	118	SLE	Sierra Leone		164	LCA	St. Lucia
	119	SOM	Somalia		165	SPM	St. Pierre Miquelon
	120	ZAF	South Africa		166	VCT	St. Vincent
	121	SDN	Sudan		167	SUR	Suriname
	122	SWZ	Swaziland		168	TTO	Trinidad and Tobago
	123	TZR	Tanzania		169	URY	Uruguay
	124	TGO	Togo		170	VEN	Venezuela
	125	UGA	Uganda				
	126	ZAR	Congo, Dem.Republic	Mediterranean	171	CYP	Cyprus
	127	ZMB	Zambia		172	MLT	Malta
	128	ZWE	Zimbabwe		173	TUR	Turkey
Latin America & Caribbean	129	ARG	Argentina		174	BIH	Bosnia and Herzegovina
	130	ATG	Antigua and Barbuda		175	CRO	Croatia
	131	BHS	Bahamas The		176	SVN	Slovenia
	132	BRB	Barbados		177	MDN	TFYR Macedonia
	133	BLZ	Belize		178	SIM	Serbia/Montenegro
	134	BMU	Bermuda	Economies in Transition			
	135	BOL	Bolivia	Eastern Europe	179	ALB	Albania
	136	BRA	Brazil		180	BGR	Bulgaria
	137	CHL	Chile		181	CZE	Czech Republic
	138	COL	Colombia		182	HUN	Hungary
	139	CRI	Costa Rica		183	POL	Poland
	140	CUB	Cuba		184	ROM	Romania
	141	DMA	Dominica		185	SLO	Slovakia

Table 1. Continued

Regions	No...	Co de	Country name	Regions	No	Code	Country name
	142	DOM	Dominican Republic	CIS	186	ARM	Armenia
	143	ECU	Ecuador		187	AZE	Azerbaijan
	144	SLV	El Salvador		188	BLS	Belarus
	146	GRD	Grenada		190	GEO	Georgia
	147	GLP	Guadeloupe		191	KAZ	Kazakhstan
	148	GTM	Guatemala		192	KYR	Kyrgyzstan
	150	GUY	Guyana		194	LTU	Lithuania
	151	HTI	Haiti		195	MOL	Republic of Moldova
	152	HND	Honduras		196	RUS	Russian Federation
	153	JAM	Jamaica		197	TJK	Tajikistan
	154	MTQ	Martinique		198	TKM	Turkmenistan
	155	MEX	Mexico		199	UKR	Ukraine
	156	MSR	Montserrat		200	UZB	Uzbekistan
	157	ANT	Netherlands Antilles				

Source: FUGI global modeling system (FGMS 200).

2.2. INTEGRATED MULTIDISCIPLINARY SYSTEMS ANALYSIS

The design concept of FUGI global modeling (FGMS200) is based upon an innovational philosophy of humankind living on the planet Earth in the ever-changing dynamic Universe. It is worth noting that Cosmos is an entirely recycling system so that there might be no wastage of resources as seen in the current civilized human societies. In the Cosmic system *everything is interdependent and changing forever.* In order to adapt with such a dynamic cosmic system, humankind should modify present civilization in the globalizing world. Consciousness of co-existence of human beings with nature and solidarity of humankinds will be needed. The more balanced progress between technological innovations and human minds may be necessary in order to create a desirable economic relationship and life support system of the Earth in the post-modern futures.

Current globalizing world economy has been affected by global syndromes that might not solved by a short-sighted profit maximizing human behavior apt to money worship. Adam Smith (1723-1790) thought that profit maximizing human behavior will eventually create a harmonized wealthy society guided by "invisible hand" of God. Such kind of "belief" has been inherited to even academic disciplines of modern economics, in particular, "free trade". He is well known author of "The Theory of Moral Sentiments" (1759) and "An Inquiry into the Nature and Causes of the Wealth of Nations" (1776).

This myth is not true in the light of experience in a globalizing world economy. We see "global syndromes" such as increasing "miserable wealth gap" between the rich and the poor as well as "digital divides" between the educated people and the non-educated in addition to increasing "ecological destructions of a harmony between the nature and human activities" all over the world. Human beings, in particular, the highly educated rich people should lean a Classical wisdom such as mercy, awaken, aspiration, ascetic self-control, moderate, tolerance and harmonization with nature in order to create a new human solidarity based on cosmic mind toward a global welfare society and peaceful world. Global enterprises also should pay much attention on SRI (socially responsible investing).

The innovational system design concept of FUGI global modeling system has been influenced by the recent advancement of systems engineering, life science, biotechnology, information/communication technology and space technology. The new keywords are given below. (1) Systems science and engineering, (2) Lifeinformatic economics, (3) Global dynamic cooperation and policy coordination among the countries, (4) Self-organization in accordance with changing environment, (5) Brain physiology economics in collaboration with right and left brain, (6) Fluctuation phenomenon (yuragi in Japanese) considering alternative composite policy scenario simulations under uncertainty world and (7) Global early warning system for geographical and global risks. It is worth noting that quick policy prescription and coordinated policy actions might be feasible through early recognition on possible global risks.

It is worth noting that FUGI global modeling system using original "integrated multidisciplinary systems analysis" (IMSA) will be able to provide "alternative futures of the Japanese economy in the global interdependence" in order to adjust orbit of the fluctuated global economy by global model simulations.

As it is known, econometrics has thus come forward as a powerful tool that radically supersedes former theoretical models based on abstract logical methodologies. Of course, the appropriately estimated structural parameters using long-term time series data will have a fairly high degree of stability over time, but econometric models nevertheless face the dilemma that certain degree of their structural environments are indeed changeable, thus posing a problem of fluctuation in forecasting. Indeed, this type of fluctuation phenomenon seen in life phenomena always threatens forecasts of the future using econometric methods.

In a similar way, the appearance of complex and interrelated global issues such as environment, energy, development, peace and security, human rights and displaced persons, and so on, has posed problems whose solution is quite impossible within the traditional frameworks of economics. It is worth noting that such historical trend toward fusion of science and technology should bring about multidisciplinary approach beyond the traditional framework of academic disciplines.

Integrated life-supporting systems require a new methodology of *Lifeinformatic economics* (life science + information technology + economics) beyond econometrics (economics + statistics). At the same time, there is increasing need for a new system design methodology on fuzzy systems that can manipulate *soft* variables that are not so easily quantified.

In this context, it is worth noting that computer simulation methodology plays a greater role in visualizing the alternative futures of human society using alternative scenarios. Futures might not be determined by destiny but could be altered by information derived from integrated global model simulations and human endeavors based on cosmic mind to promote human solidarity with the ever changing nature coexisting on the planet Earth..

These facts help explain why, since the early 1970s, research was begun on the design of *integrated global models* There has come into use an integrated global modeling which supplements weak point in econometric models. Known as System Dynamics or SD for short, it is the method used in the World System Dynamics Model developed by Jay Forrester, who gained rapid recognition for discussions of the model in the *Limits to Growth* report to the Club of Rome prepared by Dennis Meadows et al. The most distinguishing point about the SD method is it's seeing reality in terms of dynamic (i.e. active and continually developing) structures for systems. Systems used in such models have a number of variables, which govern the ways in which change *pattern recognition* methods take place in the past, present, and future.

It is a fact that SD methods are the object of various types of criticism; in particular, by econometric methods. Econometrics methods have achieved qualitative improvements through the advancement of information technology. Thus, *IT economics* (Information technology + economics) has appeared as seen in *the FUGI global modeling system.* In any case, the main distinguishing feature of econometric models is the fact that the models' structural parameters are inferred from real statistical data by stochastic methods. Compared with econometric methodology, the structural parameters used in SD models are not necessarily as appropriate, especially in the case of Forrester's world model, since his model seems to be too "deterministic," neglecting "*stochastic natures of the systems"*. Consequently, criticisms are often voiced alleging that with the relatively rough parameters used in SD models, forecasts about the future must therefore have a low credibility.

SD seems likely to be an outgrowth of old-fashioned Newtonian dynamics systems that are too deterministic to allow for stochastic fluctuations of systems. Furthermore, Forrester's world model does not classify the world into regions or country groups, so it cannot discuss *increasing global interdependence phenomena* as IPCID (International per-capita income disparities). However, it is difficult to assert that these are fundamental faults in the SD method. This method's most outstanding characteristic lies in its comprehensive, *intuitive pattern recognition* of social and economic phenomena as being a complicated loop of cause-and-effect relationships. In this process, there is the problem of how to estimate stochastic structural parameters as intermediaries in determining the cause-and-effect links among the variables.

In spite of these serious defects neglecting *stochastic natures of the systems*, the SD method, which can easily accommodate a nonlinear fuzzy system, may be said to be relatively versatile in comparison with the econometric method. Of course this is not to say that an econometric model is incapable of handling a nonlinear fuzzy system. But it cannot be denied that the econometric method is less flexible than the SD modeling method when we include non-economic and non-quantifiable *soft variables* such as terrorism, peace and security as well as human rights.

We are now faced with the task of deepening our understanding of the various methodologies and creating a new approach that includes the best features of all of them. The author should like to call such an approach, which will ideally exercise both the left and the right hemispheres of the human brain, a stochastic and fuzzy *"dynamic soft systems analysis"* (DSSA), using human-intelligence oriented modeling. For purposes of making simulations of the future global economy it is necessary to quantify reality and make analyses by means of computer-aided modeling; yet there is at the same time a need to make qualitative analyses, i.e. scenario analyses because the future should have certain *fluctuation phenomena* to be called by biotechnology and life science within the range of optimistic or pessimistic futures in accordance with human behaviors.

To gain a grasp of not just a part of economic reality but of its whole, a method of *systems engineering* is indispensable. The *dynamic soft systems analysis* (DSSA) is indispensable for the analysis of a world in which the whole of socioeconomic and environmental reality is constantly changing and developing over time. DSSA is an attempt to offer practical prescriptions by which we can respond to the *"crisis problematiques"* facing humankind, as Aurelio Peccei, founder of the Club of Rome, suggested. The prescriptions derived from a model of interdependent dynamic system structures, patterned after the real world and subjected to human-intelligence-oriented modeling, in turn allow us to elaborate probable or possible pictures of our world in the future, depending on various possible *"scenarios"* and *"policy exercises."*

Stimulated by our joint research with the United Nations University on a *"global early warning system for displaced persons"* (1986d), we have felt the need for our FUGI model has to go beyond its present capacities centered on an econometric model in the rather traditional restricted terms of academic disciplines. We have therefore developed an *integrated global model for sustainable development* that can make future simulations of *"global syndromes"* or "global complexes of symptoms," including various types of environmental problems and refugee issue (1987, 1995b, 2003a, 2003b).See Onishi A. (2003b) FUGI global model for early warning of forced migration (http://www.forcedmigration.org) Forced Migration Online, Refugee Studies Centre, University of Oxford. This is why the FUGI global model has been expanded in scope to deal with such non economic issues by using *integrated multidisciplinary systems analysis beyond the traditional framework of economics disciplines.*

The latest FUGI model 9.0 M200 treats almost all countries, regardless of how large or small, as having the possibility of being dealt with as country units. It is designed to be a comprehensive system model that can not only deal with economic problems but also incorporate subsystems to take account of environmental issues, population, energy, food, indicators of quality of life, as well as issues concerning human rights, peace, and security. Although our methodology is first and foremost based on various country or regional studies, we have felt it desirable, using these country or regional studies as a base, to adopt an orientation that further gives consideration to a highly sophisticated global modeling system.

The *"dynamic soft systems analysis"*, derived from Lifeinformatic economics, reflects the astounding development of information technology, particularly in the field of computers during the 1970s, 1980s, and 1990s. Extraordinarily sophisticated handling of information has become possible. In this regard, too, the software which computers use, that is to say utilization techniques, have made notable strides toward what we might call *"global model simulation".*

This approach is supported not only by the so-called soft sciences but also by developments in interrelated multi-disciplinary fields of the frontier human sciences. For example, our understanding of the human brain has greatly advanced through developments in *brain physiology*. As a result, it is seen that the right brain perceives images of reality, while the left brain analyzes these in logical and conceptual ways and constructs logical models. As a part of its own division of labor, the brain's central ridge facilitates high-level flows or exchanges of information between the left and right hemispheres. Through a skillful treatment of the organically linked functions of the left and right brains, one can develop a soft system model. In a similar way, what we have tried to develop for our present purpose is not merely collecting information but providing a sophisticated global information system based upon *"global model simulation"*. *Human brain is not sufficient enough to make simulation a complex dynamic global modeling system without advancement of computers and multidisciplinary sciences.*

The developments in life sciences are making ever clearer the conceitedness between individual cells of the human body and the human body as a whole organic entity. Individual cells contain information pertaining to the entire body. Thus, at times of special stress, the individual cells invoke a regulatory mechanism by which they pool their forces, working together in the face of difficulties. This is an extraordinarily important capacity, which living things possess, and we in fact need to incorporate just this sort of capacity into any global modeling system to prevent or mitigate, through international cooperation, undesirable phenomena in the global human society.

It is worth noting that first-generation modern economics is based upon *"Newtonian dynamics and Darwinism"*. Second-generation economics is *"econometrics"*, which has been greatly developed through progress with particle physics, stochastic statistics and economic modeling. The third generation might be *"integrated multidisciplinary systems analysis"*, reflecting progress in systems engineering, life sciences, biotechnology, ecology, and soft systems science and information technology.

In the twenty-first century, we may expect that economic models will come to have much *softer* dynamic systems. The information revolution, often known as the *third wave*, has had a great impact on the field of economic research, and through the extraordinary progress being made with computer hardware and software systems, great changes are being made in the traditional methods of economic research. With the advent of large-scale capabilities for data processing by personal computers, FUGI global modeling system has become accessible to economists, and as a result we look forward to greatly improved capacities for research on economic theory and trade policies. The making of policy proposals and the building of theoretical economic models, formerly dependent on professional economists with rich experience, sharp intuition, and outstanding capacities for judgment and analysis, can now, through intelligent expert systems, be achieved to a large extent by ordinary researchers. *Consequently, when* our human society *is about to enter an age of global interdependence, FUGI global modeling system can justly claim pride of place as a new frontier science of economics.*

2.3. STRUCTURE OF GLOBAL INTERDEPENDENCE

Let us explain the *broad structure of global interdependence* in FUGI global modeling system. Current world economy consists of around 200 countries/ regions where each country / region   model is increasing *global interdependence.* The most important *global interdependence variables* are world trade matrix (200 x 200), export/import prices, commodities prices in   particular, oil prices, foreign exchange rates, stock market prices, ODA, private foreign direct investment, interest rate As LIBOR, particularly the US interest rates, fiscal & monetary policies, energy and environment policies etc. Certain countries are selected from the Regional Classification of 200 courtiers /regions for illustration of broad structures of global interdependence in FUGI global modeling system (see Fig.1).

Among 200 countries /regions, it is worth noting to note that economic geographical map is rapidly changing toward the end of this century. Apart from current super powers of the US, EU and Japan, so called BRICs (China, India, Brazil and Russia) are rapidly increasing economic powers so that their shares of real GDP and or nominal GDP in terms of the US dollar in the world economy might be changing rapidly.

According to FUGI global model simulations, the US will hardly maintain the current shares, although EU15 and Japan's share will be decreasing. It is reasonably expected that enlarged EU will play a greater role of globalizing world. Among the BRICs, the Chinese share is strikingly growing and will take over Japan' position sooner or later As a matter of facts, foreseeable changes in the geo-economic map will induce structural changes in the world trade and global interdependence.

The FUGI global modeling system includes more than 170,000 structural equations so that the reader might not understand the structure of the huge model at a glance. It is surprising for the reader to recognize that such a large complex dynamic system model is operational by a personal computer, because dramatic "information technology innovation" has been occurred over the past only 40 years. It seems likely to be too hard job to find solutions of such sophisticated non-linear dynamic model using conventional mathematical formula. Instead of using the conventional mathematical formula, we have adopted computerized mathematics formula, so that system engineers might easily understand computerized modeling system and make computer simulation exercise using computer programming languages and iteration methods. *Computer simulation technology will strengthen traditional thinking of modeling; because human brain might have certain physical limitations to understand such sophisticated complex interrelated dynamic phenomenon at a glance.*

We would be better to explain very simple images of *"global interdependence"* on the FUGI global modeling system. Concept of the FUGI global modeling system is that *everything around the world is apt to change forever and interrelated.* At the same time, past historical experiences have certain effects on present situations and current human behaviors, in turn, will have impacts on the future situations of the world economy. Thus, business cycles tend to repeat similar historical *fluctuation* patterns in the major developed economies such as the US economy. In the globalizing world, every country around the world cannot survive alone segregated from the interdependent global economy but may survive in the co-existing world. Furthermore, in this uncertainty world, every country, in particular, the US may not find a proper way without a *navigation map* for operating systems of the world economy. This is why we have designed the FUGI global modeling system to provide information on globalizing world very quickly to human society.

Although the major core of the FGMS 200 is economic development subsystem, there are other related important subsystems such as population; foods, environment, human right, human health care, digital divide, peace and security for life supporting system of humankinds on the Earth. For example, population increase of the Earth depends upon birth rates and death rates in each country. These ratios are depends on education, life expectancy at birth etc. Labor force increase depends on population dynamics and labor force participation rates. Thomas Robert Malthus (1766-1834) in his book, *An Essay on the Principle of Population*, first published in 1798 believes that population explosion may bring global poverty and unemployment. But this is not true in the light of simulations using FUGI global modeling system. Unemployment rates partly depend upon increasing rate of labor force but major factors are wage cost issues. If nominal wage rate increase would lower than those of labor productivity, employment opportunities will be increased. If labor hours would be shortened by work sharing, unemployment rates could be decreased. As a matter of facts, decreases in unemployment rates may increase real GDP growth rates.

As a core subsystem of *"economic development,"* labor productivity plays a significant role to raise per-capita income level and eventually overcoming poverty. Furthermore, it is reasonably expected that labor productivity increase using robotics will provide with more free time to raise humanistic activities level and improve quality of life covering health care, digital divide in accordance with gradually shortenings of working hours in the global society in the futures. On the supply side, therefore, labor productivity increase is the most important factor to raise per-capita income and living standards. GDP growth potentials can be increased by not only labor force but also by capital assets, educational assets and technology assets. Non housing fixed investment and, in particular, R&D increase capital and technology assts to raise labor productivity in the developed market economies. On the other side, educational expenditure and ODA, in particular, technical co-operation can play greater role to increase growth potentials of the poor developing countries. Without increases in GDP growth potentials, sustainable development could not be achieved over the long-run in the global interdependent economy.

Apart from "global financial/economic crisis" as seen in the US originated *subprime loan issues* in 2007-2009, major factors to induce business cycles to interfere the sustainable development of the developed market economies seem likely to be *fluctuations* of fixed investment. For instance, increasing rates of non-housing investment in the US and Japan are explained mostly by profit rate to non-housing capital assets minus interest rates on loan. If profit rate is higher than interest rates, non- housing investment may increase while if interest rates overshoot, non-housing investments tend to shrink. Then depression period may be started. While depression periods continue, Federal Fund Rate (US) might be lowered compared with profit rates in order to escape from economic stagnation traps. Accordingly, economies will recover sooner or later and real growth rates will be accelerated toward ceilings restricted by GDP growth potentials on the supply side. Such kind of growth patterns and interest behaviors have been recorded as human historical memories so that business cycles might repeat in accordance with historical pattern recognition. It is however worth noting that the historical patterns of business cycles are not always remains same, but may be changeable in accordance with changing economic environment and policies.

For example, demand oriented Keynesian policy seems likely to be not so effective in the globalizing interdependent world economy. If the US would pursue such a policy, the US economy should be got in troubles of increasing twin deficits namely government budget and trade deficits (for reference, see simple explanatory notes on *Global Interdependence Table*). Depreciation of US dollars against the other major currencies such as EURO, Yen and Yuan may not solve the US structural trade deficits, but the US international competitiveness on price and non price should be improved by lowering employment costs and increasing R&D through technology innovations.

With regard to the sustainable development of the globalizing interdependent economy, *"fluctuations"* of the *stock market prices* also may play a significant role as seen a global coincidental market crash induced by "sub-prime loan crisis". Today the assets, in particular, financial assets are major variables to explain the movement of private consumption expenditures which have been explained by mostly disposal income, namely, compensation of employees and operating surplus after tax reduction. However, assets effects will have getting an increasing importance in the rich societies as A.C. Pigou (1877-1959) once suggested against J.M. Keynes. Fluctuations of stock market prices of the major power like the US will induce fluctuations of the world economy through information and financial flows in the interdependent global economy.

For the time being, the US will still play a significant role to sustain the global economy, but economic geographical map on a planet Earth is rapidly changing. Furthermore, there is still a hope in the global human society to strengthen a global consciousness on co-existence with nature for sustainable life support system of the Earth. For instance, through the UN, NGOs and volunteers, global consciousness and collaborations against desertification of the Earth by reclamation of forests will be increasing (see *Global Early Warning System* in *EOLSS*). Japan should take a lead on recognition of global consciousness on co-existence with nature for sustainable life support system of the Earth that will have an increasing importance in accordance with concerted progress in both cosmic mind and science & technology in the 21st space age.

2.4. GLOBAL INTERDEPENDENCE TABLE

It is worth noting that the key variable of *Global Interdependence Table* (originally designed by Onishi) is *trade matrix*. For the readers who are not familiar with mathematics, skip this mathematical note and proceed to policy implications of global interdependence table. Only for the readers who have a good knowledge of mathematics, we will show simple explanatory notes on *"Global Interdependence Table"* in the followings;

$$GDP \# = E\# - M\# + CP\# + CG\# + GFCF\# + IIS\#$$

Where *GDP#, E#, M#, CP#, CG#, GFCF#* and *IIS#* are column vectors at constant market prices in terms of millions of US dollars. In the FUGI global modeling system, variables with # denote constant market prices and those without # denote current market prices. For instance, GDP denotes gross domestic product at current domestic market prices, GDP# denotes GDP at constant market prices and GDPS denotes current GDP in terms of *current* US dollar prices.

GDP#: Gross domestic products, E#: exports of goods and services, M#: imports of goods and services, CP#: private consumption expenditures, CG#: government consumption expenditures, GFCF#: gross fixed capital formation (NHI#: non-housing investment plus HI#: housing investment), IIS#: increase in stocks including statistical discrepancies.

E#<1> = E#<1, 1> + E#<1, 2> + E#<1, 3>---------------------- + E#<1, n>

E#<2> = E#<2, 1> + E#<2, 2> + E#<2, 3>---------------------- + E#<2, n>

E#<3> = E#<3, 1> + E#<2, 2> + E#<3, 3>---------------------- + E#<3, n>

.

E#<n>= E#<n, 1> + E#<n, 2> + E#<n, 3> ----------------------+ E#<n, n>

Where <n> =200 in FGMS 200.

ETFOB# = *E# MAT<SUM J>* in E#<I, J> trade matrix elements,

MTFOB# = *E#MAT<SUM I>* in E#<I, J> trade matrix elements,

Where E#<I, J> denotes exports from a county <I> to country <J>.

E# and *M#* are linear functions of *ETFOB#* and *MTFOB#* respectively.

For simple mathematical explanations of the model, suppose that *E#* (= *ETFOB#)*, *M#* (= *MTFOB#)* and *CP#* are linear functions of *GDP#*. *GDP#* vector can be easily calculated by the following simple mathematical formula.

GDP# is obtained from inverse matrix of *(I - A + B - C)* multiplied by a predetermined column vector *(CG# + GFCF# +IIS#)*, namely,

$$GDP\# = (I - A + B - C)^{-1} * (CG\# + GFCF\# + IIS\#)$$

Where *I*: unit matrix. *A*: export coefficients n x n matrix, *B*: import coefficient diagonal matrix and *C*: private average propensity to consume coefficient diagonal matrix. From this simple mathematical formula, the readers may be able to understand that an increase in *CG#*, *GFCF#* and *IIS#* will increase in real GDP through multiplier effects $(I - A + B - C)^{-1}$ in the interdependent global economy.

This simple instructive global model is a demand oriented model. But FGMS 200 theoretical model has been designed as demand- supply integrated model. See *Appendix A: The FUGI global modeling system (FGMS200)* and *Appendix B: World trade matrix.*

It is also worth noting that FGMS is non-linear system and its mathematical solution needs more complex iteration process.

2.5. POLICY IMPLICATIONS OF GLOBAL INTERDEPENDENCE TABLE

Apart from a tiresome mathematical model, we would be better to explain *policy implications of global interdependence table.*

If the gross fixed capital formation, GFCF in the interdependent global economy would increase by adequate policy measures such as expansion of R&D to induce more advanced *"technology innovations"* and *"energy revolutions"* for developing alternative energies against global warming gas emissions, it is reasonably expect that increased GDP will not only induce world trade expansion but also reduce global CO_2 emissions through global interdependence. The more global interdependence is developed in the globalizing world, the more trade expansion is expected. Every country around the world may enjoy benefits from US expansion of imports from the rest of the world.

However, trade expansion effects may not be equally distributed to every country around world. This is particularly true in case of the China-US trade relationships. Exports from China to the US will be enlarged more than the US imports from China. As a result, China will accumulate huge trade surplus with the US. On the other side, the US trade deficits will be strikingly enlarged. This means that global trade disequilibrium will be keen issues in the globalizing world. In order to cope with such global disequilibrium, not only the US should not cutback imports from China by introducing protectionist policy, but also China should open the doors increasing imports by mitigating tariff and non-tariff barriers. Exports of China to the US have been partly interfered by safety and healthy global standard. This is an example of *"appropriate trade policy"* in the globalizing world.

It is expected that while the US will continue trade deficits by 2020, private foreign direct investment together with government sovereign financial fund such as SWF (Sovereign Wealth Fund) may offset the US trade deficits to large extent in accordance with devaluation of US dollar against major currencies such as

EURO and Yen. It is worth noting that the US dollar devaluation against other major currencies may not *"appropriate"* policy measures to improve the US trade deficits and structural disequilibrium in the globalizing world.

2.6. SOFTWARE OF FUGI GLOBAL MODELING SYSTEM

In 2000-2009, Onishi, A designed a significant new software for the integrated global modeling system (consisting of interdependent 200 countries/regions models) using a personal computer (Windows 2000/XP Professional/Vista/7). This expert software system, named as *FUGI global modeling system (FGMS 200)* has been researched and developed as a "package" for specific use in making computations for the FUGI global model 9.0 M 200PC. The *FGMS 200* software system consists of (1) *CONTROL*, data file control systems for listing, loading, printing, and updating time-series country data file (*CNT*), time-series region data file (*RGN*),cross country data file for initial conditions of the model (*CRS*),as well as variable (*VAR*) data files; (2) *DSERVE*, supplementary data servicing programs for updating and storing *RGN.DAT* file, etc;(3) *ESTIMATE*, estimating parameters of the model, using Automatic Parameter Estimating System *(APES)* to select automatically the most appropriate sets of explanatory variables; (4) *SIMULATE*, making simulations using the FUGI global model;(5) *OUTGT*, printing out simulation results in forms of 170 world tables, each country tables and world trade matrices;(6) *UTILITY*, receiving data from *FUGIDB* to initialize and overwrite the time-series data, *RGN.DAT,* as well as to create variable data files, *VAR.DAT.*

FGMS200 can carry out automatic estimation of a given set of structural parameters of the model, applying OLS (ordinary least squares method) or MLBM (maximum likely food method) by selecting the most appropriate combination of explanatory variables in a given estimation period. Automatic Error Correction System (*AECS*) allows making forecast simulations efficiently using error collection column vector "*d*" The target setting of a given variable, for instance, oil cutback requirement in a given period of the developed countries can be easily done using "*d*". This expert AI system has already entered the stage of practical application. It is hoped that the FUGI global modeling system (*FGMS 200)* can contribute to progress in the integrated global model for sustainable development. For further details of *FGMS 200,* see *Users Guide.* FUGI global model 9.0 M200, *Integrated Global Models for Sustainable Development,*

UNESCO Encyclopaedia of Life Support System, EOLSS Publisher, Oxford, UK, 2003-2008 (http://www.eolss.net).

2.7. MAIN SUBSYSTEMS: POPULATION, ENVIRONMENT AND ECONOMIC DEVELOPMENT

Population System

In the population system, there are key variables such as population, birth rates, total fertility rates (TFR), death rates, population below 15, population above 65, economically active population, 15-65, life expectancy at birth for male and female. The population changes can be explained by birth rates and death rates as well as net immigrant's rates. Both birth rates and total fertility rates tend to decrease in accordance with an increase of per-capita income, higher government education expenditures to GDP and longer life expectancy at birth. The death rates can be explained by real GDP per capita, rates of government health and welfare expenditures to GDP, the shares of population over 65 to total population, the birth rates over the past five years and life expectancy at birth. The life expectancy at birth of both male and female can be explained by real GDP per capita, rates of government health, and welfare expenditures to GDP, rates of government education expenditures to GDP as well as, total fertility rates. The ratio of the urban population to total population is estimated by (1 - (rural population / total population)) which in turn can be explained by the changes in the ratio of agricultural income to GDP.

Labor force of male, LCLEFM and female, LCLFF, are explained separately on the basis of economically active population of male and female NPMEA and NPFEA. These numbers should be adjusted by emigrant and immigrant that will have increasing importance in the enlarged EU (27 member countries in 2007) where liberalization of labor force in EU area is going on.

It is interesting to note that Japanese women enjoy the longest life expectancy at birth (in 2007) around the world, thanks to information provided with TV programs on healthy foods and health care. Biological evidence reveals that the more life expectancy at birth will be prolonged, the less incentive to fertility rate will be observed.

It is expected therefore that the world population explosion observed after immediate period of "industrial revolution" will reach a stationary population in accordance with increasing per-capita income and longer life expectancy at birth.

By the end of 21st century, the world populations tend to stabilize in accordance with an increase of per-capita income and longer life expectancy at birth, if human being would cope with "*global syndromes*" through human solidarity and global policy co-ordination inspired from cosmic mind.

Thomas Robert Malthus (1766-1834*)* in his book, *An Essay on the Principle of Population*, first published in 1798 believes that population explosion may bring global poverty and unemployment. But this is not true in the light of simulations using FUGI global modeling system. Unemployment rates partly depend upon increasing rate of labor force but major factors are wage cost issues. If nominal wage rate increase would lower than those of labor productivity, employment opportunities will be increased. If working hours and labor days might be shortening along with technological progress, unemployment rates might not be increased. As a matter of facts, decreases in unemployment rates may improve quality of life.

Energy System

In the 21st century it is expected that "energy revolution" will be appeared in the human society. Global warming issue derived from fossil energy use, in particular oil, and seems likely to confront with every country around the world co-existing on the planet Earth. Futures of oil should be reviewed in considering such historical trend toward energy revolution, strengthening consciousness of global warming issue.

Energy system should focus attention on energy requirements. Energy requirements (ENGYR) consist of fossil energy (FOSSIL) and alternative energy (ALTEGY). Fossil energy includes oil, (OIL), coal (COAL), and gas (GAS). Alternative energy includes nuclear, natural power (such as hydro, winds etc), solar, biomass, electric viewless, super conductor and all other high technology energy.

Oil requirement per real GDP will be deceased by increasing relative oil price to domestic producers prices, share of coal and gas to energy requirement, share of alternative energy to energy requirement, and IT investment over five years to non-housing capital. Same is true in the case of coal and gas requirement that will be decreased by increasing relative prices and alternative energy use.

It is reasonably expected that "green energy revolution "from oil to alternative renewable energy use will be appeared to increase in line with real GDP growth and relative oil price decrease. If global cooperation against global warming would be effectively carried out and ratio of global oil requirement to energy requirement could be decreased, oil prices might be stabilized. For further details, see FUGI global modeling system (FGMS200) in the Appendix.

Environment

Environment system deals with global ecosystem .As it is known, global warming might bring about serious influences on changes in climates and ecological system. Global changes in circulation patterns of atmosphere will cause unusual weather conditions and natural disasters brought in various phenomena such as floods, drought and desertification etc.

As FUGI global modeling system has been originally designed as " global early warning system "GEWS", environment system includes the following major indicators such as natural disasters, flood, drought, deforestation, erosion, dissertation, air pollution, water pollution, soil pollution, nuclear pollution, acid rain, SOX, NOX, CH_4 and CO_2 emissions etc. CO_2 emissions from fossil energy use are estimated from the following formula;

$$CO2 \ EMN = F \ ((+N) \ (CO2 \ ETF*(0.996*COAL + 0.804*OIL + 0.574*GAS)).$$

Economic Development System

Economic Development System is major core of FUGI global modeling system including the following sub-systems;

(1) Labor and Production at Constant Prices
(2) Expenditures on GDP at Constant Prices
(3) Income Distribution – Profits and Wages
(4) Prices
(5) Expenditures on GDP at Current Prices
(6) Money, Interest Rates and Financial Assets
(7) International Balance of Payments
(8) Official Development Assistance
(9) Foreign Exchange Rates

Labor and Production at Constant Prices

In this supply-side sub-bloc, special production functions are used in order to estimate real potential gross domestic product, i.e., GDPP# in a given country. In this supply-side system productivity trends in the developed market economies are estimated not by the traditionally used neo-classical production functions, but rather by Onish's own concept of *"Onishi production functions"* emphasized on *technology assets* and *educational assets*. It is assumed that obsolesce may be occurred in five years ago on technology assets and ten years ago on educational assets Technology assets increase by inflow of R&D and decrees by obsolesce of existing technology. Same is true in educational assets. Educational assets increase by inflow of government expenditures on education and decrease by obsolesce of existing information and knowledge. The value-added productivity per employed person, GDPP#/LCLF, is explained by non-housing capital stock per employed person, NHFCS#/LCLF, *educational assets* per employed person, EDUA#/LCLF, *technology assets* per employed person TECHA#/ LCLF, ratio of cumulative non-housing capital investment over the past 5 years to non-housing capital stock, SUMT5 (NHI#) / NHFCS#, and ratio of petroleum prices (as expressed in domestic currency) relative to WPI, namely PEO*FERSI/WPI as a dummy variable for energy inputs. *It is worth noting that technology assets will play much greater role to increase labor productivity and potential capacity of production in the 21st century.*

Value-added productivity will rise with higher ratios of capital to labor (i.e., with the advance of automation and the use of robots), and as seen in the case of high value-added products, productivity will rise with technology assets per employed person as a result of research and development expenditures. Also, a lessening of the vintage of capital stocks works to raise productivity. As for energy inputs as a factor in production, there is a tendency for production to lag when a given country's petroleum prices, expressed in its own currency (domestic energy cost), are high in comparison to its GDP deflator or WPI. Also, value-added productivity seems to be influenced by the capacity utilization rate, CUR that reflects the current demand situation.

It is worth noting that the shares of information technology investment (ITI) over the past five years to non-housing capital stock, SUMT5 (ITI#) / NHFCS#, tends to play much greater role in increasing productivity of the US and Japanese economy.

In the case of the developing market economies, production functions cannot be applied in the same way as when applied to the developed market economies. In the developing countries, expenditures on research and development are in most cases almost negligible. Instead of R&D, technical cooperation over the last 3 years, SUMT3 (ODATC), seems likely to increase labor productivity. As the education may influence on the productivity of developing countries, educational assets, EDUA# seem rather more persuasive in their impact. The same is seen in government expenditure on healthcare over the last 5 years, SUMT5 (GH#). In this context, it is interesting to note that Gunnar Myrdal (1898-1987), Swedish 1974 Novel Prize economist suggested in his book, *"Against the Stream, Critical Essays on Economics"* (1972), the needs for new production function against the traditional neo-classical production function by considering education and healthcare on his experience staying in India. In the non-oil-producing developing countries, high-energy costs have the same negative impact on productivity growth as in the developed countries.

For the economies in transition, the main explanatory variable is fixed capital stock per employed person. This is because in the countries in this category, data for expenditures on research and development, together with data for some other major explanatory variables are unavailable.

Research and development expenditures, RD#, can be explained by operating surplus, OS#, minus corporate income tax in some countries as well as by government defense expenditures and economic services. In the following examples, it is seen that in Japan, unlike the US, R&D expenditures are not notably influenced by government defense expenditures.

Unemployment rate, UNEMPR, tends to increase with rises in wage cost, WSEI/LPI, or WSEI/CPI/LPI<USA>, as well as with a decrease in overall economic climate in terms of GDP#.1/GDP#.2 and GFCF# /GDP#. Although J.M.Keynes (1833-1946) thought that unemployment rate is a function of *"Effective Demand"* in "General Theory of Employment, Interest and Money" (1935-1936), employment costs also seem likely to play a greater role in Post Keynesian age. Unemployment rate also tends to increase in line with supply of labor force, LCLF (adjusted by hours of work, HOW, in case of EU, Japan and USA). Using explanatory variables such as the above, changes in employment rates may be estimated from given time-series data.

Although Keynes introduced a positive fiscal and monetary policy to induce *"Effective Demand"* in coping with "Great Depression", his idea was too short sighted to discuss the futures of the interdependent global economy. He could not predict that the globalizing world might face a dilemma how to sustain *"affluent"* society with energy and resources constraints within the planet Earth. He could not imagine that the future human society should adopt *"recycling system"* in order to save energy and resources for sustainable development of the global economy deferred from Keynes proposal for wastage of resources to induce employment.

The FUGI global model's supply-side subsystem for looking at production with energy constraints gives special consideration to the possibility of circumstances such as a sudden cut in oil supplies due to an intensification of geographical risks, alternative simulations can be made, for example, as to what kinds of impacts on a country's domestic production might be expected under such circumstances. For instance, in the case of sudden oil supply restrictions, supply-side questions would arise with regard to alternative domestic energy sources e.g., the extent to which domestic oil production could be increased, or the degree to which alternative energy sources could be developed and the extent to which oil reserves could or should be used.

In the short run, the model indicates how, in response to rising oil energy costs; a non-oil-producing country's domestic demand is kept down. In other words, effective domestic energy demand cannot increase to an extent greater than allowed by energy supplies (domestic and foreign), and there exists, so to speak, a built-in "feedback system". If relative oil cost rise and cutbacks are made in oil use, it is likely to decline the share of oil to total energy supply, putting a brake on the oil price rise

In considering possible degrees of oil supply restriction in the longer terms, the model reflects, the "system" by which domestic prices rise in response to oil price rises and resultant cutbacks in oil use through greater efforts for technological innovations on alternative energy sources. Thus, there is a hope that although continued higher oil prices may bring temporally lowered rates of real GDP growth on the short run but higher oil prices may induce a greater opportunity to create alternative clean energy sources in the long run and sustain real GDP growth rates, improving global environment.

Production by industrial origin is classified into three major sectors: agriculture, industry, and services. Industry is furthermore classified into manufacturing and other industrial activities. First of all, we obtain theoretical curves showing nonlinear relationships between per capita real GDP and ratios of each sector's "real value added" to real GDP, by using cross-country analyses. Then, we forecast the future changes in industrial structures in each country or regional grouping using time-series analyses of deviations from the theoretical curves derived from cross country analysis.

Note on theoretical curve from cross-country analysis

Agriculture:

GDPAG#C = 0.3551436 - 0.1279891* GDPP# / NP

$\quad$ +0.01691503* (GDPP# / NP$)^{2}$ - 0.0009406098*(GDPP# / NP$)^{3}$

$\quad$ + 0.00002291084*(GDPP# / NP$)^{4}$ -0.0000002013468* (GDPP# / NP$)^{5}$

Industry:

GDPIN#C = 0.2088974 + 0.05532418 * (GDPP#/NP)   ;

$\quad$ -0.007219928 * (GDPP#/NP$)^{2}$ + 0.0003702608 * (GDPP#/NP$)^{3}$

$\quad$ -0.00000829076 * (GDPP#/NP$)^{4}$ + 0.00000006798821 *(GDPP#/NP$)^{5}$

Manufacture:

GDPMF#C = 0.1241992 + 0.0200785 * (GDPP#/NP)   ;

$\quad$ -0.002310938 *(GDPP#/NP$)^{2}$ + 0.0001191378 * (GDPP#/NP$)^{3}$

$\quad$ -0.000002766923 * (GDPP#/NP$)^{4}$ + 0.00000002371586 * (GDPP#/NP$)^{5}$

Were GDPP#/NP denotes per-capita real GDP derived from production function.
GDPAG#C: share of agriculture; GDPIN#C: share of industry; GDPMF#C: share of manufacture

It is worth noting that the higher per capita income tends to decrease shares of agriculture to real GDP, but to increase shares of industry to real GDP as well as shares of manufacture until a certain saturation point and then gradually decrease in accordance with increasing shares of service sector. However such kind of historical trends may not observe simultaneously every country around the world. As a matter of fact, a historical tempo of industrial revolution and information technology revolution might differ from country to country. Diversification of agriculture, industry and service sectors as well as international trade structures will be developing rapidly around the world. Since globalizing world market, however, will induce severe survival games on competition on prices and non-prices such as quality, design, safety and environment protection etc among players, it provides big business chance for new comers. In order to survive in the globalizing world economy, every country around the world might make greater efforts for "*export diversification*" and "*import substitution*" trade policy that might provide opportunities for increase real GDP growth rates. Such kind of "*appropriate*" trade policy might be particularly recommended to newly industrializing developing countries. Such phenomena, however, may induce complex conflicts of trade policy and anti feelings against "globalization" in the globalizing world.

Expenditures on GDP at Constant Prices

In this sub-bloc, the demand side of real GDP in each country or region is treated in terms of such major items within GDP as exports minus imports, private final consumption expenditures, government final consumption expenditures, non-housing fixed investment, housing investment, and changes in inventories. Together, these factors in the model form an organic economic system of global interdependence.

In the FUGI global model, global interdependent relationships among nations are expressed in terms of the world trade matrix, and also through a "multilateral trade coupling system" (MTCS). The Project LINK system deals with trade matrices using a linear trade coefficient matrix a (see *Project LINK System in EOLSS Encyclopedia*). The FUGI model adopts another method to use non-linear trade coefficients. The exports at constant US dollar prices of a given country I to another trading partner J, namely $E\#MAT<I,J>$ *that is each element of the world trade matrix* are explained by the most adequate combinations of variables. As a matter of fact, the total exports of each country, ETFOB#, are aggregates of row elements of the world trade matrix and the total imports in each country, MTFOB#, are aggregates of column elements of the world trade matrix. In the FUGI global modeling system, for example, the most appropriate export functions are chosen for elucidating various trade relationships, such as exports from each country to the developed market economies, to the developing market economies, and to the economies in transition. The model can also analyze trade flows between developed market economies. For example, Japan's real exports to the United States $E\#MAT<JPN, USA>$ are explained by such variables as the US real gross domestic product $GDP\#<USA>$, the ratio of Japan's export prices $PES<JPN>$ to the United States consumer price index $CPI<USA>$ (indicating conditions of price competitiveness between Japan and the US). It is worth noting that Japan's exports to the US are also influenced by Japan's research and development expenditures, $RD\#<JPN>$, over the most recent past four years. The same thing is true of US exports to Japan.

At times when Japan's price competitiveness increases due to a devaluation of the yen against the US dollar, there is a tendency for Japan's exports to the US to show a temporary increase. Even at times when US business conditions are relatively inactive and real GDP is kept down, if US domestic prices should rise in comparison to Japan's export prices, it is possible that Japan's exports to the US might not slacken but would rather increase, possibly eventuating in greater US-Japan trade imbalance. On the other hand, US exports to Japan are influenced not only by Japan's GDP and tariff and non-tariff barriers but also by US price competitiveness and non-price competitiveness, which could be strengthened by research and development expenditures.

In contrast to the case of Japanese exports to the developed countries, in the case of Japan's exports to the developing countries, the model introduces into its export functions the concept of "import capability," CAPM#. In order to determine the "import capabilities" of developing countries, their real exports, E#, adjusted by the terms of trade, PES/PMS, ought, first of all, to be considered. Also to be considered as factors in defining import capabilities of developing countries are financial inflows, FCI, such as bilateral ODA and private direct investments from developed countries, as well as multilateral development assistance from other international organizations (deflated in terms of dollar-base import prices, PMS, of the importing countries in question).

For instance, Japan's exports to a given developing country increase when that rises relatively to import prices so that there is an improvement in the terms of trade. On the other hand, if there is a worsening in the developing country's terms of trade (with drops in the prices of primary commodities under stagnant business situations), there import capabilities drop, and a "system" comes into being whereby Japan's exports to the country in question stagnate.

Similar conditions apply to Japan's exports to the economies in transition. In other words, what determines exports to the economies in transition is not just the scale of those countries' GDP# but rather considerations of import capability.

Thus Japan's total exports are derived from the trade matrices which include Japan's exports to the other countries and regional groupings of the model. Similarly, all the elements in trade matrices may be computed on the basis of estimated export functions. While trade between a given country and itself will of course be zero the diagonal elements of the matrix will indicate inter-regional trade among regions.

Private final consumption expenditures, CP#, in the case of the developed market economies, can be explained by such factors as GDP# or domestic disposable income, DFI#, compensation of employees, COMPE#, operating surplus, OS#, expected inflation rates, and short-term interest rates, IC. In this model, "private consumption functions" are classified into categories called the AME type, the Japan type, the USA type and the EU type, respectively. Both the Japan and the USA types have additional explanatory variables of financial assets.

It is worth noting that the US type of consumption function should be modified to include another explanatory variable of "housing assets" in order to explain all of a sudden impact of "subprime loan" in 2007-2008. A sharp two-step increase of housing loan interest rate called as "subprime loan" toward low income strata has suddenly turned into a "bad loan". In the globalizing world economy, some global securities are incorporated *"subprime loan"* so that the US oriented financial disturbance has simultaneously transmitted around the world.

In the FUGI global modeling system, housing real investment, HI#, in the case of the developed market economies can be mostly explained by the gross domestic product, GDP#. Other relevant explanatory variables are long-term interest rate on housing loan, IH, and housing investment price deflator, PHI. In this context, the US originated decrease in housing investment derived from *"subprime loan"* issues should induce "fluctuations" in the globalizing interdependent world economy.

In the case of most developing market economies for which a production-oriented model is used, as well as in the case of economies in transition, private consumption is calculated as what is left after subtracting savings from income. However, for some developing market economies demand oriented models are used in order to incorporate both supply and demand sides, similar to those employed for the developed economies.

The increasing rate of non-housing real investment, NHI# in most of the developed market economies, can be explained by the expected increase in operating surplus, OS# after deducting corporate income tax, TYC# divided by non-housing fixed capital stock, NHFCS# minus long-term interest rate (prime rate), IP. Other relevant explanatory variables are exports, ETFOB#, research and development expenditures, RD#, share of information technology investment to non-housing investment, ITI# / NHI# and capacity utilization rate, CUR etc. In most of the developed market economies, a nonlinear investment function is applied. It is worth noting that fixed investment is a major player of business cycles in the developed market economies.

In the case of investment functions for developing market economies, GDP#, in some cases domestic savings is used in place of "operating surplus." Also, as mentioned previously, the concept of "capability to import "with respect to capital goods is also used as a relevant explanatory variable. In importing capital goods from the developed countries for making investment in plant and equipment, most of the developing countries and economies in transition have a restricted availability of foreign currency reserves – a matter to which the model gives due consideration.

Income Distribution – Profits and Wages

In the economic system for determining income distribution, the major variables are operating surplus and wages. Factors determining real operating surplus, OS#, are GDP# (from which compensation of employees, COMPE#, is subtracted), interest rates, IP, and terms of trade, PES/PMS, etc. Factors affecting employed persons' nominal wage rates, WSEI, are rate of increase in consumer prices, CPI; rate of change in productivity, LPI; ratio of nominal operating surplus, OS, to nominal GDP; and unemployment rate, UNEMPR.

Needless to say, these variables are not all used for all countries; rather, those variables are chosen which appear to be the most appropriate and to have the highest descriptive capacity for a given country at a given time. In the above process of selecting variables, the most highly descriptive explanatory variable for nominal wages in many countries is consumer price index. This reflects the fact that in some countries "wage indexation" is a significant factor in labor-management agreements. Consequently, in such cases, changes in productivity may possibly have little effect on the determination of wages. Cases of unemployment rate affecting wages may be described by the "*Phillips Curve*" in post-Keynesian economic theory, but such would not always appear to be the reality at all times or in all developed market economies.

Prices

A number of price-related functions are incorporated into the FUGI global modeling system. These are producer price index, WPI, consumer price index, CPI, and "deflators" for private final consumption expenditures, government final consumption expenditures, non-housing investment, housing investment, exports and imports, etc. One of the most characteristic features of the FUGI global modeling system is that each country's export and import prices are endogenously determined. Export prices, PES are determined first, and then import prices, PMS are determined through the trade matrix taking into account the weighted average of each country's export prices in accordance with the volume of trade with each other country.

The percentage changes in export prices, PES are explained by those of producers price index, WPI, wage cost, WSEI/LPI, weighted average export prices of the developed countries, PESAME, foreign exchanges indices, FERSI and primary commodities prices, PEC etc. in the developed market economies. On the other side, the percentage changes in oil prices, PEO in the oil exporting developing countries may be explained by the changes in the weighted average export prices of the developed market economies, PESAME and those of shares of global oil to global energy requirement, OILG / ENGYRG, in addition to the oil shock dummy variables

On the other hand, percentage changes of non-oil commodities prices, PEC is explained by those of the weighted average export prices of the developed market economies, PESAME and the weighted average rates of interest of the developed market economies, ICAME.

In the globalizing world, domestic prices in every country around the world may be suffered from "*fluctuations*" of international commodities prices and exchange rates. For instance, sharp price increases in oil as well as bio-fuels should induce inflationary pressures on domestic prices around the world. Within a single country flame work, we could not cope with a globalized transmission of inflation. This is why international co-operation of policy should be needed in the globalizing world.

Expenditures on GDP at Current Prices

The values for the various components of nominal GDP, when multiplied by the various corresponding deflators yield the corresponding nominal values of GDP. The GDP deflator, PGDP, is thus obtained by dividing this nominal GDP by real GDP#.

Money, Interest Rates and Financial Assets

In defining M1 and M2 in the monetary "sub-bloc," the M1 money supply functions are determined first through the selective use (in response to the conditions of a given country) of such explanatory variables as nominal GDP and the central bank's official discount rate, IN.

Next, quasi-money (time and savings deposits outstanding), MTD, is determined by such explanatory variables as GDP and difference in interest rates between long-term government bonds and time deposits, (IB - ITD) / ITD. The model is "system designed" so as to be able to reflect the financial innovation that has taken place in recent years in the United States. Then, M2 is obtained from the sum of M1 and MTD.

The model allows for upper and lower limits of M1 and M2 in response to monetarist policies. At times when what can be called a policy "target zone" is mapped out to define the upper and lower limits of permissible expansion for M1 (and/or M2). Such policies are carried out to direct the economy within those limits; M1 (and/or M2) as computed from the demand side will be kept down by restrictions on supply. In such a case, changes in the speed of currency circulation will take place in response to the supply-restricted values for M1 (and/or M2). Thus, as mentioned before, the model makes allowances for such a system and its possible impact on domestic inflation.

A point that should be given attention here is the impact on interest rates from a strengthening of control over the money supply in cases where there are certain pressures to increase money supply as a result of increased credit to the government sector accompanying an expansion of government expenditures and of the resultant government debt. Interest rates are described in terms of various functions, including the following: prime rate (i.e., top preferential bank rate extended to top-ranking enterprises), IP; housing loan rate, IH; short-term interest rate, i.e., call rate or Federal Fund rate, IC; government long-term bond yield, IB; central bank's official discount rate, IN; and Euro area rate, IEURO.

It is worth noting that the FUGI global modeling system is specially designed to incorporate "*policy reaction functions*" in order to analyze what kinds of environmental conditions influence the raising or lowering of official discount rates by central banks. In other words, when setting official discount rates, central banks do not have a limitless degree of freedom in policy choice. The model indicates the realities according to which official discount rates, IN and or Federal Fund Rate in the US can be raised or lowered within a rather narrow margin of choice as a result of influence from the rates of consumer price hikes, $1 + DOT$ (CPI) - CPI / ((CPI + CPI.1) / 2); expectation of GDP# growth rates; exchange rate index, FERSI; interest rates in the US, IN<USA>; etc. What most influences short-term interest rates, IC, are rates of change in consumer prices or expected rates of inflation as well as rates of increase in money supply.

On the other hand, government long-term bond yield, IB, when government bond issues increase as a means of obtaining funds during a period of expanding government deficit, government bond yields are raised due to concern that the value of the bonds might otherwise fall, and this at the same time influences the short-term money market. If government deficits should expand during efforts to recover better business conditions, there is likely to arise a greater competitiveness with private demand for funds, with increased concern about the so-called "*crowding out*" phenomenon, which may be understood to be a result of pressures pushing for higher interest rates (or at least influences preventing a lowering of interest rates), unless there is a large-scale inflow of capital from globalizing financial market.

In the globalizing world, asset management funds as well as sovereign wealth fund (SWF) will play an increasingly greater role in the financial market.

It is worth noting that the "global financial crisis" induced by the US originated "subprime loan issues" in 2008-9 has simultaneously turned into "global economic crisis" through "global interdependence without systemic global risk management". In order to overcome such "global syndrome", international coordinated action should be necessary to build appropriate systemic global risk management.

The US originated subprime loan securities have spread to an extraordinary large extent in the globalizing world without any proper regulations against speculative activities of equity funds including hedge funds that might induce a spiral of systemic bankruptcy of financial institutions. As a result, all of a sudden decrease of subprime loan security prices has induced a global stock market crash. It is reasonably expected that sharp decreases in the capital equity ratios of major banks should bring about a chain of vicious circle of systemic collapse of financial institutions that might recollect Japan's negative exemplum of "bad loans in dark age". More restricted lending capacities of commercial banks, together with decreased capital stocks of private enterprises should induce decrease in investment activities in real sectors. As shown in the "Global Interdependence Table", Decreases in real domestic capital formation lead to shrinkage of world trade toward "global economic crisis".

International Balance of Payments

The FUGI global modeling system makes a rather detailed analysis of the international balance of payments. First of all, exports, ETFOB and imports, MTFOB are derived from the aforementioned trade matrix. The current values of "services" are calculated from both credits and debits on such items as transport, foreign travel and all others. In all other items, computer software transactions occupy greater weights in recent years. "Income" items cover returns on investment and other income transfers. Private foreign direct investment and "portfolio investment" (i.e., investment in stocks and bonds) are calculated in terms of both assets and liabilities, respectively.

Private foreign direct investments, DIA, are explained by GDPS; employment cost differentials, ratios of operating surplus to GDP and anticipated changes in foreign exchange rates. In the case of portfolio investments – expressed as PIONA (assets) and POINL (liabilities) – the principal explanatory variables are ratios of M2 to GDP#, international differences in interest rates, anticipated changes in foreign exchange rates, current balance of payments and ratios of operating surplus to GDP, etc. The FUGI global modeling system permits a comprehensive analysis of trade balances, current balance of payments, and capital accounts.

It is reasonably expected that global asset management funds will play a role of increasing importance in the globalizing world economy. If such global asset management funds guided by high technology oriented "financial engineering" would be affected by a short-sighted profit maximizing human behavior apt to money worship, the globalizing world economy might be seriously suffered from unexpected turbulences.

Official Development Assistance

The official development assistance (ODA) is determined as a function of the size of the donor country's dollar-base GDP (GDPS). It is then distributed both bilaterally and multilaterally. Bilateral assistance is distributed to developing countries in accordance with judgments made by the donor country. In its handling of such assistance, the FUGI global modeling system (FGMS) uses OECD figures of ODA matrices for the most recent years for which geographical distribution matrix data are available.

In operating multilateral assistance, the FUGI global modeling system uses the concept of a *"world pool"* whereby funds flow to the various developing countries in accordance with already existing distribution patterns. A useful characteristic of the model is its ability to estimate impacts on given developing countries from a given degree of raising or lowering the ratio of ODA to the GDPS of the DAC member countries among the OECD. In the FUGI global modeling system, it is worth noting that a complex system structure for the external debt of the developing countries has been introduced by using the World Bank data.

Foreign Exchange Rates

Various types of theoretical models have been developed for determining exchange rates. The FUGI global modeling system uses, as an indicator, an exchange rate index (1995=1). For example, in describing the index for the Japanese yen against the US dollar, we have made of the following explanatory variables. These are ratio of Japan's GDP deflator to the US GDP deflator, $PGDP<JPN> / PDP<USA>$; ratio of Japan's exports to the US vis-à-vis the US exports to Japan, $ESMAT<JPN, USA> / ESMAT<USA, JPN>$; and differences in short term interest rates between Japan and the US, $(IC<USA> - IC<JPN>) / IC<JPN>$; and Euros exchange rate index against the US dollar; FERI EUR.

Of course the explanatory capacity of these variables depends upon a given country and time span. With respect to recent trends in Japan and EU, the variable with the greatest explanatory capacity is the influence of differences in short-term interest rates with respect to the United States. Another important explanatory variable is the ratio of these countries' current balances of payments to the US balance of payments. Differences in inflation rates between these countries and the US have a consistent explanatory capacity in the determination of the exchange rates against the US dollar.

Because the scope of FUGI global modeling system is not merely the developed market economies but includes also the developing market economies and economies in transition, the model must provide a means of determining exchange rates not only for certain developed market economies representing the major currencies traded on the world market, but also for the developing economies and economies in transition. In most of the developing economies and economies in transition, the theories of supply and demand traditionally used in determining exchange rates for currencies directly traded in foreign exchange markets have little significance. Rather, there are numerous cases in which the influence of domestic inflation rate relative to the inflation rate in the US, and the "effective exchange rate" of the US dollar hold the greatest descriptive capacity. A number of countries' exchange rates are linked with the US dollar, EURO and/or "market baskets" of major currencies.

In the FUGI global modeling system, PPP (Purchasing Power Parity) exchange rates have also been introduced. For instance, we can compare GDP# at 1995 constant dollar prices with GDP#PPP at 1995 PPP dollar rates in IPCID (International Per Capita Income Disparity).

Chapter 3

EXAMPLES OF ESTIMATED
PARAMETERS OF GLOBAL MODEL

It is worth noting that through the use of FGMS200, automatic estimation of full set of parameters of the model is carried out very efficiently by automatically selecting either OLS (ordinary least squares) or MLBM (maximum likelihood method) in accordance with indicators of DW (Durbin-Watson ratio). They can make proper judgments whether Auto Correlation exist in a given time-series data. Because of constraints of spaces, we cannot show the full set of parameters of the model but illustrate only a few examples for reference purpose.

Population- Life expectancy at birth (Female)

< Japan >

E010 LOG (LIFEEXPF <JPN>) = 4.3183 + 0.0443* LOG (GDP#.1 / NP.1)
$$(4.63)$$
+ 0.0020*LOG (GH#. 1 + GSW#. 1) / GDP#. 1
(2.07)

+ 0.0068*LOG (GEDU#.1/GDP#.1) - 0.0844*LOG (TFR)
(1.18)   (-2.68)

R*R = 1.000   DW = 0.89
SE = 0.001   MLBM (1986 - 1999)

OIL

<Japan>

E0300 LOG (OIL / GDP#<JPN) = -10.80 - 0.4980* LOG (COAL.1 + GAS.1)/ENGYR.1)

(-3.56)

- 0.2165*LOG(ALTEGY.1/ENGYR.1)
(-0.035)
+ 0.0046*LOG (SUMT5 (ITI#) / (NHFCS#)
(-0.035)

R*R = 0.9945   DW = 1.035
SE = 0.033   MLBM (1980 - 1999)

<USA>

E030 LOG (OIL / GDP#<USA>) = 10.88 - 0.0698* LOG (POIL/WPI)

(-2.38)

-1.0464* LOG (COAL.1 + GAS.1)/ENGYR.1)
(-4.66)
- 0.3902*LOG(ALTEGY.1/ENGYR.1)
(-5.95)
- 0.0832*LOG (SUMT5 (ITI#) / (NHFCS#)
(-2.08)

R*R = 0.9933   DW = 1.329
SE = 0.018   MLBM (1978 - 1999)

< China- mainland>

E030 LOG (OIL / GDP#<CHN>) = -14.12 - 0.0379* LOG (POIL/WPI)

(-0.86))

-5.4508* LOG (COAL.1 + GAS.1)/ENGYR.1)
(-5,50)
- 1.1602*LOG(ALTEGY.1/ENGYR.1)
(-11.25)
R*R = 0.9650   DW = 0.6853
SE = 0.139   MLBM (1971 - 1999)

Production function:

<Japan>

E102 LOG (GDPP# / LCLF <JPN>) = 1.8504 + 0.5236* LOG (NHFCS#*
CUR / LCLF)
$$(3.75)$$
+ 0.0686*LOG (SUMT5 (ITI#) / (NHFCS#)
(0.45)

R*R = 0.9905   DW = 0.95
SE = 0.031   MLBM (1983 - 1998)

Unemployment Rate:

<Japan>

E113 UNEMPR<JPN>= - 0.5363 + 0.0298*LOG LOG (LCLF*HOW)
                        (1.59)
+ 0.2136*LOG (WSEI.1/LPI.1) - 0.0125*LOG (GFCF#. 1/GDP#. 1)
(10.69   (-1.57))

R*R = 0.9620   DW = 1.17
SE = 0.002   MLBM (1985 - 1998)

Prices
<Japan>
E250 DOT (WPI) = -0.0051 + 0.2650*DOT (PM) + 0.3976*DOT (WSEI/LPI) +
                (7.29)   (2.74)
+ 0.1008*DOT (IV#.1)
(0.69)

R*R = 0.9253   DW = 2.37
SE = 0.030   OLS (1972 - 1999)

E252 DOT (CPI) = -0.173+ 0.0282*DOT (PM) + 0.8963*DOT (WSEI/LPI) +
                (0.82)   (3.26)
+ 0.4048*DOT (TCR/100)
(2.83)

R*R = 0.7415   DW =1.11
SE = 0.008   MLBM (1985 - 1999)

<
Exports:

<Exports from Japan to USA>
E142 LOG (E#MAT<JPN, USA>) = −4.6082 + 0.6624* LOG (GDP#<USA>),
                                               (1.04)
−1.6411* LOG (PES<JPN>. 1 *FERSI<USA>. 1 / CP I<USA>. 1),
(−5.97)
+0.4377*LOG (SUMT4 (RD#<JPN>. 1)
(1.30)

R*R = 0.9834   DW = 0.5182
SE = 0.161   MLBM (1976–1999)

<Exports from USA to Japan>

E143 LOG (E#MAT<USA, JPN>) = −7.3445 + 1.2079*LOG (GDP#<JPN>),
                                                (9.31)
−0.3851* LOG (PES< USA>. 1 / PESAME.1),
(−2.08)
−0.3008*LOG (PES<USA>. 1 * FERSI<JPN>. 1 * (1 + CTR@<JPN>. 1 +
NTB@<JPN>. 1) / CPI<JPN>. 1))
(−3.08)

R*R = 0.9924   DW = 1.91
SE = 0.050   OLS (1976–1999)

Private consumption expenditures:

<Japan>

E152 LOG (CP# <JPN>) = 7.7366 + 0.4227*LOG (DFI# - (TPI# + TYC#))
                                         (4.13)
- 0.3054*LOG (CPI / (CPI + CPI.1) /2)) - 0.2757*LOG (ICC.1)
(- 0.38)   (2.63)

+ 0.0786* LOG (MTD.1 + SMV.1) / CPI.1)
(1.54)

R*R = 0.9975   DW = 0.52
SE = 0.056   MLBM (1973 - 1998)

Non-Housing Investment

< Japan >

E162 DOT (NHING# <JPN>) = - 0.6170 + 3.4881*((OS#.1 - TYC#.1) / NHFCS#.
1 - IP.1 / 100)
                                              (2.64)

+ 0.4182*DOT (ETFOB#.1)
(2.36)

+ 1.0717*DOT (RD#.1)
(3.77)

+ 1.0126*(ITI#.1 / NHI#.1)
(2.52)

R*R = 0.8479   DW = 1.998
SE = 0.041   OLS (1981 - 1997)

Foreign Exchange Rate

<Japanese yen against US dollar>

E803 LOG (FERSI<JPN>) = 0.1353 + 1.9332*LOG (PGDP.1 / PGDP<USA>)
                                  (10.84)

- 0.2845*LOG (ESMAT<JPN.USA> .1 / ESMAT<USA, JPN>. 1)
(- 3.06)

+ 0.0325*LOG (IC<USA>. 1 / IC.1) + 0.8318*LOG (FERIEUR)
(1.30)   (7.04)

R*R = 0.9709   DW = 1.93
SE = 0.076   OLS (1980-1999)

Note: Where ( ) denotes T-statistics and DOT denotes percentage changes.
(.1) denotes one year time lag. *For further details of the notations, see Appendix
A: FUGI global model 9.0 M200.*

Chapter 4

FUTURE SIMULATIONS OF
THE WORLD ECONOMY, 2009-2020

The 21st century will be an age of integrated technology innovations in the fields of information technology, biotechnology , new energy as solar and superconductor, nanotechnology, robotics, new materials, space-technology and etc. On the other hand, it is expected that this century will be an age of terrorism and refugees. Therefore, we cannot predict futures of the world economy, because the futures would have a large degree of *"fluctuation phenomenon"* that we might depict the futures as either optimistic or pessimistic images. For instance, the interdependent world economy will face not only transmission phenomenon of business cycles induced by the US economy but also global risk as such as speculations on the major currencies, oil prices and financial securities etc. Because the deficits of current balance of payments of the US economy will be enlarged, all over sudden depreciations of the US dollar against major currencies might be occurred by speculations. As a results, sharp increase in the US interest rates as long term bond yields that might induce sharp decrease of the US economic growth rates and the major engine of sustainable global economy will be lost. Same is true in the case of the US oriented sharp increase in oil prices by global "money game" speculations as well as sharp decrease in financial securities prices with regard to the US originated subprime loan issues. This is an example of the pessimistic scenario.

John Hicks (1904-89) of Oxford University presented an interesting trade cycle model in his book entitled *"A Contribution to the Theory of the Trade Cycle"* (1950). According to his theory, business cycles may be occurred by the *"fluctuations"* in induced investments based on *"acceleration principles"*. Akira Onishi verified existing traditional trade cycle theories using 200 countries database and FUGI global modeling system. *It is worth noting that the major causes of business cycles are very complex phenomenon in the globalizing interdependent world economy.* Hick's trade cycle model based on "*acceleration principles*" is *mathematically* elegant, but we hardly find out *econometrically* best significant relationships between gross fixed investments in real terms and increment of real GDP with one year time lag (GDP#.1 – GDP#.2) in most of the developed economies. Fluctuations of non housing investments in these economies can be more adequately explained by those of operating surplus, interest rates, exports and R&D rather than increments of real GDP. In this sense, econometrics method seems likely one of the most powerful tools for testing economic theories.

It is worth noting that the business cycles of the US economy, having large shares of the world economy, will tend to transmit to the rest of the world consisting of the global community through international trade, export-import prices, exchange rates, capital movements and stock market prices, etc. The gross fixed investments play a significant role to induce business cycles of the US economy and increasing rates of the investments are mostly affected by the ratios of profit/ non-housing fixed capital minus interest rates on fixed investments. In this sense, the US economy will play the most important role for the sustainable development of the global economy. However, the US economy alone may not have the responsibility in the global community but international policy coordination and co-operation might be much better in the futures of global interdependent economy.

On the other side, Karl Marx (1818-1883), well known author of "*Das Kapital*" (1867) has discovered that dynamism of the market economy is dwelt on business cycles, although he made a mistake as "labor theory of value" infected by "nightmares" of David Ricardo (1772-1823). Depression gives positive repercussion on revitalizing the private sector of the market economy though severe survival competitions as seen in the Japanese economy for the depression periods, 2001-2005. In order cope with the depression, Japanese private enterprises have made utmost efforts to increase R&D for overcoming survival games in the international markets. Marx designed "*Reproduction Schema*" that gives an image of 10 % sustainable development model through the balanced growth between the producer and consumption goods sectors. Such kind of idea has been succeeded by Wasily Leontief (1906-1999) in his "*Input-Output Model*" that seems likely to be the original roots of his Global Economic Model (See *Integrated Global Models for Sustainable Development, EOLSS*). Onishi also designed an original "*multi-nation growth model*" as "*FUGI global Model*". See [1] Onishi, A (1965) *Projections of Economic Growth and Intra-Regional Trade for the Developing ECAFE Region, 1960-1970, Developing Economies,* Vol. 3(2); pp.158-172, June 1965. This presents the original idea of *"FUGI global modeling system"*. Apart from FUGI global modeling system, Klein also has initiated his original idea on international linkages of national models as *Project Link system* (See *Integrated Global Models for Sustainable Development, EOLSS).*

Under such circumstances, we would be better to start with the scenario simulations of the global economy using the FUGI global modeling system. For instance, baseline simulations mean that what will be most likely futures, if the structural parameters of the model, estimated from the past data covering latest information, would not be drastically changed. Because of advanced modeling technology, we can efficiently carry out the baseline simulations. Every day, we input new information and data to modify the *initial values* (CRS files), so that the baselines simulation might accommodate with ever changing the world economy. It is worth noting that *the future of the world global economy is not determined by destiny but could be changed by policy co-ordination among players.* This is why we have designed the FUGI global modeling system not only to make the *baseline* but also *alternative policy scenario simulations The following Scenario A: G20 collaboration projections made in 2009 are just for reference to show an exercise of global model simulations using FUGI global modeling system, because futures will have large degree "fluctuations "depending on human behaviors and policy co-ordinations.*

SCENARIO A: G20 COLLABORATION

Everyone knows that current global economic crisis originated from the US subprime loan issue has been brought by the global "money game" on oil prices as well as sharp decrease in financial securities and stock market crash. The "global financial crisis" induced by the US originated "subprime loan issues" in 2008-9 has simultaneously turned into "global economic crisis" through "global interdependence without systemic global risk management". In order to overcome such "global syndrome", international coordinated action should be necessary to build appropriate systemic global risk management and international order.

The US originated subprime loan securities have spread to unforeseeable huge extent in the globalizing world without any proper regulations against speculative activities of equity funds including hedge funds that might induce a spiral of systemic bankruptcy of financial institutions. As a result, all of a sudden decrease of subprime loan security prices has induced a global stock market crash. It is reasonably expected that sharp decreases in the capital equity ratios of major banks should bring about a chain of vicious circle of systemic collapse of financial institutions that might recollect Japan's negative exemplum of "bad loans in dark age". More restricted lending capacities of commercial banks, together with reduced capital stocks of private enterprises should decrease in investment activities in real sectors. As shown in the "*Global Interdependence Table*", decreases in real domestic capital formation lead to shrinkage of world trade toward "global economic crisis".

It is worth noting that the economic crisis in the US economy, having large shares of the world economy, tend to transmit to the rest of the world consisting of the global community through international trade, export-import prices, exchange rates, capital movements, stock market prices, financial market and investment funds including hedge fund etc. In this sense, the US economy should play the most important role for the stabilization of financial market and sustainable development of the global economy. However, the US economy alone may not have the responsibility in the global community but international policy coordination and cooperation should be needed for coping with new phenomena of global financial/economic crisis.

The following alternative projections made in early 2009 are just reference materials for policy makers to evaluate policy exercises of global model simulations, because futures will have large degree "fluctuations" depending on human behaviors and policy co-ordinations.

It is worth noting that *the future of the world economy is not determined by destiny but could be changed by policy co-ordination.* This is why we have designed the FUGI global modeling system not only to make alternative policy scenario simulations namely, *Scenario A: G20 collaboration (see Table 1A)* but also *Scenario B: Global concerted policy for green revolution (see Table 1B).*

The US government has faced the US originated new "global financial /economic crisis" prevailing in 2009. In coping with a serious recession like "Great Depression" in 1930s, the US government has also introduced "economic recovery plan" to expand "effective demand" and create 3.5 million jobs. The government also has proposed "American recovery and reinvestment act" with public spending nearly 3.6 trillion dollars for stabilizing the financial system to be destroyed by a large amount of bad loans and stock market crash. Incredible systemic terrors have attacked the US economy such as bankruptcy of the major US banks like Bank of America and Citibank group, together with AIG, the world biggest life insurance corporation to insure US banking system. It is also striking news that the US major automobile companies such as GM and Chrysler have suffered from bankruptcy and the government set out to reconstruct. Against such terrors, in addition to the urgent economic stimulus package, the new Obama government has also stressed the long-term development policy for creating a sustainable economy supported by alternative energy (15 billion dollars in 10 years), environment, education, healthcares (633.8 billion dollars in 10 years). These are lessons from "Great Depression". According to FGMS simulations on possible impacts of the US *economic stimulus measures corresponding to 2% of GDP in 2009,* it is estimated that the real GDP growth rate in 2009 could be increased by 1.97% point compared with the Baseline figure.

Against "global economic crisis, G20 countries have introduced respectively collaborated actions to cut back of interest rates and expand "effective domestic demand" to sustain economic growth and secure employments by various safety-net measures such as tax cut and expansion of public expenditures in spite of increased government budget deficits from country to country. France and Germany in EU as a group have refrained from positive fiscal policy like the US, because of fears on increasing government budget deficits.

Japan has introduced a flat-rate benefit of 2 trillion yen to households to support private consumption expenditures. Because of a sharp fall down of exports in the amount of almost half, the Japanese real GDP in fourth- quarter of 2008 drastically decreased by 12.1 %. This is the worst record since the post-World War II, followed to "oil shock" in 1973. As a result, the export oriented Japanese economy has produced a large amount of unemployment and underemployment. The government has enforced to adopt additional business stimulus measures in 2009 fiscal year in the amount of 14 trillion yen as around 2% of GDP in spite of government debt outstanding reached to astronomical figure as 4344 trillion yen namely government debt outstanding GDP ratio as almost 150%. According to FGMS simulations on possible impacts of these fiscal policy measures, it is expected that the Japanese real GDP growth rate in 2009 will be increased by 1.87% point compared with the Baseline figure. However, nobody knows about "genuine figures" of economic stimulus measures, because 14 trillion yen is once pooled into "special account" different from "general account" of the general government budget and will allocate to each ministry and further distribute to "independent administration corporations", public administration corporations and 46 Funds including newly created 30. The Japanese constituents should know such a complex system of deficit financing as resultant astronomical figures of government debt outstanding. The more tax is increased, the more black holes are enlarging in Japan, in spite that Japan should contribute to "Green Revolution" and sustainable development of the global economy, while avoiding wastage of fiscal resources.

It is worth noting that Jimintou (Liberal democratic party) lost majority in recent general election of Syugiin (lower parliament) on August 30, 2009 so that we might reasonably expect dramatic changes in the Japanese political situation by win an overwhelming victory of Minsyutou (Democratic party) over Jimintou toward a right direction to the sustainable development of the Japanese economy avoiding black holes as wastage of fiscal resources.

On the other side, so-called BRICs such as China, India, Brazil and Russia have been affected by "global economic crisis". Unemployment figure of Russia has reached 6 millions in 2009. In the globalizing world economy, however, BRICs seem likely to become a countervailing power against the US oriented business cycles in the futures. Major cause of business cycles seems likely to be "fluctuations" of "induced fixed investment" so that government sovereign "autonomous" investment in these countries might have, to certain extent, resistance against the business cycles. For example, Chinese real GDP growth rate is hardly sustained at 6.1% for the first quarter of 2009. The Chinese government has introduced an appropriate economic policy against "global economic crisis" to expand "effective domestic demand" to sustain an 8% target economic growth rate and induce employment to large extent in 2009. It is hoped that global surveillance and regulations against unlimited freedom of speculations by global investment funds including hedge funds to induce unexpected turbulence of global interdependence economy would be realized in the futures.

It is also expected that the international organizations such as UN, UNCTAD, FAO, WHO, GATT, IMF, World Bank and OECD in line with G20 summit meeting will play a greater role in the sustainable development of the world economy in order to cope with potential risks as night mares of "*Great Depression*" initiated by stock market crash in New York in October 1929. The world economy was seriously affected from negative growth rates for the period 1930-1933. The outlet of "*Great Depression" was a road to World War II.* The emergence of newly organized international organizations after World War II seems likely to be outcome of awful experience in human history. It is worth noting that London G20 summit 2009 has announced the international joint recovery action plan in the amount of 5 trillion US dollars for the period, 2009-2010 against "global economic recession" such as strengthening IMF role, stability of financial system and introducing utmost economic stimulus measures in each country. London G20 summit has recognized an importance of terminating current Global Financial Crisis as soon as possible and further needs for international coordination of policies. For an alternative simulation on G20 collaboration against the global economic recession, it is expected that the global economy would recover by around 2% point compared with those of the baseline in 2009-2010 by global cooperation toward economic stimulus measures. Simulation results reveal that the US economic growth rate in 2009 will recover by 1.97% point compared with those of the baseline, through synergy effects of the US own economic stimulus measures plus repercussion of other G20 countries collaboration in the interdependent global economy. It is interesting to note that the US temporary decrease in GDP growth rate in 2009 will recover in 2010-2011, because of decrease in trade deficit, if adequate international collaborate policies against the depression might be introduced effectively.

According to G20 collaboration scenario simulation, average oil prices will increase at rather higher speeds with speculations and induce inflationary pressures. Increasing rates of Global CO_2 emissions will be maintained at 3.2% for the period, 2011-2020. As a result, the world economy will face serious dilemma to maintain the sustainable economy.

Table 1A. Projections of the world economy, 2009-2020

Scenario A: G20 Collaboration

GDP# - GROSS DOMESTIC PRODUCT (CONST.) (AVERAGE PERCENTAGE CHANGES)

UNIT: %	Actual 2001-2005	Estimate 2006-2010	2001-2010	Projection 2011-2015	2016-2020	2011-2020
World	2.6	2.4	2.5	2.9	3.4	3.2
Developed Economies	1.8	1.4	1.6	2	2.3	2.3
Developed Asia-Pacific	1.5	1	1.3	2.3	2.4	2.4
Japan	1.3	0.9	1.1	2.1	2.2	2.1
Australia	3.2	2.3	2.8	3.4	3	3.2
North America	2.4	1	1.7	2.1	2.7	2.4
Canada	2.5	1.6	2.1	2.6	2.8	2.7
United States	2.4	1.0	1.7	2	2.7	2.4
Western Europe	1.5	1.9	1.7	1.9	2.3	2.1
Euro Area	1.3	1.9	1.6	1.7	2.3	2
France	1.7	1.9	1.8	1.8	2.1	1.9
Germany	0.7	1.2	0.9	1.5	2.6	2
Italy	0.6	1.5	1	1.2	1.6	1.4
Non-Euro Area	2.2	1.8	2	2.2	2.3	2.3
United Kingdom	2.4	1.5	1.9	2.2	2.1	2.2
Developing Economies	4.5	5.2	4.9	4.8	5.3	5
Asia-Pacific	6.1	6.6	6.4	5.7	6.4	6
East Asia	6.9	6.7	6.9	5.9	6.7	6.3

Table 1A. Continued

GDP# - GROSS DOMESTIC PRODUCT (CONST.) (AVERAGE PERCENTAGE CHANGES)						
UNIT: %	Actual	Estimate		Projection		
	2001-2005	2006-2010	2001-2010	2011-2015	2016-2020	2011-2020
China	9.6	8.2	8.9	7.2	8	7.6
Republic of Korea	4.9	2.9	3.9	3.6	4.3	3.9
Southeast Asia	4.3	4.5	4.6	4.5	4.3	4.4
Indonesia	4.3	4.4	4.9	4.8	5.2	5
South Asia	5.9	7.2	6.5	6.2	7.1	6.7
India	6.4	7.8	7.1	6.5	7.5	7
Middle East	3.2	2.8	3	4.3	3.3	3.8
Saudi Arabia	4	3	3.5	5.1	3	4
Africa	3.7	3	3.4	2.7	2.6	2.7
North Africa	3.5	2.1	2.8	2.2	1.9	2.1
Sub-Saharan Africa	3.8	3.5	3.7	3	2.9	2.9
South Africa	3.9	3.9	3.9	3.4	3.5	3.5
Latin America and Caribbean	2.3	3.6	2.9	3.3	3.8	3.6
Argentina	1.6	5.4	3.5	5.8	6.4	6.1
Brazil	2.2	2.9	2.5	2	3.3	2.6
Mexico	1.8	2.6	2.2	2.8	1.7	2.3
Mediterranean	3.8	5	4.4	4	3.4	3.7
Turkey	4.3	6.2	5.2	4.4	3.7	4.1
Economies in Transition	5.3	5.2	5.2	4.1	4.4	4.3
South-Eastern Europe	3.6	3.9	3.7	3.3	3.1	3.2
CIS	6.5	5.6	6	4.7	5.1	4.9
Russian Federation	6.1	5.4	5.8	4.4	5.2	4.8

Source: FUGI global modeling system.

Table 2A. CO_2 emissions from fossil energy use. 2001-2020

Average Percentage Changes

Scenario A	Actual	Estimate		Projection		Unit:%
LONG TERM -	2001-2005	2006-2010	2001-2010	2011-2015	2016-2020	2011-2020
World	3.3	3.6	3.5	3	3.5	3.2
Developed Economies	1.3	0.4	0.8	1.1	1.8	1.4

Table 2A. (Continued)

Scenario A	Actual	Estimate		Projection		Unit:%
LONG TERM -	2001-2005	2006-2010	2001-2010	2011-2015	2016-2020	2011-2020
Developed Asia-Pacific	1.2	0.4	0.8	0.8	1.4	1.1
Japan	-0.7	0.1	-0.3	-0.3	0.6	0.2
Australia	5	2.2	3.6	2.8	2.7	2.8
North America	1.5	-0.5	0.5	0.8	1.7	1.3
Canada	2.2	0.6	1.4	2.6	2.9	2.8
United States	1.5	-0.6	0.4	0.6	1.5	1.1
Western Europe	1	1.8	1.4	1.6	2	1.8
Euro Area	0.9	1.7	1.3	1.5	2.2	1.8
France	1	0.9	1	0.8	1.1	0.9
Germany	-0.2	0	-0.1	-0.4	0.7	0.2
Italy	0	1.4	0.7	2.2	3	2.6
Non-Euro Area	1.4	2	1.7	1.7	1.7	1.7
United Kingdom	0.5	1.1	0.8	1.7	1.5	1.6
Developing Economies	4.8	5.6	5.2	4	4.1	4
Asia-Pacific	6.3	6.5	6.4	4.2	4.2	4.2
East Asia	7.2	6.6	6.9	3.3	3.1	3.2
China	7.6	7.3	7.4	3.3	3	3.2
Republic of Korea	7.1	3.8	5.4	2.5	3.1	2.8
Southeast Asia	4	6.6	5.3	6.1	4.9	5.5
Indonesia	5.3	5.7	5.5	5.3	8.7	7
South Asia	4.6	5.8	5.2	6.3	7.8	7
India	4.9	6	5.5	6.4	8.1	7.3
Middle East	3.8	4.4	4.1	4.4	4.6	4.5
Saudi Arabia	0.4	2.1	1.3	1.9	1.2	1.6
Africa	1.7	2.1	1.9	2.3	2.9	2.6
North Africa	2.7	1.8	2.3	2.1	2.1	2.1
Sub-Saharan Africa	1.1	2.3	1.7	2.4	3.3	2.9
South Africa	0.4	2.3	1.3	2.9	3.3	3.1
Latin America and the Caribbean	0.1	3.5	1.8	3.2	3.4	3.3
Argentina	2.1	5.6	3.9	5.8	6.4	6.1
Brazil	-2.1	2	-0.1	0.5	1	0.8
Mexico	1.9	3	2.4	3.8	2.2	3
Mediterranean	3.9	5.2	4.6	4.1	3.5	3.8
Turkey	3.4	5.4	4.4	4.3	3.7	4

Table 2A. (Continued)

Scenario A	Actual	Estimate		Projection		Unit:%
Economies in Transition	5.3	5.5	5.4	4.1	4.8	4.4
South-Eastern Europe	4.6	4.5	4.5	3.9	3.8	3.8
CIS	6.9	5.3	6.1	3.9	6	4.9
Russian Federation	5.9	4.9	5.4	3.4	6.5	4.9

Source: FUGI global modeling system.

Notes: Pre-projection was made for the period, 1995-2008. .Projection periods are 2009-2020. This projection has been made at the end of June 2009 but has a large degree of "fluctuations" under uncertainty futures.

Chapter 5

ALTERNATIVE PATH OF GLOBAL ECONOMY AGAINST CO$_2$ EMISSIONS

5.1. GLOBAL ENVIRONMENT INDICATORS: CO2 EMISSIONS

In order to make the baseline projections of the global economy and CO2 emissions, we have to face one of the most key issues on average oil price trends that might have a large degree "fluctuations" by speculations. In the FUGI global modeling system, average oil prices are explained by weighted average export prices of developed economies, shares of global oil consumption to global energy requirement and dummy variables as geographical risks etc. so that development of alternative energy such as solar, biomass, nuclear as well as fossil energy savings technology such as EV (electric vehicles), super conductor might oppress sharp increase in oil price in the long-run.

Of course, average oil prices may be modified in accordance with alternative scenarios. For instance, it would be possible to assume that development of alternative energy and energy saving technologies will be accelerated by global policy coordination against global warming on the planet Earth. This is an optimistic scenario. On contrary, we can adopt more pessimistic scenario that each nation would not take into account of international co-ordination polices against global warming and continue current pattern of fossil energy consumption without taking care of futures.

Alternative energy consists of all sort of energy excluding fossil energy. For instance, it includes nuclear, biomass, solar, batteries, other renewals and superconductor etc. At this time (2009), *nuclear energy* plays a greater role in the developed countries such as France and Japan. In Japan nuclear power plants are not so popular, because of nightmare of Hiroshima-Nagasaki but nuclear energy deems as one of the important transition energy sources until new clean energy age will appeared. In place of nuclear, *solar energy* will play much greater role in Japan and Germany where new technology frontiers in HC (*hybrid cars*) and *EV (electric vehicles)* will rapidly expanding. It is also worth noting that Japan and Germany will take lead in the development of innovational energy savings technology such as *super conductor*. Super conductor uses natural electric phenomena of super conductivity where electric resistance of materials becomes zero in very low absolute temperature, for example, in outer space. Intensive research for *super alloy* to induce superconductivity in relatively moderate temperature is also going on. Experimental super express trains using super conductor have been already succeeded in Japan and Germany. There is a hope that *super conductor seems likely play ultimate energy saving technology in the futures of global human society.*

Among the developing countries, Brazil like agricultural resource rich country will play greater role in using *biomass* in place of fossil energy. On the other side, China has been not only succeeded in high economic growth performance, enjoying extraordinary large foreign exchange reserves but also will become the world largest CO_2 emission country by 2010 and confront serious environment issues if proper policy measures for environment protection would not be introduced as soon as possible.

5.2. ALTERNATIVE PATH OF GLOBAL ECONOMY AGAINST CO_2 EMISSIONS. SCENARIO B: GLOBAL CO-OPERATION FOR "GREEN REVOLUTION"

In order to cut back global CO_2 emissions, we should confront dilemma of sustainable development of the global economy. A surprising proposal made by *Limits to Growth (1972)* is zero growth of the global economy. If the global economy will confront with zero growth, it seems likely to induce global crises such as *Great Depression* in 1930s. Unemployment will become serious issues. Global issues such as poverty, international per-capita disparity, peace and security could not solve in the human society. Zero growth may cutback CO_2 emissions but could not solve trade-off between environment issues and desirable development of the global economy.

Alternative simulation by FGMS (FUGI global modeling system) reveals that cutbacks of global CO_2 emissions should be prerequisite against global warming.

In order to cutback global CO_2 emissions, it should be needed for international co-operation and co-ordination of development strategy. Even if EU and Japan will co-operate and co-ordinate the policies toward cut back of CO_2 emissions by technology innovations for developing alternative energy and energy savings, it could not achieve the global targets without co-operation with the major CO_2 emission nations such as US, China, Russian Federation. In order to decrease global CO_2 emissions, it is desirable to join the developing countries as a group. This is a very difficult job, because most of the developing countries should have keen interest and priority to develop their economies in order to overcome poverty rather than environment protection. This is why the developed countries should promote official development assistance (ODA), in particular, technical co-operation to the developing countries. Technology transfer from the advanced to developing countries are pre-requisite for achieving the target of cut back global CO_2 emissions.

Advanced economies should make utmost efforts to increase R & D as well as investments for alternative energy and energy savings. *The FUGI global model simulations affirm that not only increased R&D together with investments will increase rates of development of global economy but also decrease global CO_2 emissions.* There is a hope that global warming could be protected if information on early warning for possible fears on the planet Earth would be shared beyond differences between culture, race, and religion on common conscious of cosmic minds.

Scenario B: Global Cooperation and Concerted Policy for Green Revolution

Although a set of policy mixtures may be modified in any ways in the *Scenario B: global cooperation and coordination of polices for sustainable development of the interdependent global economy toward "green revolution"* after immediate short-term recovery policy measures in 2009-2010, we have assumed the followings for a policy exercise starting from 2011 to 2020;

*Developed Economies**

(1) Average oil prices will be stabilized at reasonable levels by cutting back oil energy use by 5% per year in 2011-2005 and 10% per year in 2016-2020 (in the case of Japan, 5% in 2011-2005 and 20% in 2016-2020). It is reasonably expected that electric vehicles (EV) will replace the

traditional internal conversion engines

(2) Alternative energies other than fossils will be expected to increase 5% (10% in Japan) per year in 2011-2006 and 10% (20% in Japan) per year in 2006-2020. In addition to more safety nuclear, new entries of renewable energy such as solar, wind and superconductor and batteries for EV.

(3) *A new innovative investment together with research and development expenditures (R&D)* improving labor productivity and global environment will be expected to increase by 3% per year in 2011-2020.

(4) Private foreign direct investment (PFDI) will be expanded by 3% per year in 2011-2020.

(5) Official development assistance (ODA), in particular technical cooperation for renewable energy, energy savings and recycling technology transfer to developing countries will be increased by 2% per year in 2011-2020.

(6) In order to cope with unemployment issues, developed economies should greater efforts for "work sharing" shortening regular labor hours and days in order to expand employment opportunities and improve quality of life,

(7) Global collaboration solidarity might be needed for enhancing cosmic mind to live on the planet Earth in order to realize the above scenario overcoming current economic crisis.

(* In this exercise, *developed economies* cover FGMS country code 1-23).

Developing Countries + Economies in Transition

(1) Oil requirements will be cutback by 2.5% per year in 2011-2015 and 5, 0% per year in 2016-2020.

(2) Alternative energy will be increased by 2.5% per year in 2011-2015 and 5.0% per year in 2016-2020.

According to the FUGI global model simulation, both the Japanese and US economy will be able to sustain real GDP growth performance of 2.6% for the period 2011-2020. Japan should take an initiative to cutback CO_2 emissions 25% compared with those of 1990 level by 2020 in accordance with Kyoto protocol. The US also will be able to cutback CO_2 emissions around 20% compared with those of 2010 level by 2020.

It is worth noting that China as the biggest CO_2 emission country will sustain rather high GDP growth rate of 7.5% and low CO_2 emission increasing rate of

1.0% for the period, 2011-2020 according to Global co-operation scenario (see Table 1B – 3B). It is reasonably expected that average oil prices will be stabilized for the period, 2011-2020, because of oil requirements will be expected to decrease to a large extent by green energy revolution, in particular, in Japan and the US (see Table 4B). It is worth noting that alternative energy will be likely to increase by more than 10 times by 2020 compared with those of 2005 (see Table 5B)..

Table 1B. Projections of the world economy, 2011-2020

Scenario B: Global Co-operation for "Green Revolution"

GDP# GROSS DOMESTIC PRODUCT (CONST.) (AVERAGE PERCENTAGE CHANGES)

UNIT: %

- LONG TERM -	Actual 2001-2005	Estimate 2006-2010	2001-2010	Projection 2011-2015	2016-2020	2011-2020
World	2.6	2.3	2.4	2.9	3.6	3.2
Developed Economies	1.8	1.1	1.5	2	2.7	2.4
Developed Asia-Pacific	1.5	0.5	1	2.4	2.9	2.6
Japan	1.3	0.3	0.8	2.3	2.9	2.6
Australia	3.2	2.7	2.9	3.4	3	3.2
North America	2.4	0.6	1.5	2	3.3	2.6
Canada	2.5	1.4	2	2.6	3.1	2.8
United States	2.4	0.6	1.5	1.9	3.3	2.6
Western Europe	1.5	1.8	1.7	1.8	2.1	2
EU	1.5	1.8	1.7	1.8	2.1	2
France	1.7	1.9	1.8	1.8	2	1.9
Germany	0.7	1.1	0.9	1.4	2.2	1.8
Italy	0.6	1.4	1	1.2	1.4	1.3
United Kingdom	2.4	1.5	1.9	2.3	2	2.1
Developing Economies	4.5	5.2	4.9	4.7	5.3	5
Asia-Pacific	6.1	6.5	6.3	5.7	6.4	6
East Asia	6.9	6.9	6.9	5.9	6.7	6.3
China	9.6	9.2	9.4	7.1	7.9	7.5
Republic of Korea	4.9	4	4.4	3.5	4.3	3.9

Table 1B. Continued

GDP# GROSS DOMESTIC PRODUCT (CONST.) (AVERAGE PERCENTAGE CHANGES)

UNIT: %	Actual	Estimate		Projection		
Southeast Asia(ASEAN)	4.3	4.9	4.6	4.5	4.5	4.5
Indonesia	4.3	5.3	4.8	4.7	5.2	5
South Asia	5.9	7.2	6.5	6.3	7.5	6.9
India	6.4	7.8	7.1	6.7	8	7.3
Middle East	3.2	2.8	3	4	2.7	3.3
Saudi Arabia	4	3	3.5	5.1	3	4
Africa	3.7	3	3.4	2.7	2.6	2.7
North Africa	3.5	2.1	2.8	2.2	1.9	2.1
Sub-Saharan Africa	3.8	3.5	3.7	3	2.9	3
South Africa	3.9	3.9	3.9	3.4	3.5	3.5
Latin America and the Caribbean	2.3	3.6	2.9	3.3	3.7	3.5
Argentina	1.6	5.4	3.5	5.8	6.4	6.1
Brazil	2.2	2.9	2.5	1.9	3.2	2.6
Mexico	1.8	2.4	2.1	2.9	1.8	2.4
Mediterranean	3.8	5	4.4	4	3.5	3.8
Turkey	4.3	6.2	5.2	4.4	3.7	4.1
Economies in Transition	5.3	5.2	5.2	4.1	4.4	4.3
South-Eastern Europe	3.6	3.9	3.7	3.4	3.4	3.4
CIS	6.5	5.6	6	4.7	5.1	4.9
Russian Federation	6.1	5.4	5.8	4.4	5.2	4.8

Source: FUGI global modeling system.

Table 2B. CO$_2$ emissions from fossil energy use. 2011-2020

Scenario B: Global Co-operation for Green Revolution

UNIT: % - LONG TERM -	Estimate 2006-2010	Estimate 2001-2010	Projection 2011-2015	2016-2020	2011-2020
World	1.9	3.5	1.5	1.8	1.7
Developed Economies	1.7	0.8	-1.1	-2.2	-1.6
Developed Asia-Pacific	2.4	0.8	-0.5	-4.2	-2.4

Table 2B. (Continued)

UNIT: % - LONG TERM -	Estimate 2006-2010	Estimate 2001-2010	Projection 2011-2015	2016-2020	2011-2020
Japan	1.9	-0.3	-1.3	-7.3	-4.3
Australia	4.1	3.6	0.9	0.5	0.7
North America	1.6	0.5	-0.8	-2.5	-1.7
Canada	2.4	1.4	0.8	-0.5	0.2
United States	1.6	0.4	-1	-2.8	-1.9
Western Europe	1.4	1.4	-1.5	-0.8	-1.1
EU	1.4	1.4	-1.5	-0.7	-1.1
France	1.2	1	-2	-1.7	-1.8
Germany	3	-0.1	-2.9	-0.7	-1.8
Italy	0.3	0.7	-1.8	-1.3	-1.5
United Kingdom	-0.1	0.8	-2.1	-0.2	-1.2
Developing Economies	1.1	5.2	2.8	3.2	3
Asia-Pacific	5.1	6.4	2.9	3.1	3
East Asia	5.9	6.9	1.7	1	1.4
China	5.3	7.4	1.6	0.5	1
Republic of Korea	5.1	5.4	1.6	3.2	2.4
Southeast Asia(ASEAN)	9.9	5.3	5	7.2	6.1
Indonesia	9.5	5.5	5.1	7.6	6.3
South Asia	7.8	5.2	6	6.7	6.4
India	10.1	5.5	6.3	6.9	6.6
Middle East	8.7	4.1	3.1	4.5	3.8
Saudi Arabia	11.1	1.3	1	2.8	1.9
Africa	11.1	1.9	1.5	2.5	2
North Africa	13.3	2.3	1.3	1.9	1.6
Sub-Saharan Africa	5.8	1.7	1.7	2.8	2.2
South Africa	5.8	1.3	2.6	3.3	2.9
Latin America and the	3.8	1.8	2.3	3.3	2.8
Argentina	5.9	3.9	5.3	6.4	5.9
Brazil	8.2	-0.1	-0.5	0.9	0.2
Mexico	1.9	2.4	3	2.4	2.7
Mediterranean	3.7	4.6	3.3	3.3	3.3
Turkey	4	4.4	3.6	3.8	3.7
Economies in Transition	1.1	5.4	2.9	4.2	3.6

Table 2B. (Continued)

UNIT: % - LONG TERM -	Estimate 2006-2010	Estimate 2001-2010	Projection 2011-2015	2016-2020	2011-2020
South-Eastern Europe	0.7	4.5	3.1	3.3	3.2
CIS	3.6	6.1	3.4	5.4	4.4
Russian Federation	5	5.4	3.3	6.1	4.6

Source: FUGI global modeling system.

Table 3B. CO_2 emissions from fossil energy use. 2011-2020

Scenario B: Global Co-operation for Green Revolution

CO2EMN - CO2 EMISSION FROM FOSSIL ENERGY USE

UNIT: MTCE - LONG TERM -	Actual 1990	Projection 2010	2015	2020
World	21408.84	36261.28	39108.89	43031.93
Developed Economies	9944.37	12763.17	12128.71	11074.57
Developed Asia-Pacific	1350.43	1858.01	1807.63	1663.71
Japan	1061.77	1239.43	1160.95	796.32
Australia	262.99	557.98	584.07	598.29
North America	5302.03	6547.13	6281	5523.45
Canada	428.67	622.5	646.94	632.18
United States	4873.36	5924.63	5634.06	4891.27
Western Europe	3291.91	4358.03	4040.09	3887.41
EU	3247.67	4301.79	3983.48	3838.72
France	378.31	559.15	506.52	465.11
Germany	981.43	1005.48	866.38	837.59
Italy	408.15	431.6	394.38	369.76
United Kingdom	585.28	702.01	631.08	623.35
Developing Economies	6702.12	18338.69	21018.72	24634.56
Asia-Pacific	3993.92	13140.06	15138.31	17623.88
East Asia	2893.37	9431.89	10277.9	10828.21
China	2362.04	7936.12	8588.85	8789.31
Republic of Korea	233.66	1016.79	1101.22	1288.51
Southeast Asia(ASEAN)	414.51	1722.26	2201.15	3120.25
Indonesia	155.21	564.33	722.11	1041.97
South Asia	683	1981.28	2654.63	3670.8
India	599.78	1791.65	2426.83	3387.23

Table 3B. (Continued)

CO2EMN - CO2 EMISSION FROM FOSSIL ENERGY USE				
UNIT: MTCE	Actual	Projection		
- LONG TERM -	1990	2010	2015	2020
Middle East	644.18	1713.44	1994.1	2490.25
Saudi Arabia	168.56	421.66	443.27	509.68
Africa	715.84	1044.05	1126.16	1273.78
North Africa	205.45	370.05	393.95	433.85
Sub-Saharan Africa	510.39	674	732.21	839.93
South Africa	296.08	363.7	413.9	485.8
Latin America	1124.98	1924.01	2152.67	2533.09
Argentina	97.31	232.44	301.09	411.01
Brazil	218.38	382.52	373.63	390.85
Mexico	302.41	577.41	670.63	753.23
Mediterranean	223.21	517.14	607.48	713.56
Turkey	138.38	330.11	394.15	474.52
Economies in Transition	4762.34	5159.42	5961.46	7322.8
South-Eastern Europe	312.12	408.67	475.01	559.58
CIS	3847.09	3741.6	4413.74	5732.06
Russian Federation	2336.9	2346.67	2753.81	3694.7

Source: FUGI global modeling system.

Table 4B. Oil requirement. 2011-2020

Scenario B: Global Co-operation for Green Revolution

OIL - OIL REQUIREMENT					
UNIT: MT					
	Actual	Estimate	Projection		
- LONG TERM -	2000	2005	2010	2015	2020
World	3933.92	4496.35	5302.54	5209.89	5240.00
Developed Economies	2073.02	2147.21	2186.06	1887.02	1503.12
Developed Asia-Pacific	346.9	360.23	364.7	326.97	262.25
Japan	289.05	277.95	283.61	243.68	182.59
Australia	49.58	61.54	73.04	76	72.67
North America	1031.47	1038.35	983.86	817.13	526.74
Canada	89.98	95.77	92.4	87.53	49.84
United States	941.49	942.58	891.46	729.6	476.9
Western Europe	694.66	748.63	837.5	742.92	714.13

Table 4B. (Continued)

OIL - OIL REQUIREMENT
UNIT: MT

- LONG TERM -	Actual 2000	Estimate 2005	Projection 2010	2015	2020
EU	680.71	733.92	821.49	727.28	701.47
France	116.48	124.85	133.34	120.88	107.25
Germany	155.03	159.36	167.35	146.69	143.21
Italy	91.29	88.42	89.68	63.58	35.97
United Kingdom	90.96	102.07	109.86	93.97	86.99
Developing Economies	1648.04	2065.07	2737.02	2872.49	3183.43
Asia-Pacific	820.65	1180.01	1699.24	1813.03	1976.77
East Asia	462.87	769.9	1153.09	1149.96	1111.3
China	262.57	502.22	836.12	807.85	712.72
Republic of Korea	148.59	208.67	245.6	258.53	296.08
Southeast Asia(ASEAN)	220.31	247.92	343.49	422.14	623.93
Indonesia	57.02	66.67	88.01	104.8	111.1
South Asia	134.35	158.9	198.43	235.75	234.63
India	108.42	135.19	171.09	203.62	188.07
Middle East	240.38	255.28	294.81	288.64	316.84
Saudi Arabia	84.52	72.89	78.93	72.45	85.65
Africa	128.86	148.11	172.1	173.26	186.25
North Africa	54.98	62.51	70.87	76.21	87.05
Sub-Saharan Africa	73.88	85.6	101.23	97.05	99.2
South Africa	6.14	5.4	4.32	2.23	0.92
Latin America and the Caribbean	402.9	415.18	485.26	501.62	592.68
Argentina	24.57	26.93	37.54	49.58	70.31
Brazil	110.17	100.02	107.63	107.47	120.19
Mexico	110.33	119.94	133.33	146.48	160.04
Mediterranean	55.25	66.49	85.6	95.95	110.89
Turkey	39.36	48.11	62.32	71.65	84.5
Economies in Transition	212.86	284.08	379.46	450.38	553.44
South-Eastern Europe	25.45	31.71	41.58	45.21	54.15
CIS	147.97	204.39	256.89	311.61	416.99
Russian Federation	94.54	127.55	168.59	217.25	298.91

Source: FUGI global modeling system.

Table 5B. Alternative energy. 2011-2020

Scenario B: Global Co-operation for Green Revolution

ALTEGY - ALTERNATIVE ENERGY SUPPLY(METRIC TON)

UNIT: MTOE	Actual	Estimate	Projection		
- LONG TERM -	2000	2005	2010	2015	2020
World	1104.99	1614.37	2058.5	3328.14	5410.84
Developed Economies	771.77	943.09	1065.13	1777.62	3142.36
Developed Asia-Pacific	108.5	135.21	161.64	491.93	1285.59
Japan	103.3	122.6	142.3	463.26	1249.85
Australia	1.06	5.7	10.14	16.66	22.09
North America	305.63	379.27	397.01	486.53	700.51
Canada	61.63	78.9	95.03	124.54	167.75
United States	244	300.37	301.98	361.99	532.76
Western Europe	357.65	428.62	506.47	799.16	1156.26
EU	349.8	420.63	498.29	789.87	1146.68
France	132.11	157.31	190.39	340.51	561.14
Germany	53.03	61	69.26	111.78	159.09
Italy	46.86	56.02	72.65	106.01	140.36
United Kingdom	31.7	40.37	47.22	81.03	119.36
Developing Economies	217	443.59	693.79	1047.25	1497.01
Asia-Pacific	90.26	132.16	195.1	296.05	454.14
East Asia	64.1	88.26	122.93	171.28	237.96
China	22.97	39.16	63.14	94.6	141.05
Republic of Korea	27.09	33.89	43.11	56.28	71.42
Southeast Asia(ASEAN)	13.52	16.77	20.29	27.99	39.06
Indonesia	3.49	4.99	7.38	12.81	21.23
South Asia	12.03	26.11	50.19	94.22	173.62
India	6.72	17.8	41.06	81.96	158.53
Middle East	7.03	13.4	17.75	23.72	28.35
Saudi Arabia	2.48	3.7	4.37	6.36	7.43
Africa	19.52	58.39	94.89	130.71	162.22
North Africa	0.93	5.42	8.81	12.82	15.62
Sub-Saharan Africa	18.59	52.98	86.08	117.88	146.6
South Africa	4.78	23.49	43.48	62.39	79.4
Latin America and the Caribbean	90.43	223.43	362.93	563.58	810.56
Argentina	4.67	9.91	20.92	37.46	60.25
Brazil	50.11	157.69	249.01	372.21	499.31

Table 5B. (Continued)

ALTEGY - ALTERNATIVE ENERGY SUPPLY(METRIC TON)				
UNIT: MTOE - LONG TERM -	Actual 2000	Estimate 2005	Projection 2010	2015	2020
Mexico	12.36	15.3	19.7	27.14	31.6
Mediterranean	9.76	16.21	23.12	33.19	41.75
Turkey	5.98	10.38	15.35	23.11	29.76
Economies in Transition	116.22	227.69	299.58	503.28	771.48
South-Eastern Europe	10.91	16.53	23.03	29.46	37.64
CIS	94.84	198.54	256.8	447.36	702.43
Russian Federation	44.94	124.34	154.21	307.88	528.91

Source: FUGI global modeling system.

Chapter 6

POLICY EXERCISE AND
SIMULATIONS OF FUTURES

The 21st century is an age of humankind challenge for *global syndrome* that is not so easily resolved in a single country framework. It is worth noting that the 21st century is also an age of *integrated technology innovations* in the fields of information technology, biotechnology, new energy as solar and superconductor , nanotechnology, robotics, new materials, space-technology and etc. On the other hand, it is expected that this century might be an age of *terrorism and refugees* if future human society would not awaken by cosmic mind to create a new international order toward global citizenship and human solidarity on the planet Earth.

It is widely known among economists that the word of *"innovation"* has been brought by J. Schumpeter (1983-1950), author of *Capitalism, Socialism and Democracy* in economics. His idea has been derived from Dwain's findings in Bioscience. This is a good example that the science of economics has been affected by the progress of science and technology in other related fields.

It is clear now that main roots of terrorism and refugees seem likely to be poverty and international per capita income disparity (See *global early warning system for displaced persons* (Onishi 1986, 1987, 1990) and *FUGI global model for early warning of forced migration* (http://www.forcedmigration.org) Forced Migration Online, Refugee Studies Centre, University of Oxford. It is worth noting that global risks on peace and security such as terrorism might not be resolved by mere oppression by military forces. The more oppression by military powers increase, the more terrorist powers against oppression might increase. This might induce a vicious circle of poverty and refugees as well as battles against terrorism without outlets.

According to FUGI global model simulation, *international per capita income disparity* (IPCID) will be increasing in the coming decades, although the position of both China and India will be improved very rapidly in Asia. Major poor hardcore in Africa, however, will remain at almost standstill states. In terms of IPCID indicators (average per capita income of whole world = 100 expressed by 1995 constant prices in terms of US dollars), Japan enjoyed as No. 3 position next to Luxembourg and Switzerland in 1995. But the reader should not misunderstand that Japan is a paradise country. During the period, 2001-2006, so called "*black age*" for the Japanese economy, average nominal wage rate per worker was decreased while nominal GDP was registered minus growth, although real GDP growth rates were maintained hardly plus because of decreasing GDP deflator. As a result, Japan's per capita income in terms of *current US dollars* was strikingly dropped from No.2 in 1993 to 18th in 2006. Such situation is improved to a large extent in 2009 on account of Yen appreciation against the US dollar as 1995 Yen equivalent to one US dollar.

It is worth noting that Japan is not paradise for immigrants because of very poor capacity to absorb refugees, although the population growth rates are decreasing. The official unemployment rate statistics of 4.4% (in 2005), 4.9% (in 2008) and 5.7% (in 2009) do not include unemployed youngsters called as *NEET* (Not in Employment, Education or Training) and unemployment of increasing irregular workers. If Japanese unemployment figures would be recalculated based on German standard, they will nearly correspond to French and German unemployment rates.

The Japanese economic situation was worst for the period, 2008-9, because of "Global economic crisis". As a result, tax revenues of the government have drastically decreased on account of slowing down of GDP (real/nominal) growth rate as the FUGI global model policy simulations show. As a result, government deficits could not be improved. This is a good example of *pessimistic scenario.* Therefore, The Japanese should recognize the needs for changes in policies for revitalization of the Japanese economy for coping with global risks in the globalizing world. There is a hope for Japan to escape from "Japan syndrome" if *appropriate* policies would be introduced in the coming near futures. It is worth noting that the Japanese should have potential capacities and talents for not only technology innovations but also progress in human minds toward "*Cosmic age*" beyond "*Global age*" in the coming centuries.

Table 6. IPCID – International Per-Capita Income Disparities

AVERAGE PER CAPITA INCOME OF WHOLE WRD = 100   Unit: 1995 constant prices in terms of US dollars

	1990	1995	2000	2005	2010	2015	2020
World	100	100	100	100	100	100	100
Developed Economies	508.9	522.5	539.8	550.1	561.5	563.9	569.5
Developed Asia-Pacific	670.6	690.4	661.2	669.2	669.8	660.3	672.9
Japan	720.8	741.5	706.1	710.8	710.6	694.3	705.6
North America	499.5	514.1	552.6	572	602.7	622	645.8
Canada	393.3	387.9	404	419.2	450.6	473.3	490.1
United States	511.2	528.1	569.1	588.7	619.1	637.7	662.1
Western Europe	454.3	464.6	482.8	486.5	486.1	478.9	466.8
EU15	443.8	454.5	473.4	477.3	476.7	469.3	457.6
France	526.2	530.1	559.4	560.3	557.4	537.9	529.3
Germany	580	589.4	596.7	578.8	570.7	547.8	533.1
Italy	370.4	380.1	378.9	377.2	368.8	356.1	334.5
United Kingdom	370.1	380.4	397.8	415.3	413.9	423.9	416.5
Developing Economies	23.8	27	28.1	30.2	32.2	35.3	38
Asia-Pacific	14.5	18.9	21	24.7	28.3	32.8	37.4
East Asia	17.8	24.9	29.7	37	43.5	51.4	60.2
China: Mainland	7	11.5	15.2	21.5	27.3	34.7	43.5
Southeast Asia(ASEAN)	24.7	31.4	31.2	33.5	37.2	40.7	43
Indonesia	15.6	20.5	18	19.5	21.5	24	25.6
Malaysia	66.2	87	88.7	94.6	104.8	115.5	123.5
Philippines	22.5	21.7	21.3	22.7	23.8	25.1	26
Singapore	367.6	504.4	587.1	609	698.7	760.6	830.3
Thailand	41.2	57.5	51.8	57.5	67.4	78	87.7
South Asia	6.8	7.7	8.4	9.6	11.1	13	15.4
India	6.8	7.8	8.7	10.3	12.3	15	18.3
Middle East	66.9	62.1	57.9	57	58.2	56.1	53.9
Africa	15.5	14.3	13.9	13.4	12.3	11.4	10
North Africa	27.7	26.7	27.1	27	24.8	23.3	20.9
Sub-Saharan Africa	12.6	11.5	10.9	10.4	9.6	9	7.9
Latin America and the Caribbean	71.6	76.4	74.9	72.1	70	75	77.2
Brazil	83.7	88.5	84.9	80.9	79	78.4	83.1
Mediterranean	82.5	80.4	83.2	86.4	86.6	90.1	88.3
Economies in Transition	58.2	39.6	38.7	46.4	52.6	57.9	61.1
Eastern Europe	60.9	58.1	63.1	70.5	77.1	81.3	81.6
CIS	57.2	33	30	38	44.1	49.8	54.2
Russian Federation	75.3	45.7	40.2	51.1	60.1	68.3	76.6

Table 6. Continued

AVERAGE PER CAPITA INCOME OF WHOLE WRD = 100   Unit: 1995 constant prices in terms of US dollars

	1990	1995	2000	2005	2010	2015	2020
1 Japan	720.8	741.5	706.1	710.8	710.6	694.3	705.6
2 Australia	373.9	407.5	429.6	467	479.3	515	544
3 New Zealand	315.4	327.5	315	328.4	328.8	331.3	324.9
4 Canada	393.3	387.9	404	419.2	450.6	473.3	490.1
5 United States	511.2	528.1	569.1	588.7	619	637.7	662
6 Belgium	529.4	543.5	567.2	565.4	571.8	561.9	519.5
7 Denmark	639.3	693.8	722.6	742.3	751.5	707.4	697
8 France	526.2	530.1	559.4	560.3	557.4	537.9	529.3
9 Germany	580	589.4	596.7	578.8	570.7	547.8	533.1
10 Greece	219.1	221.6	236.8	268	257.5	258.4	253.3
11 Ireland	285.7	364.3	523.8	639.2	773	893.3	1071.9
12 Italy	370.4	380.1	378.9	377.2	368.8	356.1	334.5
13 Luxembourg	727.7	866.5	986.6	1050.2	1098.1	1117.5	1092.3
14 Netherlands	492.9	516.3	553.3	531.6	546.9	538.5	501.9
15 Portugal	199.6	212.8	230.7	226.3	220.2	227.6	231.4
16 Spain	273.5	283.4	309	330	339.6	350.9	343.2
17 United Kingdom	370.1	380.4	397.8	415.3	413.9	423.9	416.5
18 Austria	561.1	578.4	580.2	587.2	591.1	597.3	588.3
19 Finland	532.8	493.9	563.9	609.2	612.7	595.8	558.1
20 Iceland	544.2	521	572.9	575	615.8	611.1	597.3
21 Norway	592	675.3	693.8	709.4	753	742.7	711.2
22 Sweden	541.9	526.6	559.7	576.4	562.4	548.7	537.9
23 Switzerland	926.4	862.2	834.9	817.7	795.9	799	779.8
24 China: Mainland	7	11.5	15.2	21.5	27.3	34.7	43.5
25 China: Hong Kong	386.2	448.2	454.9	485.9	482.1	479.3	442.8
26 China: Macau	303.5	343.4	285.8	279.5	259.5	257.3	232.6
27 Taiwan(Province of china)	189.8	244.1	274.3	282	313.1	332.9	338
28 Korea: Republic of	163.6	218.1	237.7	270.6	287.1	304.8	319.5
29 Korea: North	40.3	36.1	31	29.9	28	27.4	26.4
30 Brunei	384.2	355.2	337.3	321	284.4	249.9	199.8
31 Indonesia	15.6	20.5	18	19.5	21.5	24	25.6
32 Malaysia	66.2	87	88.7	94.6	104.8	115.5	123.5
33 Philippines	22.5	21.7	21.3	22.7	23.8	25.1	26
34 Singapore	367.6	504.4	587.1	609	698.7	760.6	830.3
35 Thailand	41.2	57.5	51.8	57.5	67.4	78	87.7
36 Cambodia	5.2	5.9	5.8	6	5.8	5.6	5

Table 6. Continued

AVERAGE PER CAPITA INCOME OF WHOLE WRD = 100 Unit: 1995 constant prices in terms of US dollars

	1990	1995	2000	2005	2010	2015	2020
37 Lao P. D. Rep	6.4	7.4	8	8.8	8.1	7.6	6.8
38 Myanmar (Burma)	40.6	49.8	59.6	65.2	71.1	76.5	76.6
39 Viet Nam	4.2	5.5	6.5	7.9	9.3	10.4	10.6
40 Afghanistan	0.4	0.3	0.2	0.2	0.2	0.2	0.2
41 Bangladesh	5.7	6.4	6.9	7.8	8.8	10.4	12.2
42 Bhutan	2.8	3.3	3.5	3.8	3.4	3.2	2.8
43 India	6.8	7.8	8.7	10.3	12.3	15	18.3
44 Mongolia	10.2	7.8	7.6	8.2	9.1	10.1	10.5
45 Nepal	3.7	4.1	4.2	4.3	4.2	4.3	4.2
46 Pakistan	8.3	9	8.5	8.2	7.6	7.4	6.8
47 Sri Lanka	12.1	14.6	16.2	16.9	17.5	18.8	19.5
48 Fiji	49	51	44.7	42.5	40.7	40.5	38.7
49 French Polynesia	351.3	358.4	350.1	356.1	343.6	336.1	313.5
50 Guam	49.1	49.5	48.4	48.1	45.8	45.5	43.5
51 Kiribati: Rep. of	11.4	11.5	11.1	10.2	9	8.2	7.2
52 Maldives	18.6	21.8	24.1	26	26	27.2	26.7
53 Nauru	49	49.9	46.6	46.3	43.3	41.3	37.5
54 New Caledonia	383.8	373.2	353.1	331	283.6	296.2	287.4
55 Papua New Guinea	18.2	23	19.6	17.3	16.3	15.7	14.5
56 Solomon Islands	16.1	17.3	11.2	9.1	8.1	7.5	6.8
57 Tonga	29.4	34.5	28.4	28.6	30	32.1	32.7
58 Tuvalu	49	49.9	47.2	45.7	41.9	39.5	35.7
59 Western Samoa	19.1	18.5	18.7	21.8	25.3	33.3	42.3
60 Vanuatu	32.3	28.1	26.7	24.4	21.9	20.3	18.1
61 Bahrain	180.2	197.1	195.5	216	225.1	240.4	246.1
62 Iran: I.R. of	20.9	23	23.3	26.2	28.4	31	32.8
63 Iraq	106.3	49.7	45.2	34.8	31.5	28.4	25.7
64 Israel	278.5	312.7	306.7	279.4	263.6	254.4	234.7
65 Jordan	20.2	22.7	20.1	19.4	17	18	20.5
66 Kuwait	213.7	314.9	261.1	238	210.6	181.6	141.3
67 Lebanon	50.3	74	70.9	74.4	76.5	79.2	77.5
68 Oman	104.5	112.5	97.7	85.1	79	78.7	71.9
69 Qatar	311.3	297.5	329.7	377.1	359.7	336.5	311.9
70 Saudi Arabia	143.6	140.3	119.7	119.4	130	120	116.7
71 Syrian Arab Rep	19.2	23.3	20.4	19.9	18.2	17.2	15.5
72 United Arab Emirates	413.7	388.1	382.6	441.7	520.3	528	533.9

Table 6. Continued

AVERAGE PER CAPITA INCOME OF WHOLE WRD = 100   Unit: 1995 constant prices in
terms of US dollars

	1990	1995	2000	2005	2010	2015	2020
73 Yemen Rep	5.6	4.9	5	4.6	4	3.5	2.9
74 Algeria	33.7	29.5	28.1	28	24.2	21.6	18.5
75 Egypt	18.6	19.4	21.1	21	19.8	19.1	17.4
76 Libya	95.8	85.8	74.1	64.5	52.9	44.5	35.5
77 Morocco	27	25.5	25.2	26.3	24.6	23.5	21.2
78 Tunisia	37.4	40.3	45.3	46.7	45.8	45.9	43.5
79 Angola	13.7	9.2	9.6	10.5	9.6	9	8.2
80 Benin	7.2	7.5	7.9	7.7	7.4	6.7	5.4
81 Botswana	64.1	66.6	70.8	77.4	83	80.9	68.7
82 Burkina Faso	4.5	4.5	4.6	4.5	4.1	3.8	3.4
83 Burundi	4.2	3.3	3	3.2	3.2	3.2	2.8
84 Cameroon	15.7	12.1	12.2	11.4	9.6	8.3	6.9
85 Cape Verde	23	25.9	26.8	28.2	28.6	29.7	29.6
86 Central African Rep.	7.5	6.8	6.2	5.6	4.9	4.3	3.7
87 Chad	4.7	4.3	4.3	3.9	3.4	3.1	2.6
88 Comoros	8.7	7.1	5.9	5.4	4.8	4.4	4
89 Congo	19.1	16.6	14.3	12.4	10.6	9.8	8.7
90 Djibouti	21.6	16.4	13.9	12.3	10.6	10.2	9.1
91 Eritrea	3.6	3.6	3.6	3.4	2.9	2.6	2.2
92 Equatorial Guinea	6.9	8.2	20	19.9	19.2	14.9	13.2
93 Ethiopia	2.2	2.1	2.2	2.2	2	1.9	1.6
94 Gabon	93.7	92.2	84.8	77.1	67.8	61.5	53.7
95 Gambia	7.7	6.9	6.4	5.9	5.2	4.8	4.2
96 Ghana	7.1	7.3	7.2	7	6.8	6.1	5.2
97 Guinea	10.9	10.3	11.2	12.5	13.4	14.3	14.7
98 Guinea Bissau	4.6	4.7	3.1	2.8	2.3	2	1.7
99 Ivory Coast	16.2	14.8	14.6	14.1	12.4	11.1	9.4
100 Kenya	7.3	6.7	6	5.3	4.6	4	3.5
101 Lesotho	7.6	8.9	9.9	10.4	9.9	9.5	8.5
102 Liberia	9.1	12	8.5	7.5	6.4	5.4	4.2
103 Madagascar	5.7	4.6	4.2	3.6	3	2.7	2.3
104 Malawi	2.9	3.1	3.1	2.9	2.6	2.3	2
105 Mali	4.9	5	4.9	4.5	3.8	3.4	2.8
106 Mauritania	9	9.2	8.9	8.1	7	6	4.9
107 Mauritius	60.7	71.5	81.5	85.1	85.3	92.7	91.4
108 Mozambique	2.9	2.8	3.3	3.3	3	2.7	2.2
109 Namibia	40	43.3	39	35.2	30.6	27.5	23.6

Table 6. Continued

AVERAGE PER CAPITA INCOME OF WHOLE WRD = 100 Unit: 1995 constant prices in terms of US dollars

	1990	1995	2000	2005	2010	2015	2020
110 Niger	4.8	4.1	4.3	4.6	4.3	4.2	4.2
111 Nigeria	5.9	5.7	5.3	5.3	5.2	5.1	4.9
112 Reunion	221	252.6	260.8	263.1	255.6	258	250.3
113 Rwanda	6	4.9	5.2	5.2	4.4	3.8	3.1
114 St. Helena	6	3.1	2.8	2.7	2.5	2.5	2.4
115 Sao Tome & Principe	7.5	6.9	5.2	4.5	3.8	3.3	2.8
116 Senegal	11.7	10.8	10.7	9.7	8.3	7.2	6
117 Seychelles	129.3	135.2	126.5	115.4	99.3	87.2	72.7
118 Sierra Leone	5.7	4.1	3.1	2.9	2.6	2.5	2.2
119 Somalia	0.9	0.9	0.8	0.7	0.7	0.6	0.6
120 South Africa	87.4	80.8	78.1	80.6	79.9	78.9	72.3
121 Sudan	4.1	5.4	5.7	5.3	4.7	4.2	3.7
122 Swaziland	30.4	29.1	28	27.6	25.8	24.2	19.7
123 Tanzania	3.6	3.3	3.3	3.1	2.7	2.4	2.1
124 Togo	7.7	6.5	6.2	5.7	5	4.5	3.9
125 Uganda	5.1	6.1	6.5	5.7	5.5	5.3	4.8
126 Zaire	5.1	2.8	2.4	1.8	1.7	1.6	1.6
127 Zambia	9.9	8.5	8	7.4	6.6	6	5
128 Zimbabwe	14.3	13.1	12.2	9	7.9	7.2	6.2
129 Argentina	118.7	148.8	145.5	139.3	152.9	179.8	209.2
130 Antigua and Barbuda	143.3	151.9	155.3	155.9	145.8	148	129
131 Bahamas The	286.5	247.2	232.9	228	203.5	198.2	174.3
132 Barbados	151.2	140.5	147.1	142.4	130.9	123.9	111.3
133 Belize	52.7	55.6	55.7	59.2	59.5	61.7	60.8
134 Bermuda	660.7	659.4	617.8	581.6	526.4	488.1	432.5
135 Bolivia	17.2	18.1	17.5	16.8	17.5	18.9	19.9
136 Brazil	83.7	88.5	84.9	80.9	79	78.4	83.1
137 Chile	61.3	83.7	88.4	97	109.9	126.7	137.3
138 Colombia	43.5	48.1	41.7	41.7	40.9	41.3	39.8
139 Costa Rica	48.4	50.8	50.8	52.6	51.4	51.3	48.5
140 Cuba	48.6	53.2	48.9	49.3	46.9	45.7	42.4
141 Dominica	58.8	61.1	64.3	59.2	51.1	47.7	41.5
142 Dominican Republic	28	30.6	37.6	36.3	38.3	38.9	27.4
143 Ecuador	30.3	31.4	26.2	27.8	25.9	25.1	23.3
144 El Salvador	28.3	33.6	32.4	30.6	30	30.8	30.4
145 Greenland	412.9	434.2	419.4	436.6	424.2	418.5	390.2
146 Grenada	59.5	58.2	68.6	70.7	67.8	66.6	62.2

Table 6. Continued

AVERAGE PER CAPITA INCOME OF WHOLE WRD = 100 Unit: 1995 constant prices in terms of US dollars

	1990	1995	2000	2005	2010	2015	2020
147 Guadeloupe	195.8	173.7	160.3	161.1	153.8	151.9	141.8
148 Guatemala	27.9	29.4	28.7	26.2	24.8	25.1	25.3
149 Guiana: French	117.1	91.4	84.4	76.3	67.6	59.2	47.5
150 Guyana	11.4	15	17.3	19.4	22	24.9	25.4
151 Haiti	9.3	7	6.5	6.1	5.5	5	4.4
152 Honduras	14	14	13.1	12.8	11	10.6	9.4
153 Jamaica	34.4	33.9	29.3	27	24.9	23.9	22.4
154 Martinique	280.3	301.6	310.2	315	299.8	290.7	267.2
155 Mexico	83.1	79.9	87.6	83.1	69.3	82.8	80.8
156 Montserrat	28.4	30.9	31.3	31.2	29.1	27.8	25.3
157 Netherlands Antilles	141.6	138.9	132.4	129.5	120.3	115.4	105.6
158 Nicaragua	9.4	8.6	8.7	8.3	7.7	7.4	6.8
159 Panama	51.8	60.2	62.5	64.9	64.7	64.7	59.9
160 Paraguay	37.3	37.3	31.1	28.2	25.6	24	21.4
161 Peru	41.3	50.2	48.2	50.3	56.8	66.1	72.9
162 Puerto Rico	213.3	228.5	238.1	261.9	266.6	277.5	257.5
163 St. Kitts Nevis	91.9	113.6	133.2	133.6	123.4	123.6	112.7
164 St. Lucia	65.4	72	76.4	85.3	88.5	91.5	86.7
165 St. Pierre Miquelon	28.4	30.9	34.1	31.5	27.8	26.1	23.4
166 St. Vincent	44.5	47.6	52.5	51.1	44.9	44.9	43.6
167 Suriname	16.2	16.4	16.5	22	26.8	30.9	32
168 Trinidad and Tobago	84.1	84.5	92.5	102.9	109.1	119.6	123.6
169 Uruguay	94.7	106.8	104.4	107.5	102.6	111.6	109
170 Venezuela	68.8	70.9	60	55.7	60.6	59.9	59.1
171 Cyprus	213.7	237.7	242.4	242.3	229.2	232.7	219.1
172 Malta	144.1	173.4	172.9	193.9	208	230.3	244.4
173 Turkey	53.2	55.6	56.9	58.6	58.4	59.7	58.1
174 Bosnia and Herzegovina	97.5	81.6	94.5	97.9	94.5	92.6	85.3
175 Croatia	118	83.9	92.3	107.1	116.1	121.6	122.8
176 Slovenia	206.6	188.7	201.7	224.3	235.8	254.5	263.9
177 TFYR Macedonia	27.2	25.8	26.4	26.5	26.5	27.9	27.7
178 Serbia/Montenegro	198.3	198.1	213.8	229.4	241.1	270.1	278.1
179 Albania	17.3	15.3	18	21.7	22.6	21.9	19.4
180 Bulgaria	35.2	30.9	27.3	32.6	35.9	37.3	37.9
181 Czech Republic	108.8	101	97.8	108.5	113.8	117.8	114.1
182 Hungary	99.7	87.5	100.1	113.5	124.6	139.7	157.4

Table 6. Continued

AVERAGE PER CAPITA INCOME OF WHOLE WRD = 100 Unit: 1995 constant prices in terms of US dollars

	1990	1995	2000	2005	2010	2015	2020
183 Poland	59.5	65.5	76.8	82.7	90	92.8	91.2
184 Romania	32.4	28.9	24.4	29.2	32.2	34.4	35.5
185 Slovakia	78.9	65.1	73.1	83.7	97.9	105.4	106.9
186 Armenia	31.6	16.2	19.3	25.7	23.8	23	21.5
187 Azerbaijan	21.9	7.7	9.6	14.3	18.7	21.6	21.6
188 Belarus	56.7	35.3	44	54.5	71.7	96.3	111.8
189 Estonia	92.1	64.6	79.7	92.7	95.2	107.5	113.8
190 Georgia	43.4	11.6	14.7	19.1	22.5	27.3	31.7
191 Kazakhstan	41.6	24.2	25	34.4	43	50.2	55.9
192 Kyrgyzstan	32.1	14.6	16.9	18.5	19.1	19.5	18.9
193 Latvia	75.6	38.7	47.2	63.4	75.8	83.4	87.4
194 Lithuania	65.2	37	40.5	53.2	60.1	59.6	50.7
195 Republic of Moldova	36.4	14.2	10.7	13.1	11	10.9	9.8
196 Russian Federation	75.3	45.7	40.2	51.1	60.1	68.3	76.6
197 Tajikistan	14.7	6.9	7	9.2	10.3	10.4	10.3
198 Turkmenistan	23.7	13	13	21.5	24.8	28.6	32
199 Ukraine	40.6	19.1	16.1	23.3	27.6	31.5	33.3
200 Uzbekistan	27.5	19.8	19.6	19.2	17.9	17.2	15.8

Source: FUGI global modeling system.

The 21st century is an age of humankind challenge for *global* c*risis* that is not so easily resolved in a single country framework. This is why we have to collaborate in the globalizing world. As a Japanese proverb says "Wazawai tennjite fukutonasu" (Disasters may turn into fortunes). The same is true in the case of current "global economic crisis" as shown by policy simulations using FUGI global modeling system.

1. Impacts of Oil Saving Technology on Oil Prices in the Futures

The uncertain "fluctuations" of global oil prices will provide an opportunity to develop alternative energy sources and energy saving technology in order to open the doors to use renewable energy and curve CO_2 emissions against global warming. For instance, the Japanese economy has become much stronger against oil shocks after the oil crisis in 1970s because we have made greater efforts for creating alterative energies such as solar, super conductor and safety use of nuclear power plants, etc as well as energy saving technologies such as LED, robotics, super express train using super conductor and innovative electric vehicles (EV) etc. By the midst of the 21st century, it is reasonably expected that electric vehicles, including hybrid cars, will replace the present internal combustion engine vehicles. As a result, uncertain *"fluctuations"* of oil prices induced by money games as well as geographical risks will be mitigated as FUGI global model simulation shows.

2. Impacts of New Technology Investment Supported by R&D on the World Economy

In order to increase *GDP growth potentials* the developed countries should increase research and development expenditures (R&D) to induce technology innovations for the long run. In 2005, Sweden takes lead to attain the highest R&D ratios to GDP, around 4.0%. Then Finland, Japan, the US, Germany and France follow as 3.5%, 3.2%, 2.6 %, 2.5% and 2.2% respectively. *FUGI global model simulation suggests that diffusion of technology innovations at the global level through increased R&D and technology transfer from the developed to developing countries should be much more stressed in the globalizing world as most effective means against a new "global economic crisis".*

3. Appropriate Trade Policy against a New Global Economic Crisis

According to *"Global Interdependence Table"* originally designed by Onishi, *appropriate trade expansion policy by* mitigating tariff and non-tariff barriers will be needed to cope with global economic crisis It is worth noting that one of the major reasons of Chinese success story in economic development should depend upon higher increasing rates of exports on account of higher competitiveness with lower employment costs and stability of exchange rates. Without trade expansion on account of joining GATT, China could not become "a factory in the world" and take over the position of the Japanese economy in the globalizing world. Increasing global disequilibrium issues have appeared as a result of China success story. China continues to accumulate a huge amount of trade surplus and foreign exchange reserves, while the US trade deficit with China continues. In the coming near future, China should face the policy dilemma whether mitigating tariff and non-tariff barriers to increase imports, together with introducing more flexible foreign exchange rates against the US dollars. Because trade imbalances between the US and China will be very rapidly expanding, rather than those of the US and Japan trade relationships as well as those of EU. *FUGI global model simulation reveals that the US should face serious policy dilemma to solve the twin deficits both trade and fiscal budget, if the US alone would fight against "Global financial/economic crisis".*

4. Expansion of Private Foreign Direct Investment Coupled with ODA

Expansion of private foreign direct investment coupled with ODA; in particular, appropriate technical co-operation should be increased in coping with poverty at the global level. FUGI global model simulation shows that the international per-capita income disparity will increase rather than decrease. This is one of the major causes of international instability for peace and security in this planet. Without sharp inflows of private foreign direct investment, China could not rapidly catch up advanced technology for exports so that China might narrow the international per-capita income disparities. As FUGI global model simulation suggests, expansion of both trade and private foreign direct investment will play a greater role of recovering economic growth rates of the world economy. China represents a success story of high economic performance and India will follow the Chinese pattern of economic growth if peace and security will be maintained. It is hoped that in Africa as well as Latin America, anti-feeling sentiments of nightmares against private foreign direct investment in the colonial age will be gradually turned into friendlier host country sentiments in the interdependent global economy.

5. Needs for Shortening Regular Labor Hours and Days to Improve Unemployment and Quality of Life

FUGI global model simulation suggests that a global mass unemployment issues may not be solved by defunct "Keynesian economics". Although J.M.Keynes (1833-1946) thought that unemployment rate is a function of "*Effective Demand*" in "General Theory of Employment, Interest and Money" (1935-1936), employment costs also seem likely to play a greater role in Post Keynesian age. Unemployment rate also tends to increase in line with higher employment cost and increased supply of labor force, LCLF (adjusted by hours of work in case of EU, Japan and USA). Keynes introduced a positive fiscal and monetary policy to induce *"Effective Demand"* in coping with "Great Depression". However, his idea was too short sighted to discuss the unemployment issues. He could not imagine that the globalizing world might face a dilemma how to sustain *"affluent"* society with energy and resources constraints within the planet Earth. He could not imagine that the future human society should adopt *"recycling system"* in order to save energy and resources for sustainable development of the global economy differed from Keynes proposal for any wastage of resources to induce employment. In the post Keynesian age, *lower employment cost and shortening regular labor hours as well as days will improve unemployment and quality of life (QOL). As FUGI global model simulation suggests that diffusion of technology innovations at the global level through increased R&D and technology transfer from the developed to developing countries should be much more stressed in the globalizing world as most effective means against "global unemployment issues improving QOL". Robotics to be appeared by technology innovations will play much greater role in place of labor force in the futures. It is expected that Japan will take a lead in robotics, because robotics has been already invented during Edo era. Foreigners might be surprised to notice the Japanese innovative idea on creating robotics.*

6. Role of Education and Healthcare

FUGI global model simulation confirms that the role of *education and healthcare* should be more emphasized for improving labor productivity in the poor countries as Swedish economist, G. Myrdal once suggested in the light of his experience in India. There is a hope that not only India but also the rest of developing countries should improve education and healthcare situation by self reliance efforts and global collaboration. *It is worth noting that the highly educated people may have higher probability to become the rich people of the society in the globalizing world. Unfortunately, the non educated poor people may have little opportunity to enter the rich strata in the globalizing world. This is why globalization might induce disparity between the rich and the poor not only at country level but also global level.*

However, the main objective of higher education in the future generations should not enlarge income disparities between the rich and the poor in the interdependent globalizing world but share common consciousness of cosmic mind toward solidarity of human beings irrespective of differences in culture, religion and race co-existing with ever changing nature on the planet Earth. It is hoped that such cosmic mind will eventually strengthen global citizenship.

In the globalizing highly technology oriented society, it is reasonably expected that obsolesce of knowledge will be going on rapidly so that people might learn in total life time span. In accordance with speed up of technology innovation, objective of higher education might be dwelt upon cultivating specific talent to induce "creativity". This is why the author emphasizes the need for advancement of human spirit in line with technological progress.

7. Needs for Cosmic Mind

It is worth noting that FUGI global modeling system is designed by "*cosmic mind*". "*Cosmic mind*" means human solidarity to create common cosmic conciseness living on the planet Earth in the ever changing infinite dynamic cosmos by overcoming predilections on differences among races, cultures and religions. *Cosmic mind for peace and security with harmonization with nature at the planet level might be needed for coping with global warming and risks of terrorism. Harmonized progress of human spirit with technology should be needed at this planet Earth.*

Chapter 7

CONCLUSION

The FUGI global modeling system (FGMS200) has been developed as a scientific tool of policy simulations for providing global information to the human society and finding out possibilities of policy coordination among countries in order to achieve sustainable development of the world economy in coping with global warming. The development of both hardware and software systems of high-technology computer has supported FUGI global modeling and policy simulations. The FUGI global modeling system represents a new frontier in economic science stimulated by information technology and life science.

It is worth noting that mutual understanding can be expected to increase through global information exchanges, in particular, on global warming phenomenon and we can seriously talk about possibilities for *increasing international cooperation and policy coordination.*

In the futures of interdependent global economy, policy simulations using global modeling system should be needed to evaluate impacts of policy exercises. Nobody could estimate the possible impacts of policy mixtures. The globalizing world will be getting more and more complex system structure so that human brain might have a limit of reasoning about possible cause and effect relationships at a glance. Therefore, we have to largely depend upon advanced computer simulation technology. For instance, various policy scenario simulations should be tested in order to evaluate *"synergy effects of appropriate policy mixtures".*

We need a navigation map to travel unknown globalizing world. This is particularly true to envisage development policy in the globalizing world. For instance, in the globalizing world, the *"appropriate"* trade policy might be desirable. In the textbook of trade policy, there are two extreme disciplines, namely *free trade* vis à vis *protectionism.* It is widely known that Classical economist; David Ricardo advocated "free trade" against *"protectionism"* in his book *"On the Principles of Political Economy and Taxation* "(1810). His original idea is that every country around world can enjoy "comparative advantage" through international trade and division of labor, even if it is inefficient to produce all products. His idea has been inherited in modern economics and reformed as Heckscher-Olin theorem.

However Neo-Classical "free trade" policy might be modified in the light of reality of globalizing world. Globalizing world economy consists of multi-dimensional countries/regions where there are different stages of development and resources are not equally distributed. Every country all over the world cannot alive on self-sufficiency. It is clear that every country need international trade and division of labor that might support "free trade".

Since globalizing world market, however, will induce severe survival games on competition on not only prices but non-prices such as quality, design, safety, recycling, energy savings and ecology etc among players, it provides big business chance for new comers with talent. In order to survive in the globalizing world economy, every country around the world might make greater efforts for *"export diversification"* and *"import substitution"* trade policy that might provide opportunities for increase real GDP growth rates. Such kind of policy might be particularly recommended to newly industrializing developing countries. It is worth noting that traditional "free trade" theorem based on "comparative advantage" could not be applicable to the all over the countries. *Everything around the world is apt to change forever and interrelated* so that a concept of "comparative advantage" might not be considered as a given permanent interrelationship in the globalizing world.

For example, immediate after the Pacific War, everyone could not believe that Toyota would be able to overcome GM, since Toyota was far behind GM in all aspect such as technology and sales management power. Same thing is true in the case of Japanese origin global enterprises such as Honda, Sony, Panasonic, Canon, Nikon, Mitsubishi heavy industry, Hitachi, Toshiba, Sharp, Nintendo and many others that have created brand image of "made in Japan". Today Japan brand takes a lead in many *technology innovation* fields such as information technology, biotechnology, energy savings, more safety nuclear plant, solar and superconductor, nanotechnology, robotics, new materials, space-technology and etc. Nowadays, such defunct "myth" of "comparative disadvantage" of enfant Japanese industry has turned into "comparative advantage" in the globalizing world. This is a lesson of Japanese experience for the late coming developing countries.

On the other hand, globalizing world, "disparity phenomena" will simultaneously proceed. Not only increasing IPCID and appearing "the richest strata" but also "working poor" is increasing important social issue. For instance, Japanese economy suffered from stagnant domestic demand for the period, 2001-2010. This means that domestic demand oriented enterprises face severe cutthroat survival games. Big global enterprises like Toyota could survive by making large profits from exports to the global market. Even smaller enterprises having specific skills and advanced technology such as "animated cartoon" have also fortunes to expand exports in the globalizing world, in spite that most of small and medium-scale businesses have faced increasing risks of bankruptcy. Labor share as well as wage cost is continuously decreasing and working poor has become usual phenomenon.

In the case of agriculture, situation is different from manufacturing sector. Japan depends upon imports to the large extent, although self sufficiency of rice is maintained by subsidy policy. For foods security and environment protection reasons, agriculture and forest industry will play a much important role in the futures, apart far from "comparative advantage" reformed by Heckscher-Olin theorem. It is of interest that there is a recent success story of Japanese agriculture to cultivate most expensive exportable products such as brand beef, fruits even rice and etc... Thanks to original idea and utmost efforts, the Japanese farmers have succeeded to produce delicious organic agricultural products, irrespective of the myth as "comparative disadvantage". Although Japan is foods importing country, it has increasing power for diversified exports of specific agricultural products in the globalizing world market.

Therefore it is worth noting that the *"appropriate"* trade policy might be desirable. In this sense some *"appropriate"* policy measures might be acknowledged, although "endless" diversification of "new" exportable goods and substitution of import goods by introducing new substitute goods. Such kind of *"appropriate"* trade policy should vitalize the globalizing dynamic world economy in the futures.

However, it is worth noting that "Global financial/economic crisis" in 2009, originated from the US subprime loan issues, has shown as a typical global syndrome where every country around the world might be involved in the globalizing world.

Metaphorically speaking, in the globalizing world, the world's around 200 countries including the UN and non-UN members can be thought of as *"cells"* which, when separate and isolated should only act in a disconnected way, each in its own fashion. But when given information concerning the global human society, the possibility arises that each country can take in information on what it ought to best to do, with the result that through a sort of feedback system the global economy will operate more smoothly. This is one of the hints given by the recent development of life science.

The transmission of information is an important aspect of life functions, absolutely essential for the existence and continuation of life. Humans furthermore have a capacity by which some information is consciously perceived as signals from outside as a result of which new and useful information can then be generated from inside "*human genome*" information, taking on, in other words, takes on a *self-organizing capacity*. There are vital characteristics of the life phenomenon.

The FUGI global modeling methodology has also received a large impact from of *brain physiology*. The human brain is made up of around 6 billion neurons, or nerve cells. The "right brain" has to do with what we call "*pattern recognition*," and specializes in the ability to grasp "images" and perceive things as a totality. The "left brain" displays an outstanding capacity to think logically in terms of symbols and words.

A thick belt of the inter-brain ridge links the information inputs handled by the left and right brains. Images taken in by the right brain are sent to the left brain, where they are logically analyzed and checked out to see if they correspond with reality, and are then fed back again into the right brain. In this way, the brain can make judgments and produce new information.

The working of the human brain, in which the neurons not only form a network through synapse but recognize each other, has provided some very useful hints for the construction of global models. This is because global models have the role of offering global information. If this information undergoes a feedback process reflecting itself in each country's actual policies, the future image of the world economy will change with the emergence of global information. In the future, mutual understanding can be expected to increase through global information exchanges, and it is only with this base that we can begin to talk about possibilities for *international cooperation and policy coordination*.

The functioning of the individual cells that support human life depends on both genetic information and non-genetic information generated through "*creative*" endeavors such as learning. It is still in the future for a global model to be developed that will in fact have a similar capacity for "*self-organization*." Perhaps we will first have to develop a global system that will be conducive to the employment of such an *avant garde* model. But in this process, it may nevertheless be expected that current global models can give useful policy suggestions. An important phenomenon discovered through research in biotechnology is the so-called "*fluctuation phenomenon*." It may be appropriately said that the presence of fluctuations seems to be a basic and necessary element for the evolution of life. And again, this is a very important element in thinking about the global economy. Forecast simulations based on present baseline scenarios accommodate a large degree of "fluctuation" in light of the current unstable situation.

At the same time, there is of course the possibility of controlling this situation and changing its course through more energetic international policy coordination, or, in the terminology of biotechnology, "*dynamic cooperation*" among countries. *There are indeed many kinds of possibilities for invigorating the global economy, raising its growth rate, greatly reducing CO_2 emissions promoting innovations opening up new 21st century frontiers. It is reasonably expected that* the 21st century will be an age of integrated technology innovations in the fields of information technology, biotechnology, new energy as solar and superconductor, nanotechnology, robotics, new materials, space   technology and etc.

By demonstrating these possibilities of *integrated technology innovations* through future simulations using the latest FUGI global modeling system, we can exercise alternative policy scenario simulations for the global economy and can offer suggestions to those responsible for policy-making in the world's various countries. In keeping with these innovations, it will no doubt advance to new frontiers in economic science, while keeping much of its heritage of traditional economics. We ought to actively pursue this vision in *new frontier of economic science*, and in this regard we see FUGI global modeling system as one of the important intellectual challenges in the 21st century.

In conclusion, it is worth noting that not only moderate harmonized adjustments of policies but wise cosmic mind to promote human solidarity with the ever changing nature will be desirable to adjust orbit of the ever changing futures of global interdependent economy. It is worth noting that Cosmos is an entirely recycling system so that there might be no wastage of resources as seen in the current civilized human societies. In the Cosmic system everything is interdependent and changing forever. In order to adapt with such a dynamic cosmic system, humankind should modify present civilization in the globalizing world. Consciousness of co-existence of human beings with nature and solidarity of humankinds will be needed. The more harmonized progress between technological innovations and human minds will be necessary in order to create a desirable human society and life support system of the Earth in the post-modern futures.

APPENDIX A: FUGI GLOBAL MODELING SYSTEM (FGMS200)

I: POPULATION: (E001-E019)

E001	LOG (BIRTHR)	= F ((+ N) LOG (TFR), (+N) LOG (NPFEA.1 / NP.1)) If TFR would not be available, use the following:
E002	LOG (BIRTHR)	= F ((- N) LOG (GDP#. 1 / NP.1)), (- N) LOG (GEDU#. 1 / GDP#. 1), (+N) LOG (SUMT5 (DEATHR.1) / 5), (-N) LOG (LIFEEXP. 1), (-) DWAR)
E003	LOG (DEATHR)	= F ((- N) LOG (GDP#. 1 / NP.1), (-N) LOG (GSW#. 1) / GDP#. 1), (+N) LOG (NPMO65.1 + NPFO65.1)/ NP.1), (+N) LOG (SUMT5 (BIRTHR.1) / 5), (+) DWAR)
E004	LOG (NPM)	= F ((+N) LOG (NP), (-) DWAR)
E005	LOG (NPMEA)	= F ((+N) LOG (NPM))
E006	LOG (NPFEA)	= F ((+N) LOG (NPF))
E007	LOG (NPMO65 / NPM)	= F ((+N) LOG (LIFEXPM.1))
E008	LOG (NPFO65 / NPF)	= F ((+N) LOG (LIFEXPF 1))
E009	LOG (LIFXPM))	= F ((+) LOG (GDP#. 1 / NP.1), (+) LOG ((GH#. 1+GSW#. 1) / GDP#. 1), (+) LOG (GEDU#. 1 / GDP#. 1), (-) LOG (TFR))

Table. Continued

E010	LOG (LIFEXPF)	= F ((+) LOG (GDP#. 1 / NP.1), (+) LOG ((GH#. 1+GSW#. 1) / GDP#. 1), (+) LOG (GEDU#. 1 / GDP#. 1), (-) LOG (TFR))
DEF	LIFEEXP	= (NPM/NP)*LIFEXPM +(NPF/NP)*LIFEXPF
E011	LOG (TFR)	= F ((-N) LOG (GDP#. 1 / NP.1), (-N) LOG (GEDU#. 1 / GDP#. 1), (+N) LOG (SUMT5 (DEATHR.1) / 5), (-N) LOG (LIFEEXP. 1), (-) DWAR)
E012	LOG (NRR)	= F ((+) LOG (GRR))
E013	LOG (GRR)	= F ((+) LOG (TFR))
E014	LOG (GFR)	= F ((+) LOG (TFR))
E015	LOG (NETMGTR)	= F ((+N) LOG (IPCID.1), (- N) LOG (UNEMPR.1)
E016	LOG (NPRURAL/NP)	= F ((+N) LOG (GDPAGR#. 1 / GDP#. 1), ((+N) LOG (TFR.1))
DEF	NP	= NP.1* (1 + (BIRTHR - DEATHR +NETMGTR)/ 1000)
DEF	NPF	= NP - NPM
DEF	NPFU15	= NPF - NPFEA - NPFO65
DEF	NPMU15	= NPM - NPMEA - NPMO65
DEF	NPFU15	= NPF - NPFEA - NPFO65
DEF	NATY	= (BIRTHR /1000)* NP
DEF	MORTY	= (DEATHR /1000)* NP
DEF	NETMGT	= (NETMGTR /1000) * NP
DEF	NPURBAN	= NP - NPRURAL
DEF	NPO65	= NPMO65 + NPFO65
DEF	NPDOT	= NP / NP.1 * 100

II: Foods: (E020-E029)

E020	LOG (EXFOOD#)	= F ((+N) LOG (ETFOB#), (+N) LOG (GDPAGR#. 1))
E021	LOG (IMFOOD#)	= F ((+N) LOG (CAPM#), (+N) LOG (FOODR# / NP))
E022	LOG (IMPCERL)	= F ((+N) LOG (IMFOOD#))

Table. Continued

E023	LOG (FPROPCI)	= F ((+N) LOG (GDPAGR# /NP),
		(+N) LOG (NPRURAL / NP), (+N) LOG (CULTIVA / NP))
E024	LOG (CULTIVA)	= F ((+N) LOG (ARABLE), (+N) LOG (FOODR#. 1), (+N) LOG (EXFOOD#. 1 + IMFOOD#. 1), (-) LOG (EROSION)
E025	LOG (ARABLER)	= F ((+N) LOG (FOODR#. 1), (+N) LOG (EXFOOD#. 1 + IMFOOD#. 1), (-) LOG (EROSION))
E026	LOG (XPDFOOD)	= F ((-) LOG (GDP# / NP), (-) LOG (GDPMF# / GDP#))
E027	LOG (XPDSTPL)	= F ((-) LOG (GDP# / NP), (-) LOG (GDPMF# / GDP#))
E028	LOG (XPDPROT)	= F ((-) LOG (GDP# / NP), (+) LOG (LIFEEXP.1))
E029	LOG (TFOODR)	= F ((+N) LOG (FOODR#))
DEF	ARABLE	= ARABLE.1 (1+ ARABLER /100)
DEF	FOODR#	= XPDFOOD*GDP#
DEF	TFOODS	= TFOODS.1* (1 + DOT (FPROPCI)+ DOT (NP))+ IMFOOD
		+ FOODAID@
DEF	FOODPOP	= (TFOODR - TFOODS) / NP
DEF	NMFOOD	= IMFOOD# * PMS - EXFOOD# * PES

*CALTIVAT < ARABLE < TLAND.

III: ENERGY: (E030-069)

< Energy Requirement >		
E030	LOG (OIL/GDP#)	= F ((- N) LOG (POIL / WPI), (- N) LOG ((COAL.1 + GAS.1) / ENGYR.1), (- N) LOG (ALTEGY.1 / ENGYR.1), (-N) LOG (SUMT5 (ITI#) / NHFCS#))
E031	LOG (COAL/GDP#)	= F ((- N) LOG (PCOAL / WPI), (- N) LOG (ALTEGY.1 / ENGYR.1), (-N) LOG (SUMT5 (ITI#) / NHFCS#)))

Table. Continued

E032	LOG (GAS / GDP#)	= F ((- N) LOG (PGAS / WPI), (- N) LOG (ALTEGY.1 / ENGYR.1), (-N) LOG (SUMT5 (ITI#) / NHFCS#))
E033	LOG (ALTEGY)	= F ((+N) LOG (GDP#), (+) LOG (POIL.1 / WPI.1))
DEF	ENGYR	= OIL + COAL + GAS + ALTEGY
*If TFCE data are available, use the following sub-system		
< Total Final Consumption of Energy: TFCE >		
E034	LOG (TFCOILI)	= F ((+N) LOG (GDP#), (- N) LOG (POIL / WPI), (-N) LOG ((TFCOAL.1 + TFCGAS.1) / TFCE.1), (- N) LOG (ALTEGY.1 /TFCE.1))
E035	LOG (TFCOILT)	= F ((+N) LOG (GDP#), (- N) LOG (POIL / WPI), (-N) LOG (TFCELC.1 / TFCE.1), (-N) LOG (BATT.1 / TFCOILT.1))
E036	LOG (TFCOILO / GDP#)	= F ((- N) LOG (POIL / WPI), (-N) LOG (TFCELC.1 / TFCE.1), (- N) LOG (ALTEGY.1 /TFCE.1), (-N) LOG (SUMT5 (ITI#) / NHFCS#))
DEF	TFCOIL	= TFCOILI + TFCOILT + TFCOILO
E037	LOG (TFCOALI)	= F ((+N) LOG (GDP#), (- N) LOG (PCOAL / WPI), (-N) LOG (TFCELC.1 / TFCE.1), (- N) LOG (ALTEGY.1 /TFCE.1))
E038	LOG (TFCOALT)	= F ((+N) LOG (GDP#), (- N) LOG (PCOAL / WPI), (-N) LOG (TFCELC.1 / TFCE.1), (- N) LOG (ALTEGY.1 /TFCE.1))
E039	LOG (TFCOALO / GDP#)	= F ((- N) LOG (PCOAL / WPI), (-N) LOG (TFCELC.1 / TFCE.1), (- N) LOG (ALTEGY.1 /TFCE.1), (-N) LOG (SUMT5 (ITI#) / NHFCS#))
DEF	TFCOAL	= TFCOALI + TFCOALT + TFCOALO
E040	LOG (TFCGASI)	= F ((+N) LOG (GDP#), (- N) LOG (PGAS / WPI), (-N) LOG (TFCELC.1 / TFCE.1), (- N) LOG (ALTEGY.1 /TFCE.1))
E041	LOG (TFCGAST)	= F ((+N) LOG (GDP#), (- N) LOG (PGAS / WPI), (-N) LOG (TFCELC.1 / TFCE.1), (-N) LOG (BATT.1 / TFCOILT.1))

Table. Continued

E042	LOG (TFCGASO/ GDP#)	= F ((- N) LOG (PGAS / WPI), (-N) LOG (TFCELC.1 / TFCE.1), (- N) LOG (ALTEGY.1 /TFCE.1), (-N) LOG (SUMT5 (ITI#) / NHFCS#))
DEF	TFCGAS	= TFCGASI + TFCGAST + TFCGASO
E043	LOG (TFCELCI)	= F ((+N) LOG (GDP#), (- N) LOG (PELC / WPI), (-N) LOG (ALTHTEC .1))
E044	LOG (TFCELCT)	= F ((+N) LOG (GDP#), (- N) LOG (PELC / WPI), (-N) LOG (ALTHTEC .1))
E045	LOG (TFCELCO)	= F ((+N) LOG (GDP#), (- N) LOG (PELC / WPI), (-N) LOG (ALTHTEC .1))
DEF	TFCELC	= TFCELCI + TFCELCT + TFCELCO
DEF	TFCE	= TFCOIL + TFCOAL + TFCGAS + TFCELC + TFCALT@
<< Total Intermediate Consumption of Fossil Energy >>		
E046	LOG (TICOIL)	= F ((+N) LOG (TFCOIL), (- N) LOG (POIL / WPI), (-N) LOG (NUCL.1 / TFCE.1), (- N) LOG (ALTEGY.1 /TFCE.1))
E047.	LOG (TICCOAL)	= F ((+N) LOG (TFCOAL), (- N) LOG (PCOAL / WPI), (-N) LOG (NUCL.1 / TFCE.1), (- N) LOG (ALTEGY.1 /TFCE.1))
E048.	LOG (TICGAS)	= F ((+N) LOG (TFCGAS), (- N) LOG (PGAS / WPI), (-N) LOG (NUCL.1 / TFCE.1), (- N) LOG (ALTEGY.1 /TFCE.1))
<<Total Energy Requirements>>		
E049	LOG (NUCL)	= F ((+N) LOG (TFCELC), (+) LOG (POIL / WPI))
E050	LOG (HYDRO)	= F ((+N) LOG (TFCELC))
E051	LOG (SOLAR)	= F ((+N) LOG (TFCELC))
E052	LOG (BIOMASS)	= F ((+N) LOG (TFCELC))
E053	LOG (BATT)	= F ((+N) LOG (TFCELC))
E054	LOG (ALTHTEC)	= F ((+N) LOG (TFCELC))
DEF	ALTEGY	= NUCL + HYDRO + SOLAR + BIOMASS + BATT + ALTHTEC

Table. Continued

DEF	OIL	= TFCOIL + TICOIL
DEF	COAL	= TFCOAL + TICCOAL
DEF	GAS	= TFCGAS + TICGAS
DEF	ENGYR	= OIL + COAL + GAS + ALTEGY
DEF	FOSSIL	= OIL + COAL + GAS
DEF	ENGYS	= ENGYR + NENGYTB@
<< ENERGY INDICATORS >>		
DEF	ALTEGYR	= (ENGYR - FOSSIL) / ENGYR
		< Alternative <Alternative Energy Rate >
DEF	EPC	= (ENGYR / NP) * 1000
		< Energy per <Energy per capita >
DEF	ESR	= ENGYR / GDP#
		< Energy Savings Rate: Energy Intensity >
DEF	AETR	= CO2EMN / ENGYR
		< Alternative Energy Technology Rate: CO2 Efficiency >
DEF	CO2PC	= (CO2EMN / NP) * 1000
		<CO2 per capita>
DEF	CO2ESR	= CO2EMN /CO2 EMN.1995 * 100
		< CO2 emission stabilization rate >

IV: ENVIRONMENT: (E070 – E099) (ECOSYSTEM)

< Country / Regional Level >		
E070	LOG (NDISAST)	= F ((+N) LOG (DFAWC@), (+N) LOG (FLOOD), (+N) LOG (DROUGHT))
E071	LOG (FLOOD)	= F ((+N) LOG (DEFORES), (+N) LOG (DFAWC@), (+N) LOG (ESWARM)
E072	LOG (DROUGHT)	= F ((+N) LOG (DEFORES), (+N) LOG (DFAWC@))
E073	LOG (DEFORTR)	= F ((+N) LOG (NP), (+N) LOG (ARABLE), (+N) LOG (ACRAIN), (+N) LOG (EXTIM@))

Table. Continued

E074	LOG (EROSION)	= F ((+N) LOG (DROUGHT), (+N) LOG (DEFORES))
E075	LOG (DESERT)	= F ((+N) LOG (EROSION), (+N) LOG (DEFORES))
E076	LOG (AIRPOL)	= F ((+N) LOG (FOSSIL), (-N) LOG (SUMT5 (APNHI#. 1))
E077	LOG (WATPOL)	= F ((+N) LOG (NPURBAN), (-N) LOG (SUMT5 (APNHI#. 1))
E078	LOG (SOILPOL)	= F ((+N) LOG (LANDCON), (+N) LOG (WATPOL), (+N) LOG (INTWAR), (+N) LOG (INTLWAR))
E079	LOG (NUCLPOL)	= F ((+N) LOG (NUCL), (+N) LOG (INTWAR), (+N) LOG (INTLWAR))
E080	LOG (APNHI#)	= F ((+N) LOG (NHI#))
E081	LOG (ACRAIN)	= F ((- N) LOG (SOX), (- N) LOG (NOX)
		(0 (MAX) < pH < 7 (MIN))
E082	LOG (SOX)	= F ((+N) LOG (FOSSIL), (-N) LOG (ALTEGY), (-N) LOG (TECHA#), (-N) LOG (SUMT5 (APNHI#. 1)))
E083	LOG (NOX)	= F ((+N) LOG (FOSSIL), (-N) LOG (ALTEGY), (-N) LOG (TECHA#), (-N) LOG (SUMT5 (APNHI#. 1)))
E084.	LOG (CH4)	= F ((+N) LOG (NPRURAL))
E085	CO2EMN	= F ((+N) (CO2ETF*(0.996 * COAL + 0.804 * OIL + 0.574 * GAS))
E086	LOG (CO2ETF)	= F ((-N) LOG (TECHA#))
E087	LOG (CO2)	= F ((+N) LOG (CO2EMN), (- N) LOG (FOREST), (- N) LOG (BIOTEC@))
E088	LOG (ESWARM)	= F ((+N) LOG (ESWARMG))
DEF	FOREST	= FOREST.1 - DEFORES
DEF	DEFORES	= DEFORES.1* (1 + DEFORTR/1000)
< Global level >		
DEF	CO2 G	= CO2<SUM>
DEF	FORESTG	= FOREST <SUM>

Table. Continued

E089	LOG (CO2PPMG)	= F ((+N) LOG (CO2G), (- N) LOG (FORESTG), (- N) LOG (BIOTECG@))
E090	LOG (ESWARMG)	= F ((+N) LOG (CO2G), (+N) LOG (CH4G), (+N) LOG (O3G@), (+N) LOG (CFCG@))
<< GEWS INDICATORS >>		
I	ENVI	Destruction of Environment
I-1	NDISAST	Natural Disasters
I-2	WATPOL	Water Pollution
I-3	AIRPOL	Air Pollution
I-5	NUCLPOL	Nuclear Pollution
I-6	DESERT	Ecological Imbalance

V: ECONOMIC DEVELOPMENT: (E100 – E899)

1. Labor and Production < At Constant Prices >: (E100 – E139)

E100	LOG (GDPP# / LCLF) <AME>	= F ((+N) LOG (NHFCS# / LCLF), (+N) LOG (EDUA# / LCLF), (+N) LOG (TECHA#)/LCLF), (+N) LOG (SUMT5 (NHI#) / NHFCS#)) Type A
E101	LOG (GDPP# / LCLF) <AME>	= F ((+N) LOG (NHFCS# / LCLF), (+N) LOG (TECHA# / LCLF), (+N) LOG (SUMT5 (NHI#) / NHFCS#)) Type B (BEL, DEU, IRL, LUX, GBR, SWE)
* If NHFCS# data are not available, NHFCS# should be estimated by using the definition on NHFCS# where NHFCS# (at 1995 prices) is assumed as 1.20*GDP# (at the estimation starting year 1970).		
*If CUR and ITI# data are available, use the following equation		
E102	LOG (GDPP# / LCLF) <AME>	= F (((+N) LOG (NHFCS#*CUR / LCLF), (+N) LOG (SUMT5 (ITI#) / NHFCS#)) Type C (JPN, USA)

Table. Continued

E103	LOG (GDPP# / LCLF) <DME>	= F ((+N) LOG (NHFCS# / LCLF), (+N) LOG (EDUA# / LCLF), (+N) LOG (SUMT5 (GH#. 1) / LCLF), (+N) LOG (SUMT3 (ODATCR.1 / PMS.1), (-N) LOG (PEO.1*FERSI.1 / WPI.1)) Type A (Non-Oil Ex.)
E104	LOG (GDPP# / LCLF) <DME>	= F ((+N) LOG (NHFCS# / LCLF), (+N) LOG (EDUA# / LCLF), (+N) LOG (SUMT5 (GH#. 1) / LCLF), (+N) LOG (SUMT3 (ODATCR.1) / PMS.1), (+N) LOG (PEO.1*FERSI.1 / WPI.1)) Type B (Oil-Ex.)
E105	LOG (RD#)	= F ((+N) LOG (GDP#. 1), (+N) LOG (GES#. 1))
E106	LOG (RD#) <USA>	= F ((+N) LOG (OS#. 1-TYC#. 1), (+N) LOG (GES#. 1), (+N) LOG (GDF#. 1)
E107	LOG (RD#)<JPN>	= F ((+N) LOG (OS#. 1-TYC#. 1), (+N) LOG (GEST#. 1))
*If data on RDBE# and RDGOV# are available, use the following equations		
E108	LOG (RDBE#)	= F ((+N) LOG ((OS#. 1-TYC#. 1), (+) LOG ((OS#. 2-TYC#. 2))
E109	RDGOV#	= F ((+N) GES#. 1)
E130	RDGOV# < JPN>	= F ((+) GEST#. 1)
E110	DNHC#	= F ((+) NHFCS#. 1)
*If DNHC# data are not available, DNHC# should be estimated by 0.07 *NHFCS#. 1		
E111	UNEMPR<AME>	= F ((+N) LOG (LCLF), (- N) LOG (GDP#. 1 / GDP#. 2), (+N) LOG (COMPE#. 1 / GDP#. 1), (- N) LOG (GFCF#. 1 / GDP#. 1)) Type A
E112	UNEMPR<AME>	= F ((+N) LOG (LCLF*HOW), (- N) LOG (GDP#. 1 / GDP#. 2), (+N) LOG (WSEI.1 / CPI.1/ LPI.1), (- N) LOG (GFCF#. 1 / GDP#. 1)) Type B. USA

Table. Continued

E113	UNEMPR<AME>	$= F ((+N) \text{ LOG } (LCLF*HOW), (- N) \text{ LOG } (GDP\#. 1 / GDP\#. 2),$ $(+N) \text{ LOG } (WSEI.1 / LPI.1),$ $(- N) \text{ LOG } (GFCF\#. 1 / GDP\#. 1))$ Type C. EU (FRA, DEU, GRC, IRL, ITA, GBR, AUT, SWE)
E114	UNEMPR<DME>	$= F ((+N) \text{ LOG } (LCLF), (- N) \text{ LOG } (GDP\#. 1 / GDP\#. 2),$ $(- N) \text{ LOG } (GFCF\#. 1 / GDP\#. 1))$
E115	UNEMPR<EIT>	$= F ((+N) \text{ LOG } (LCLF), (- N) \text{ LOG } (GDP\#. 1 / GDP\#. 2),$ $(- N) \text{ LOG } (GFCF\#. 1 / GDP\#. 1))$
DEF	GDPAG#C	$= 0.3551436 - 0.1279891* GDPP\# / NP$ $+0.01691503* (GDPP\# / NP)^2 -$ $0.0009406098*(GDPP\# / NP)^3$ $+ 0.00002291084*(GDPP\# / NP)^4$ $-0.0000002013468* (GDPP\# / NP)^5)$
DEF	GDPMF#C	$= 0.1241992* + 0.0200785*GDPP\# / NP$ $-0.002310938* (GDPP\# / NP)^2$ $+0.0001191378*(GDPP\# / NP)^3$ $-0.000002766923*(GDPP\# / NP)^4$ $+0.00000002371586* (GDPP\# / NP)^5)$
DEF	GDPIN#C	$= 0.2088974 + 0.05532418 \, GDPP\# / NP$ $- 0.007219928* (GDPP\# / NP)^2 +$ $0.000370202608*(GDPP\# / NP)^3$ $- 0.00000829076*(GDPP\# / NP)^4$ $+0.00000006798821* (GDPP\# / NP)^5)$
E116	GDPAGR# / GDPP#	$= F ((N) \, GDPAG\#C), \; (+) \, PEC.1*FERSI.1 / PGDP.1)$
E117	GDPMF# /GDPP#	$= F ((N) \, GDPMF\#C, (+) \, NHI\# / GDPP\#)$
E118	GDPIND# /GDPP#	$= F ((N) \, GDPIN\#C, (+) \, NHI\# / GDPP\#)$
DEF	GDPSER# / GDPP#	$= 1 - GDPAG\# / GDPP\# - GDPIND \# / GDPP\#$

Table. Continued

E119	LOG (IPI)	= F ((+N) LOG (GFCF#), (+N) LOG (E#), (+N) LOG (GDP# - GFCF# - E#))
E120	LOG (CUR)	= F ((+) LOG (IPI.1), (+) LOG (IPI.1 / (SUMT3 (IPI.1) / 3))
E121	LOG (TECHM#)	= F ((+) LOG (GDP#. 1), (+) LOG (ETFOB#. 1*PES.1/PMS.1))
E122	LOG (TECHE#)	= F ((+N) LOG (SUMT5 (RDBE#. 1)))
E123	LOG (LCLFM)	= F ((+N) LOG (NPMEA))
E124	LOG (LCLFF)	= F ((+N) LOG (NPFEA), (+N) LOG (GEDU#. 1 / NP.1), (+) LOG (CP#. 1 / NP.1), (-) LOG (UNEMP.1))
E125	LW	= F ((+N) CEMP, (+) LW.1)
E126	LOG (HOW)	= F ((-N) LOG (LPI.1), (+) LOG (GDP#. 1 / GDP#. 2))
E127	LOG (ITI# / NHI#)	= F ((+N) LOG (TECHA#)) Type A (JPN)
E128	LOG (ITI# / NHI#)	= F ((+N) LOG (TECHA#), (+) LOG (ITI#. 1/NHI#)) Type B (USA)
E129	LOG (LCLFF) <DME>	= F ((+N) LOG (NPFEA))
DEF	LCLF	= LCLFM + LCLFF
DEF	UNEMP	= UNEMPR * LCLF
DEF	CEMP	= LCLF - UNEMP
DEF	NHFCS#	= NHFCS#. 1 + NHI# - DNHC#
DEF	RDOTH#	= RD# - RDBE# - RDGOV#
DEF	EDUA#	= EDUA#. 1 + GEDU# – OBEDU#
DEF	OBEDU#	= 0.025* EDUA#. 1
DEF	TECHA#	= TECHA# .1 + RD# + TECHM# - OBTECH#
DEF	OBTECH#	= 0.05* TECHA# .1

* If data on NHI# are not available, use GFCF# in place of NHI#.

<AME>: DEVELOPED MARKET ECONOMIES
<DGE>: DEVELOPING ECONOMIES
<EIT>: ECONOMIES IN TRANSITION.
<DME>: DGE + EIT

2. Expenditure on GDP < at Constant Prices >: (E140 – E199)

E140	LOG (E#MAT <AME, AME>)	= F ((+N) LOG (GDP#<J>), (- N) LOG (PES<I>.1 / PESAME.1), (- N) LOG (PES<I>.1*FERSI<J>.1 /CPI<J>.1)) Type A
E141	E#MAT <AME, AME>	= F ((+N) GDP#<J>, (- N) PES<I>.1 / PESAME.1, (- N) PES<I>.1*FERSI<J>.1 /CPI<J>.1)) Type B
E142	LOG (E#MAT<JPN, USA>)	= F (+N) LOG (GDP#<J>),
		(-N) LOG (PES<I>.1*FERSI<J>.1 / CPI<J>.1), (+N) LOG (SUMT4 (RD#<I>.1))
E143	LOG (E#MAT<USA, JPN>)	= F ((+N) LOG (GDP#<J>), (- N) LOG (PES<I>.1 / PESAME.1),
		(- N) LOG (PES<I>.1*FERSI<J>.1*(1+CTR@<J>.1+NTB@<J>.1) / CPI<J>.1), (+N) LOG (SUMT4 (RD#<I>.1))
E144	E#MAT<DME, AME>	= F ((+N) MTFOB#<J>.1, (+N) GDP#<J>, (- N) PES<I>.1 / PMS<J>.1)
E145	E#MAT < ANIES, AME>	= F ((+N) GDP#<J>, (- N) PES<1>.1 / PMS<J>.1, (- N) PES<I>.1*FERSI<J>.1 / CPI<J>.1)
E146	E#MAT <CHN, AME>	= F ((+N) GDP#<J>, (- N) PES<1>.1 / PMS<J>.1, (- N) PES<I>.1*FERSI<J>.1 / CPI<J>.1)
E147	E#MAT <WORLD, DME>	F (+N) ETFOB#<J>.1 *PES<J>.1/PMS<J>.1, (+N) GDP#<J>, (-N) (PES<I>.1 / PMS<J>.1)
E148	E#MAT<WRD, CHN>	= F ((+N) GDP#<J>, (- N) PES<I>.1*FERSI<J>.1* (1+CTR@<J>.1+NTB@<J>.1) / CPI<J>.1)
E149	E#MAT<VEC, CHN>	= F ((+N) GDP#<J>, (- N) PES<I>.1*FERSI<J>.1* (1+CTRV<J>.1+NTB@<J>.1) / CPI<J>.1)
*E#MAT<I, J> relates to exports from COUNTRY<I> to COUNTRY<J>		
E150	LOG (CP# <AME>)	= F ((+N) LOG (GDP#), (- N) LOG (CPI / ((CPI + CPI.1) / 2), (- N) LOG (IC.1), (+) LOG (CP#. 1)) < Type A >

Table. Continued

E151	CP# <AME>	= F ((+N) GDP#, (- N) (CPI / ((CPI + CPI.1) / 2))*1000, (- N) ICC.1*1000, (+) CP#. 1) < Type B>
E152	LOG (CP# <JPN>)	= F ((+N) LOG (DFI# - (TPI# +TYC#)), (- N) LOG (CPI / ((CPI+CPI.1) /2), (- N) LOG (ICC.1), (+N) LOG (MTD.1 + SMV.1)/ CPI.1)) <Type C> JPN
E153	LOG (CP# <USA>)	= F ((+N) LOG (COMPE# - TPI#), (+N) LOG (OS# - TYC#), (- N) LOG (CPI / ((CPI+CPI.1) /2), (- N) LOG (ICC.1), (+N) LOG (SMV.1/ CPI.1)) <Type D> USA
E154	LOG (CP# <EU>)	= F ((+N) LOG (COMPE# - TPI#), (+N) LOG (OS# - TYC#), (- N) LOG (CPI / ((CPI+CPI.1) /2), (-N)LOG(ICC.1),(+N)LOG(CP#.1)) CPI.1)) <Type E > EU
E155	CP# <EU>	= F ((+N) (COMPE# - TPI#), (+N) (OS# - TYC#), (- N) (CPI / ((CPI+CPI.1) /2)) *1000, (- N) ICC.1*1000, (+) CP#. 1) < Type F > Remaining members of EU
E156 *	CP# <DME>	= F ((+N) GDP#, (+) CP#. 1)
E157	CP # <NIES &ASEAN>	= F ((+N) GDP#, (- N) (CPI / ((CPI + CPI.1) / 2)*1000, (- N) ICC.1*1000, (+) CP#. 1)
E158	CP# <EIT>	= F ((+N) GDP#, (+) CP#. 1)
E159	LOG (NHI#<AME>)	= F ((+N) LOG (OS#. 1 - TYC#. 1), (-N) LOG (IP.1), (+N) LOG (ETFOB#. 1), (+N) LOG (SUMT3 (RD#. 1)) Type A (AUS, NZL, BEL, DNK, FRA, GRC, LUX, PRT, AUT, FIN)

Table. Continued

E160	DOT (NHI# <AME>)	= F ((+N) (OS#. 1 - TYC#. 1) / NHFCS#. 1 - IP.1/100,
		    (+N) DOT (ETFOB#. 1),
		    (+N) DOT (RD#. 1))
		
		Type B (CAN, DEU, IRL, ITA, NLD, GBR,
		                 NOR, SWE, CHE)

E161	DOT (NHI# <AME>)	= F ((+N) (OS#. 1 - TYC#. 1) / NHFCS#. 1 - IP.1/100,
		    (+N) DOT (ETFOB#. 1),
		    (+N) DOT (RD#. 1),
		    (+N) ITI#. 1 / NHI#. 1,
		    (-N) DOT (CUR.1)
		                  Type C (USA)

E162	DOT (NHING# <JPN>)	= F ((+N) (OS#. 1 - TYC#. 1) / NHFCS#. 1 - IP.1/100,
		(+N) DOT (ETFOB#. 1),
		    (+N) DOT (RD#. 1),
		    (+N) ITI#. 1 / NHI#. 1)
		                  Type D (JPN)

E163	NHI# <DME>	= F ((+N) GDP#. 1,
		    (+N) ETFOB#. 1*PES.1 / PMS.1,
		    (+N) FCI.1 / PMS.1)

E164	NHI# <NIES & ASEAN>	= F ((+N) GDP#. 1,
		    (- N) IP.1*1000, (+N) ETFOB#. 1*PES.1/PMS.1,
		    (+N) FCI.1 / PMS.1)

E165	LOG (HI#)	= F ((+N) LOG (GDP#), (-N) LOG (IH.1), (-N) LOG (PHI.1))
E166	IIS#	= F ((+N) GDP#, (-) IP.1*1000, (+) ((WPI / ((WPI+WPI.1) / 2)))*1000)
*In case of production oriented model in DME and PME, IIS# should be treated as residual variables		
E167	E#	= F ((+) ETFOB#)
E168	M#	= F((+) MTFOB#)
E174	LOG (CG#)	= F ((+) LOG (GDP#. 1)) Type A
E169	LOG (CG#)	= F ((+) LOG (GE#)) Type B

Table. Continued

E170	LOG (CG#)<JPN>	= F ((+) LOG (GE#.1)) Type C
E171	LOG (PFCF#)<JPN>	= F ((+) LOG (GE#.1 - CG#.1))
DEF	NHI#<JPN>	= NHING# + PFCF#
DEF	GDP#	= E# - M# + CP# + CG# + NHI# + HI# + IIS#
DEF	IS#	= IS#. 1 + IIS#
DEF	GFCF#	= NHI# + HI#
*If HI# data are not available, HI# should be treated as nil	
DEF	GFCF#	= NHI#
DEF	CAPM#	= (ETFOB#*PES+ FCI)/ PMS
DEF	ETFOB#	= E#MAT<SUMJ>
DEF	MTFOB#	= E#MAT<SUMI>

*Notes:

1) If projected GDP# is larger than GDPP#, GDP# should be replaced by GDPP#. In this case IIS# should be obtained as residual using the identity on GDP#. The system seems likely to be behaved as production oriented model.

2) If there are needs to convert to GDP# components at constant prices to original data based on national currency unit, they should be multiplied by FERS.1995.

3. Income Distribution: Profit - Wage: (E200 – E249)

E200	OS#	= F ((+N) GDP#, (- N) IP.1*1000, (+N) (PES.1 / PMS.1)*1000
E201	OS# <JPN>	= F ((+N) (GDP# - COMPE # - DNHC#), (- N) IP.1*1000, (+N) (PES.1 / PMS.1)*1000, (+N) (ETFOB.1 + ICII.1) *FERSI .1/ WPI.1)
E202	CQE#	= F ((+N) OS#, (+) CQE#. 1)
E203	PUE#	= F ((+) OS#, (+) PUE#. 1)
E204.	HPI#	= F ((+) OS#, (+) HPI#. 1)
E205	DOT (WSEI <AME>)	= F ((+N) DOT (CPI.1), (+N) DOT (LPI), (+N) DOT2 (OS.1, GDP.1), (- N) UNEMPR.1)
E206	DOT (WSEI <DME>)	= F ((+N) DOT (CPI.1), (+N) DOT (LPI))
E207	DOT (WSEI<EIT>)	= F ((+N) DOT (CPI.1), (+N) DOT (LPI))
DEF	LPI	= (GDPP# / CEMP) / (GDPP#. 1995 / CEMP.1995)

Table. Continued

DEF	OS	= OS# * PNHI
DEF	GGO#	= OS# - CQE# - PUE#
DEF	COMPE	= WSEI * LW * (COMPE.1995 / LW.1995)
DEF	COMPE#	= COMPE / CPI
DEF	DFI#	= COMPE# + OS#
DEF	DFI	= COMPE + OS
DEF	STDC#	= GDP# - DFI# - DFC# - TI# + SUB#
DEF	PUE	= PUE# /PGDP
DEF	HPI	= HPI# /PGDP
DEF	COE	= COE#/PGDP

4. Prices: (E250 – E299)

E250	DOT (WPI)	= F ((+N) DOT (PM), (+N) DOT 2(WSEI, LPI), (+N) DOT (IV#. 1), (+) DOT (WPI.1))
E251	DOT (CPI)	= F ((+N) DOT (PM), (+) DOT (WSEI), (+) DOT (IV#. 1), (+) DOT (CPI.1))
E252	DOT (CPI \<JPN\>)	= F ((+N) (DOT (PM) + DOT (CTR@) + DOT (NTB@)), (+N) DOT (WSEI), (+N) DOT (IV#. 1), (+N) TCR@/100)
E253	DOT (PCP)	= F ((+N) DOT (CPI))
E254	DOT (PCG)	= F ((+N) DOT (CPI.1))
E255	DOT (PNHI)	= F ((+N) DOT (WPI), (+N) DOT2 (NHI#. 1, GDP#. 1), (+) DOT (PNHI.1))
E256	DOT (PHI)	= F ((+N) DOT (PNHI), (+N) DOT (WSEI), (+) DOT (PHI.1))
E257	DOT (PEO)	= F ((+N) DOT (PESAME.1), (+N) DOT 2 (OILG.1, ENGYRG.1), (+) DY74, (+) DY79, (+) DY90, (+) DY2000)
*DY74: DUMMY VARIABLE, 1974 =1, REST OF THE YEARS = 0		
*DY79: DUMMY VARIABLE, 1979 =1, REST OF THE YEARS = 0		
*DY90: DUMMY VARIABLE, 1990 =1, REST OF THE YEARS = 0		
*DY2000: DUMMY VARIABLE, 2000=1, REST OF THE YEARS = 0		

Table. Continued

E258	DOT (PEC)	= F ((+N) DOT (GDP#G.1), (- N) (ICAME.1), (-N) DOT (FERIAME.1), (+) DOT (PEC.1))
E279	DOT (PEGOLD)	= F ((+N) DOT (PESAME), (+N) DOT (PEC), (+) DY80)
E259	DOT (PES <AME>)	= F ((+N) DOT2 (WPI.1, FERSI.1), (+N) DOT2 (WSEI, LPI), (+N) DOT (PESAME.1), (- N) DOT (FERSI.1))
E260	DOT (PES <CEAME>)	= F ((+N) DOT2 (WPI.1, FERSI.1), (+N) DOT2 (WSEI, LPI), (+N) DOT (PESAME.1), (+N) DOT (PEC), (- N) DOT (FERSI.1))
E261	DOT (PES <USA>)	= F ((+N) DOT (WPI.1), (+N) DOT 2 (WSEI, LPI), (+N) DOT (PESAME.1), (+N) DOT (PEC), (+N) DOT (FERIAME.1))
E262.	DOT (PES <DME>)	= F ((+N) DOT (PEC), (+N) DOT (PESAME.1), (+N) DOT2 (WPI.1, FERSI.1), (+N) DOT2 (WSEI.1, FERSI.1)) <NON-OIL EXPORTING DME>
E263	DOT (PES <OILEXP>)	= F ((+N) DOT (PEO), (+N) DOT2 (WPI.1, FERSI.1), (+N) DOT 2 (WSEI.1, FERSI.1))
E264	DOT (PES <EIT>)	= F ((+N) DOT (PEC), (+N) DOT (PESAME.1), (+N) DOT2 (WPI.1, FERSI.1), (+N) DOT2 (WSEI.1, FERSI.1))
E265	DOT (PECOAL)	= F ((+N) DOT (PEO), (+N) DOT2 (COAL<SUM>.1, ENGYRG.1))
E266	DOT (PEGAS)	= F ((+N) DOT (PEO), (+N) DOT2 (GAS<SUM>.1, ENGYRG.1))
E267	DOT (POIL)	= F ((+N) (DOT (PEO) + DOT (FERSI)), (+N) DOT (WPI.1), (+N) DOT2 (OIL.1, ENGYR.1))
DEF	POIL	= POIL * (1 + CTAXRO@ / 100)
E268	DOT (PCOAL)	= F ((+N) (DOT (PECOAL + DOT (FERSI)), (+N) DOT (WPI.1) (+N) DOT2 (COAL.1, ENGYR.1))
DEF	PCOAL	= PCOAL * (1 + CTAXRC@ / 100)

Table. Continued

E269	DOT (PGAS)	= F ((+N) (DOT (PEGAS + DOT (FERSI)), (+N) DOT (PELC), (+N) DOT (WPI.1) (+N) DOT2 (GAS.1, ENGYR.1))
DEF	PGAS	= PGAS * (1 + CTAXRG@ / 100)
E270	DOT (PNUCL)	= F ((+N) DOT (WPI.1))
E271	DOT (PELC)	= F ((+N) DOT (WPI.1))
E272	DOT (SPI)	= F ((+N) (OS- TYC) / NHFCS#*PNHI – IP / 100, (+N) DOT2 (M2,GDP), (+N)) (OS.1- TYC.1) / SMV.1 – IB.1 / 100, (+ N) DOT (GDP#) – DOT (GDP#. 1), (+N) DOT (CPI) – DOT (CPI.1), (-N) DOT (FERSI) – DOT (FERSI.1), (+ N) DOT (SPI<USA>)
E273	DOT (SPI <USA>)	= F ((+N) (OS- TYC) / NHFCS#*PNHI – IP / 100, (+N) DOT2 (M2, GDP), (+N)) (OS.1- TYC.1) / SMV.1 – IB.1 / 100, (+N) DOT (CPI) – DOT (CPI.1), (+N) DOT2 (ITI#, NHI#), (- N) DOT (SPI.1))
E274	DOT (SPI <AME>)	= F ((+N) (OS- TYC) / NHFCS#*PNHI – IP / 100, (+N) DOT 2(M2,GDP), (+N)) (OS.1- TYC.1) / SMV.1 – IB.1 / 100, (+ N) DOT (GDP#) – DOT (GDP#. 1), (+N) DOT (CPI) – DOT (CPI.1), (+N) DOT2 (ITI#, NHI#), (+N) DOT (SPI <USA>))
E275	DOT (PLAND<J PN>)	= F ((+N) DOT (M2), (+ N) DOT (GDP#) – GDP# / (GDP#+GDP#. 1) / 2, (- N) DOT (FERSI) - FERSI / ((FERSI+FERSI.1) / 2), (+N) DOT (GFCF#. 1), (+N) DOT (SPI.1))
DEF	PE	= PES * FERSI
DEF	PMS	= ESMAT<SUM I> / (E#MAT <SUM I>)
*PMS data should be obtained from trade matrices, using PES. Do not make any adjustment.		
DEF	PM	= PMS * FERSI

Table. Continued

E276	DOT (PENA)	= F ((+N) DOT (PE)
E277	DOT (PMNA)	= F ((+N) DOT (PM))
E278	DOT (PPFCF)<J PN>	= F ((+N) DOT (WPI), (+N) DOT2 (NHI#. 1, GDP#. 1), (+) DOT (PPFCF))
E280	DOT (PNHING) <JPN>	= F ((+N) DOT (WPI), (+N) DOT2 (NHI#. 1, GDP#. 1), (+) DOT (PNHING))
DEF	PGDP	= GDP / GDP#
DEF	PEOB	= PEO*PEOB.95

5. Expenditure on GDP < at Current Prices >

DEF	E	= PENA * E#
DEF	M	= PMNA * M#
DEF	CP	= PCP * CP#
DEF	CG	= PCG * CG#
DEF	NHI	= PNHI * NHI#
DEF	PFCF<JPN>	= PPFCF*PFCF#
DEF	NHINP<JPN>	=PNHINP*NHINP#
DEF	NHI<JPN>	NHINP + PFCF
DEF	HI	= PHI * HI#
DEF	IIS	= WPI * IIS#
DEF	GFCF	= NHI + HI
*If HI data are not available, HI should be zero.		
DEF	GFCF	= NHI
DEF	GDP	= E - M + CP + CG + NHI + HI + IIS

* If there are needs to convert to current GDP components to original data based on national currencies, they should be multiplied by FERS.1995. If there are needs to convert them in terms of current US dollars, they should be divided by FERSI. If you want to reconvert them in terms of current EURO, they should be further divided by FEREURO.

*Note: E300 – E 399 are allocated to the merchandise trade model.   (See Annex – FUGI Global Merchandise Trade Model).

6. Money, Interest Rates and Financial Assets: (E400– E499)

E400	M1	= F ((+N) GDP, (-N) IN.1*1000) <div align="right">Type A</div>
E401	LOG (M1)	= F ((+N) LOG (GDP#), (+N) LOG (PGDP), (- N) LOG (IN.1)) <div align="right">Type B: JPN</div>
E402	MTD	= F ((+N) GDP, (-N)(((IB.1 – ITD.1) / ITD.1)*1000, (+) MTD.1)
DEF	M2	= M1 + MTD
E403	CCG	= F ((+N) (GE – GR), (+) CCG.1
E404	LOG (CPS)	= F ((+N) LOG (NHI + HI +IIS), (-N) LOG (IN.1), (+N) LOG (MTD.1 / GDP.1), (-N) LOG (IB.1 – IP.1) / IP.1)
DEF	IV#	= (M2 / GDP#) / (M2 .1995 / GDP#. 1995)

E405	IN <AME>	= F ((+N) (1 + DOT (CPI) – CPI / ((CPI + CPI.1) / 2)),
		    (+N) (1 + DOT (GDP#)-GDP# / ((GDP# + GDP#. 1) / 2)),
		    (+N) (1 + DOT (FERSI)), (+N) IN.1)

E406	IN <USA>	= F ((+N) (1+ DOT (CPI) – CPI / ((CPI + CPI.1) / 2)),
		    (+N) (1+ DOT (GDP#) – GDP# / ((GDP# + GDP#. 1) / 2)),
		    (- N) (1 + DOT (FERIAME), (+N) IC.1)

E407	INEU	= F ((+N) (1+ DOT (CPIEU) – CPIEU / ((CPIEU + CPIEU.1) / 2)),
		    (+N) (1+ DOT (GDP#EU)-GDP#EU/ ((GDP#EU + GDP#EU.1) / 2)),
		    (+N) (1+ DOT (FERIEUR)), (+N) INEU.1)

E408	IN<DME>	+ F (IN.1)
E409	IN<EU>	= F ((+N) INEU
DEF	IN<EU11>	= INEU (After 2001)
E410	IC	= F ((+N) IN, (+N) DOT (CPI), (- N) DOT (M2), (+N) IC.1) <div align="right">Type A</div>
E411	IC< AME>	= F ((+N) IN, (+N) DOT (CPI), (- N) DOT (M2), (+N) DOT (CCG + CPS), (+N) IC.1) <div align="right">Type B: JPN, USA</div>
E412	ICEU	= F ((+N) INEU, (+N) DOT (CPIEU), (+N) ICEU.1)
E413	IC<EU>	= F ((+N) ICEU)

Table. Continued

E414	IB <AME>	= F ((+N) IN, (+N) IC, (+N) IB.1)
E415	IB <JPN>	= F ((+N) IN, (+N) IC)
E416	IB <USA>	= F ((+N) IN, (+N) IC, (+N) IB.1)
E417	IBEU	= F ((+N) IN, (+N) ICEU, (+N) IBEU.1)
E418	IB <EU>	= F ((+N) IBEU)
E419	IP	= F ((+N) IC)
E420	IH	= F ((+N) IP)
E421	ITD	= F ((+N) IP)
E422	ISEURO	= F (+N) IC<USA>)
E423	LIBOR	= F ((+N) ISEURO)
E424	LOG (SMV)	= F ((+) LOG (SPI))
E425	ICC	= F ((+N) IP)

* In case of DME, IN may be treated as exogenous variable as IN@.

7. Government Finance: (E500 – E599)

Type A

<< REVENUE >>		
E500.	GR#	= F ((+N) (GDP#.1), (+) ((E#.1 + M#.1))
*Detailed	Data on	Government finance GR are available, use the followings;
E501	TPI#	= F ((+) (COMPE#. 1 + PUE#. 1 + HPI#. 1))
E502	TYC#	= F ((+N) OS#. 1)
E503	SSC#	= F ((+N) (COMPE#. 1 + OS#. 1)
E504	TP#	= F ((+N) GDP#. 1)
E505	TDGS#	= F ((+N) GDP#. 1)
E506	TITT#	= F ((+N) (MMFOB.1*FERSI.1/ PM.1)
		If CTR@ data are available, use the following equation.
E509	TITT#	= F ((+N) (MMFOB.1*FERSI.1/ PM.1)*CTR@)
E507	TIR#	= F ((+N) GDP#. 1)
E508	NTR#	= F ((+N) GDP#. 1)
DEF	TD#	= TPI# + TYC# + TP#
DEF	TID#	= TDGS# + TITT# + TIR#

Table. Continued

DEF	TR#	= TD# + TID#
DEF	GR#	= TR# + NTR# + SSC# + GRANT#@
DEF	GR	= GR#*PGDP
DEF	TITT	= TITT# *PM
<< EXPENDITURE BY FUNCTION >>		
E510	GE#	= F ((+N) GR#))
*Detailed data on government finance GE are available, use the followings;		
E511	GPS#	= F ((+N) GR#)
E512	GDF#	= F ((+N) GR#)
E513	LOG (GDF#)<USA>	= F ((+N) LOG (GR#), (+N) DY8186)
		* DY8186: 1981 – 86 =1, Rest of years =0
E514	LOG (GDF#)<RUS>	= F ((+N)(LOG (GDF#<USA>.1 / GDP#<USA>.1), (+N) DY8186)
E515	LOG (POS#)	= F ((+) LOG (GR#))
E516	LOG (GEDU#)	= F ((+) LOG (GR#))
E517	LOG (GH#)	= F ((+) LOG (GR#))
E518	LOG (GSW#)	= F ((+) LOG (GR#))
E519	LOG (GHC#)	= F ((+) LOG (GR#))
E520	GSS#	= F ((+) GR#)
E521	GES#	= F ((+) GR#)
E522	GEOP#	= F ((+) GR#)
DEF	GTE#	= GPS# + GDF# + GEDU# + GH# + GSW# + GHC# + GSS #+ GES# + GEOP#
DEF	GE#	= GTE# + GLMR#@
DEF	GE	= GE#*PGDP
DEF	GDOS	= GR - GE
DEF	GDOS#	= GR# - GE#
E523	DGD	= F ((+) (GE - GR))
E524	GBR	= F ((+) (DGD)
DEF	GDO	= GDO.1 + DGD
DEF	GDOGDP	= (GDO /GDP)*100
DEF	GBRGE	= (GBR /GE)*100
<< EXPENDITURE BY ECONOMIC TYPE >>		
E525	GCE#	= F ((+) GE#)
E526	GIP	= F ((+) GDO.1 * IB.1 / 100)
E527	CAE#	= F ((+) (GHC#+GES#))

Type B <JPN>Type

<< REVENUE >>		
E551	LOG (TPI)	= F ((+N) LOG (COMPE + PUE + HPI))
E552	LOG (TYC)	= F ((+N) LOG (OS))
E553	LOG (TP)	= F ((+N) LOG (GDP.))
E554	LOG (TC)	= F ((+N) LOG (GDP*TCR@)/100))
E555	TITT	= F ((+N) MMMOB*FERSI*CTR@)
E556	LOG (TIR)	= F ((+N) LOG (GDP))
E557	LOG (NTR)	= F ((+N) LOG (GDP))
E558	LOG (SSC)	= F ((+N) LOG (COMPE + OS))
DEF	TD	= TPI + TYC + TP
DEF	TID	= TC + TITT + TIR
DEF	TR	= TD+ TID
DEF	GR	= TR + NTR
DEF	GBR	= GE – GR
DEF	RG	= GR + GBR
DEF	GR#	=GR/PGDP
DEF	RG#	=RG/PGDP
DEF	TPI#	=TPI/PGDP
DEF	TYC#	=TYC/PGDP
<< EXPENDITURE BY FUNCTION >>		
E561	GDS	= F ((+N) (GDO.1 * IB.1 / 100))
E562	LOG (GLPF)	= F ((N) LOG (GR))
E563	LOG (GSW)	= F ((N) LOG (GR))
E564	LOG (GH)	= F ((+N) LOG (GSW))
E565	LOG (GEDU)	= F ((N) LOG (GR))
E566	LOG (GEST)	= F ((+N) LOG (GEDU))
E567	LOG (GDF)	= F ((N) LOG (GR))
E568	LOG (GPW)	= F ((N) LOG (GR))
E569	LOG (GEOP)	= F ((N) LOG (GR))
E570	GBPREP	= F ((+N) GDO.1, (-N) GDS.1)
DEF	GDOS	= GR – GE
DEF	GE	= GDS + GLPF + GSW + GEDU + GDF +GPW + GEOP
DEF	GBR	= GE – GR
E571	GDO	= F ((+N) (GDO.1 + GBR – GBPREP))
DEF	GDOGDP	= (GDO/GDP)*100

Table. Continued

DEF	GBRGE	= ((GDS - GBR)/GDP)*100
DEF	GDS#	= GDS/PGDP
DEF	GLPF#	= GLPF /PGDP
DEF	GSW#	= GSW /PGDP
DEF	GH#	= GH/ PGDP
DEF	GEST#	= GEST /PGDP
DEF	GDF#	= GDF/PGDP
DEF	GPW#	= GPW /PGDP
DEF	GEOP#	= GEOP /PGDP
DEF	GDOS#	= GDOS /PGDP
DEF	GE#	= GE /PGDP

8. International Balance of Payments: (E600 – E659)

E600	EMFOB	= F ((+) ETFOB)
E601	MMFOB	= F ((+) MTFOB)
E602	SC	= F ((+) ETFOB)
E603	SD	= F ((+) MTFOB)
*If data are available, use the following equations.		
E604	SCTPN	= F ((+) ETFOB)
E605	SDTPN	= F ((+) MTFOB)
E606	SCTR	= F ((+N) FERSI*1000, (+N) DOT (GDP#. 1)*1000, (- N) DOT (CPI)*1000, (+N) GDPS.1 / NP.1)
E607	SDTR	= F ((- N) FERSI*1000, (+N) GDPS.1 / NP.1, (+N) GDP#. 1*CPI.1 / FERSI.1))
E 608	LOG (SCOTH)	= F ((+N) LOG (GDPS.1 / NP.1), (+N) LOG ((RD#. 1 / GDP#. 1))
E609	LOG (SDOTH)	= F ((+) LOG (GDPS.1 / NP.1))
E610	DIA <AME>	= F ((+N) GDPS, (+N)) (WSEI / FERSI / LPI) / (WSEIAME/ FERIAME/ LPIAME)* 1000) (- N) (OS# / GDP#) / (OS#AME / GDP#AME)* 1000, (- N) (FERSI / (FERSI + FERSI.1) / 2) *1000)

Table. Continued

E611	DIA<DME>	= F ((+N) GDPS, (- N) (OS# / GDP#) / (OS#AME / GDP#AME)*1000, (- N)(FERSI / (FERSI + FERSI.1) / 2))*1000)
E612	DIL	= F ((+N) GDPS, (- N) ((WSEI / FERSI / LPI) / (WSEIAME/ FERIAME / LPIAME)) *1000, (+N) ((OS# / GDP#) / (OS#AME / GDP#AME))*1000, (+N) DIA<SUM>)
E613	DIL <USA>	= F ((+N) GDPS, (+N)((OS# / GDP#) / (OS#AME / GDP#AME)) *1000, (+N) FERIAME*1000, (+N) DIA <SUM>)
E614	POINA	= F ((+N) GDPS, (+N) (ICAME / IC) * 1000, (+N) ((OS# / GDP#) / (OS#AME / GDP#AME))*1000, (- N)((1 / FERSI) / ((1 / FERSI+1 / FERSI.1) /2))*1000)
E615	POINL	= F ((+N) GDPS, (- N) (ICAME / IC)* 1000, (+N) SPI*1000)
E616	POINL <USA>)	= F ((+N) (GDP# / GDP#AME)*1000, (- N) (ICAME / IC)*1000, (+N) SPI*1000, (+N) FERIAME *1000)
E617	ICIIDIA	= F ((+N) DIAO.1)
E618	IDIIDIL	= F ((+N) DILO.1)
E619	ICIIPI	= F ((+N) (POINA.1+POINA.2)*ISEURO.1)
E620	IDIIPI	= F ((+N) (POINL.1+POINL.2)*IB.1)
E621	INCOMEC	= F ((+N) ICII)
E622	INCOMED	= F ((+N) IDII)
DEF	ICII	= ICIIDIA + ICIIPI
DEF	IDII	= IDIIDIL + IDIIPI
DEF	ETFOB	= ESMAT<SUM I>
DEF	MTFOB	= ESMAT<SUM J >
DEF	TB	= ETFOB – MTFOB
DEF	TBB	= EMFOB – MMFOB

Table. Continued

DEF	EMFOB\<SUM\> = MMFOB\<SUM\>	
	* EMFOBD and MMFOBD should control the world total.	
DEF	SC	= SCTPN + SCTR + SCOTH
DEF	SD	= SDTPN + SDTR + SDOTH
DEF	SC\<SUM\> = SD\<SUM\>	
	* SCD and SDD should control the world total.	
DEF	INCOMEC \<SUM\> = INCOMED \<SUM\>	
	*INCOMECD and INCOMEDD should control the world total.	
DEF	CBT	= TBB + SC – SD
DEF	CTC	= CTCGG@ + CTCOS@
DEF	CTD	= CTDGG@ + CTDOS@
DEF	CUT	= CTC – CTD
DEF	DEF	CTC\<SUM\> = CTD\<SUM\>
		* CTCD and CTDD should control the world total
DEF	CBP	= CBT + INCOMEC – INCOMED + CUT
DEF	DIB	= DIL – DIA
DEF	POINB	= POINL – POINA
DEF	ESMAT \<I, J\>	= E#MAT\<I, J\> * PES\<I\>
DEF	GDPS	= GDP / FEERSI
DEF	DIAO	= DIAO.1 + DIA + FADEDIA@
DEF	DILO	= DILO.1 + DIL+ FADEDIL@

9. International Finance: (E700 – E799)

\<\< OFFICIAL DEVELOPMENT ASSISTANCE \>\>		
E700	ODA	= F ((+) GDPS)
E701	ODAB	= F ((+) ODA)
DEF	ODAM	= ODA - ODAB
E702	ODAMAT \<AME, WRD\>	= F ((+) ODAB\<I\>)
DEF	ODABR	= ODAMAT\<SUM I\>)
E703	ODAMR	= F ((+) ODAM \<SUM\>)
* If ODA MAT are not available, use the following E704		
E704	ODABR	= F ((+) ODAB \< SUM \>)
DEF	ODAR	= ODABR + ODAMR

Table. Continued

E705	ODATC	= F ((+) ODA)
E706	ODATCR	= F ((+) ODATC<SUM>)
<< PRIVATE FOREIGN DIRECT INVESTMENT TO DME >>		
E707	PFDIMAT <WRD, WRD>	= F ((+) PFDI<I>)
DEF	PFDIR	= PFDIMAT<SUM I>
E708	PFDI	= F ((+N) DIA)
* If PFDI MAT are not available, use the following E709		
E709	PFDIR	= F ((+N) PFDI<SUM>)
DEF	PFDIO	= PFDIO.1 + PFDI - FADEPIA@
DEF	PFDIL	= PFDIL.1 + PFDIR - FADEPIL@
DEF	FCI	= ODABR + ODAMR + PFDIR
<< EXTERNAL DEBT >>		< for DME >
- LONG - TERM DEBT -		
< PUBLIC AND PUBLICLY GUARANTEED (PPG)>		
E710	DISBOC	= F ((+N) ODAR)
E711	DISBPC	= F ((+N) NHI / FERSI, (-N) DSR.1, (-N) CBP, (-N) PFDIR.1)
E712	PREPOC	= F ((+N) DODOC.1)
E713	PREPPC	= F ((+N) DODPC.1, (-) DSR.1)
E714	IDEBTOC	= F ((+N) LIBOR)
E715	IDEBTPC	= F ((+N) ISEURO)
E716	INTOC	= F ((+) (DODOC.1 * IDEBTOC/100))
E717	INTPC	= F ((+) (DODPC.1 * IDEBTPC/100))
E718	DODOC	= F ((+) (DODOC.1 + DISBOC - PREPOC))
E719	DODPC	= F ((+) (DODPC.1 + DISBPC - PREPPC))
DEF	DISB	= DISBOC + DIBPC
DEF	PREP	= PREPOC + PREPPC
DEF	INT	= INTOC + INTPC
DEF	TDS	= TDSOC + TDSPC
DEF	TDSOC	= INTOC + PREPOC
DEF	TDSPC	= INTPC + PREPPC
DEF	DOD	= DODOC + DODPC
< PRIVATE NONGUARANTEED (PNG)>		
E720	DISBPNG	= F ((+N) NHI / FERSI, (-N) DSR.1, (-N) CBP, (-N) PFDIR.1)
E721	PREPPNG	= F ((+N) DODPNG.1, (-) DSR.1))
E722	IDEBTPN	= F ((+N) ISEURO)

Table. Continued

E723	INTPNG	= F ((+N) DODPNG.1 * IDEBTPN/100)
E724	DODPNG	= F ((+N) (DODPNG.1 + DISBPNG - PREPPNG))
DEF	TDSPNG	= PREPPNG + INTPNG
< SHORT-TERM DEBT >		
E725	DODS	= F ((-N) SUMT2 (CBP.1), (-N) IMFCRE.1)
< USE OF IMF CREDIT >		
E726	IMFCRE	= F ((-N) CBP)
< TOTAL EXTERNAL DEBT >		
DEF	EDT	= DOD + DODS + IMFCRE
< DEBT INDICATORS >		
- PUBLIC -		
DEF	DER	= DOD / (EMFOB + SC)
DEF	DGR	= DOD / GDPS
DEF	DSR	= TDS / (EMFOB + SC)
- TOTAL -		
DEF	DERT	= EDT / (EMFOB + SC)
DEF	DGRT	= EDT / GDPS
DEF	DSRLT	= (TDS + TDSPNG) / (EMFOB + SC)

10. Foreign Exchange Rate: (E800-849)

<<PER DOLLAR RATE>>		
E800	FERSI<AME>	=F ((+N) PGDP.1/PGDP<USA>.1, (+N) FERSIAME.1, (+) FERSI.1)
E801	LOG (FERIEUR)	= F ((+N) LOG (PGDPEU.1 / PGDP<USA>.1), (- N) LOG (ESMATEA.1 /ESMATAE.1), (+N) LOG ((IC<USA>.1 / ICEU.1), (+) LOG (FERIEUR.1))
E802	DOT (FERSI <EEA>)	= F ((+N) DOT (FERIEUR)
E803	LOG (FERSI <JPN>)	= F ((+N) LOG (PGDP.1 / PGDP<USA>.1), (- N) LOG (ESMAT<JPN, USA>.1 /ESMAT<USA, JPN>.1), (+N) LOG ((IC<USA>.1 / IC.1), (+) LOG (FERIEUR))

Table. Continued

E804	DOT (FERSI <EU>)	= F (+N) DOT (FERIEUR)) (Before 2001)
DEF	FERSI <EU11>	= (1+ DOT (FERIEUR))* FERSI.1 (After 2001)
E805	FERSI <DME>	= F ((+N) PE.1 / PE.1<USA>.1, (-N) CBP.1 / GDPS.1, (+N) FERIAME.1, (+) FERSI.1)
DEF	FERSI <DME>	= 1 US Dollar direct link type >
E806	FERSI <EIT>	= F ((+N) PE.1 / PE<USA>.1, (+N) FERIAME.1, (+) FERSI.1)
DEF	FERS	= FERSI * FERS.1995
DEF	FEREURO	= FERIEUR* FEREURO.1995
DEF	FERE	= FERS / FEREURO
DEF	FERE<EU11>	=EUROCR@ @ (After 2002)
DEF	FERSI <USA>	= 1.00
DEF	FERS <USA>	= $1.00
DEF	TERRA	= PEO/3 + PEC/3 + PEGOLD/3
DEF	TERRA.1995	= $1.00 (TERRA exchange rate per US dollar = TERRA 1.00 in 1995)
DEF	TERRAS	= 1 / TERRA (TERRA exchange rate per US dollar)
DEF	TERRASI	= TERRAS / TERRA.1995
<< DEFINITIONS>>		
DEF	CPIAME	= WEIGHT (CPI, GDP#, <AME>)
DEF	CPIEU	= WEIGHT (CPI, GDP#, <EU>)
DEF	EGYRG	= ENGYR <SUM>)
DEF	EMTFOB#	= ETFOB# + MTFOB#
DEF	ESMATEA	= ESMAT <EU, USA>
DEF	ESMATAE	= ESMAT < USA, EU >
DEF	FERIAME	= WEIGHT (FERSI, GDP#, <AME>)
DEF	FERIEUR	= WEIGHT (FERSI, GDP#, <EU>)
DEF	PESAME	= ETFOB <SUMA> / ETFOB# <SUMA>
DEF	GDP#AME	= GDP# <SUMA>
DEF	GDP#E	= GDP# * FERS.1995 / FEREURO.1995
DEF	GDP#EU	= GDP# <SUMEU>
DEF	GDP#DGE	= GDP# <SUMD>
DEF	GDP# G	= GDP# < SUM>
DEF	GDP#N	= GDP# * FERS.1995 / NCUCR@ (GDP#N<USA> = GDP#<USA>)

Table. Continued

DEF	GDP#PPP	= GDP# / FERS*FERSPPP.1995 (GDP#PPP\<USA> = GDP#\<USA>)
DEF	GDPE	= GDP * FERS.1995 / FEREURO
DEF	GDPN	= GDP * FERS.1995 / NCUCR@ (GDPN\<USA> = GDP\<USA>)
DEF	GDPS	= GDP / FERSI (GDPS\<USA> = GDP\<USA>)
DEF	GDPSPPP	= GDPS / FERS* FERSPPP.1995 (GDPSPPP\<USA> = GDPS\<USA>)
DEF	GDPSG	= GDPS \<SUM>
DEF	ICAME	= WEIGHT (IC, GDP#, \<AME>)
DEF	ICEU	= WEIGHT (IC, GDP#, \<EU>)
DEF	IBEU	= WEIGHT (IB, GDP#, \<EU>)
DEF	INEU	= WEIGHT (IN, GDP#, \<EU>)
DEF	LPIAME	= GDPP#\<SUMA> / CEMP\<SUMA>
DEF	NPG	= NP \<SUM>
DEF	NPAME	= NP \<SUMA>
DEF	NPDGE	= NP \<SUMD>
DEF	OILG	= OIL \<SUM>
DEF	OS#AME	= OS# \<SUMA >
DEF	PGDPEU	= WEIGHT (PGDP, GDP#, \<EU>)
DEF	WSEIAME	= WEIGHT (WSEI, GDP#, \<AME>)

Note: NCU is national currency unit. NCU \<US> is set at Millions of US dollars = 1. If a given country's currency unit is Billions, NCU should be 1000.

11. Development indicators: (E850 – E869).

\<DOMESTIC AND INTERNATIONAL INCOME DISPARITY>		
E850	LOG (MPSED)	= F ((-N) LOG (RICH20))
E851	LOG (POOR20)	= F ((- N) LOG (RICH20.1), (+N) LOG (GDP#. 1 / NP.1))
E852	LOG (RICH20)	= F (+ N) LOG (MPSED.1), (- N) LOG (IPCIDG.1)
DEF	IPCIDG	= (GDP# / NP) / (GDP#G / NPG)
DEF	IPCIDA	= (GDP# / NP) / (GDP#AME/ NPAME
DEF	IPCIDD	= (GDP# / NP) / (GDP#DGE/ NPDGE)

Table. Continued

<< GEWS INDICATORS >>		
II DEVI		Failures in Development
II-1	GDP#DOT	Poor Economic Growth
II-2	PCIDOT	Stagnant Per Capita Income Growth
II-3	IPCIDG	International Per Capita Income Disparities
II-4	CPIDOT	High Domestic Prices
II-5	UNEMPR	High Unemployment Rate
II-6	CBPGDP	CBP TO GDPS
II-7	FERSIDOT	Depreciated Foreign Exchange Rate
II-8	DSR	High Debt Service Ratio
II-9	DILGDP	Decreased Capital Inflow to GDPS
II-10	CAPMGDP	Capacity to imports to GDP#
II-11	FOODPOP	Food Population Imbalance
II-12	MPSED	Mass Poverty

VI: PEACE AND SECURITY: (E870 – E879)

E870	LOG (POLCNFL)	= F ((+N) LOG (MPSED), (+N) LOG (UNEMP))
E871	LOG (AOROL)	= F ((+N) OG (POLCNFL), (+N) LOG (UNEMP))
E872	LOG (INSURGE)	= F ((+N) LOG (AOROL.1), (+N) LOG (UNEMP.1))
E873	LOG (INTWAR)	= F ((+N) LOG (INSURGE), (+) LOG (IOED), (+) LOG (EDED@), (+) LOG (ROED@))
E874	LOG (INTLWAR)	= F ((+) LOG (INTWAR), (+) LOG (MILAID@))

<< GEWS INDICATORS >>		
III	PSI	Absence of Peace and Security
III-1	POLCNFL	Political Conflicts and Violence
III-2	AOROL	Absence of Rule of Law
III-3	GDFGDP	Military Expenditures to GDP
III-4	INSURGEN	Insurgency
III-5	INTWAR	Internal War
III-6	INTLWAR	International Conflicts and War

VII: HUMAN RIGHTS: (E880 – E889)

E880	LOG (BHENEED)	= F ((+N) LOG (GSW# / GDP#), (+N) LOG (GHC#/GDP#), (+N) LOG (IFEEXP))
E881	LOG (IOED)	= F ((+N) LOG (POLCNFL))
E882	LOG (AHLCR)	= F ((+N) LOG (GEDU# / GDP#))
E883	LOG (DPNPR)	= F ((-N) LOG (ENVI), (-N) LOG (DEVI), (-N) LOG (PSI), (-N) LOG (HRI), (+ N) LOG (DP<SUM>.1 / NP <SUM>.1))
E884	LOG (DPRNPR)	= F ((+N) LOG (IPCIDG.1), (-N) LOG (UNEMP.1))
DEF	DP	= DPNPR * NP
DEF	DPR	= DPRNPR * NP
DEF	CLDP	= CLDP.1 + DP - DDP@

<< GEWS INDICATORS >>		
IV	VHRI	Violation of Human Rights
IV-1	BHENEED	Basic Human Existence Needs
IV-2	IOED	Ideology Oppression
IV-3	EDED	Ethnic Differentiation
IV-4	ROED	Religious Oppression
IV-5	GEDGDP	Educational Expenditures to GDP
IV-6	GSWGDP	Social Security Expenditures to GDP
IV-7	AHLCR	Human and Cultural Rights

*VIII: HEALTH CARE : (E900 – E919)

E900	LOG (HLTH)	= F ((+N) LOG (GH#. 1 GDP#. 1), (+N) LOG (GDP#. 1 / NP.1))
E901	LOG (ACCH)	= F ((+N) LOG (GH#. 1 /NP.1), (+N) LOG (GSW#. 1 / GDP#. 1))
E902	LOG (H2OSAFE)	= F ((+N) LOG (GDP#. 1 / NP.1), (-N) LOG (WATPOL.1))

Table. Continued

E903	LOG (SAFERU)	= F ((+N) LOG (GDP#. 1 / NP.1), (-N) LOG (WATPOL.1))
E904	LOG (PHYS)	= F ((+N) LOG (HLTH.1), (+N) LOG (GH#. 1 / GDP#. 1))
E905	LOG (NURS)	= F ((+N) LOG (PHYS.1), (+N) LOG (GH#. 1+ GSW#. 1) /GDP#. 1,
		(+N) LOG (NPO65.1 / NP.1))
E906	LOG (BEDS)	= F ((+N) LOG (NURS.1), (+N) LOG (GH#. 1 + GSW#. 1) /GDP#. 1,
		(+N) LOG (NPO65.1 / NP.1))
E907	LOG (BRTC)	= F ((+N) LOG (NURS.1 / NATY.1), (+N) LOG (HLTH.1))
E908	LOG (BRTW)	= F ((- N) LOG (GDP#. 1 / NP.1), (- N) LOG (GH#. 1/ GDP#. 1))
E909	LOG (MMRT)	= F ((- N) LOG (GDP#. 1 / NP.1), (- N) LOG (GH#. 1/ GDP#. 1))
E910	LOG (MALN)	= F ((- N) LOG (GDP#. 1 / NP.1), (- N) LOG (GH#. 1/ GDP#. 11))
E911	LOG (ITKPROT)	= F ((+ N) LOG (HLTH))
E912	LOG (IMMIDPT)	= F ((+ N) LOG (HLTH))
E913	LOG (IMMMEAS)	= F ((+ N) LOG (HLTH))
E914	LOG (ORTH)	= F ((+ N) LOG (HLTH))
E915	LOG (TEOHR)	= F ((+ N) LOG (GDP#. 1 / NP.1), (+ N) LOG (GH#. 1/ GDP#. 1))
E916	LOG (PEOHR)	= F ((+N) LOG (GH#. 1 / GDP#. 1))
DEF	TEOHPC	= (TEOH# / NP) * 1000
DEF	PEOHPC	= (PEOH# /NP) * 1000
DEF	TEOH#	= TEOHR*GDP#
DEF	PEOH#	= PEOHR*GDP#
DEF	TEOH	= TEOH# * PGDP
DEF	PEOH	= PEOH# *PGDP

* IX: DIGITAL DIVIDE (INFORMATION TECHNOLOGY):
(E920 – E939)

<<DIGITAL DIVIDE INDICATORS>>		
E920	LOG (PCPTP)	= F ((+N) LOG (GDP# / NP), (+N) LOG (EDUA# / NP), (+N) LOG (TECHA# / NP), (+N) LOG (NHI# / GDP#))
E921	(LOG (TELMPTP)	= F ((+N) LOG (GDP# / NP), (+N) LOG (EDUA# / NP), (+N) LOG(TECHA#/NP),(+N)LOG(NHI#/GDP#.1))
E922	LLOG (INTSPTP)	= F ((+N) LOG (PCPTP), (+N) LOG (EDUA# / NP), (+N) LOG(TECHA#/NP),(+N)LOG(NHI#/GDP#.1))
E923	LOG (INTHPTP)	= F ((+N) LOG (INTSPTP), (+N) LOG (NHI#. 1 / GDP# .1))
E924	LOG (LLPTP)	= F ((+N) LOG (GDP# / NP), (+N) LOG (TECHA# / NP), (+N) LOG (NHI# / GDP#), (+N) LOG (PCPTP.1))
E925	LOG (MTELPTP)	= F ((+N) LOG (GDP# / NP), (+N) LOG (EDUA# / NP) (+N) LOG (TECHA# / NP), (+N) LOG (NHI# / GDP#), (+N) LOG (PCPTP.1))
E926	LOG (TVSPTP)	= F ((+N) LOG (GDP# / NP), (+N) LOG (EDUA# / NP), (+N) LOG (TECHA# / NP, (+N) LOG (NHI# / GDP#))
<< QOL	(Quality of Life)	SELECTED INDICATORS>>
DEF	EDUA#PC	= EDUA# / NP
DEF	TECA#PC	= TECHA# / NP
DEF	GSW#PC	= GSW# / NP
DEF	GH#PC	= GH# / NP
DEF	GDP# PPC	= GDP#PPP / NP
DEF	IPCIDP	= (GDP#PPP / NP) / GDP#PPP<SUM> / NP<SUM>
DEF	CEMPR	= (CEMP / LCLF)*100
DEF	LIFEEXP	= (NPM/NP)*LIFEXPM + (NPF/NP)*LIFEXPF

* Important Note: We have made reservations for equations; E940-E999.They may be used for extension of sub-systems.

GLOSARY NOTES

@	: EXOGENOUS VARIABLE (Ex. GEITI@)
#	: VARIABLES AT CONSTANT PRICES (Ex. GDP#)
.1	: ONE-YEAR TIME LAG (EX. GDP#. 1)
(.1995	: VALUE IN BASE YEAR OF 1995 (Ex. GDP#. 1995)
*	: MULTIPLY (Ex. GDP = GDP#*PGDP
(+)	: PLUS SIGN CONDITIONS OF ESTIMATED PARAMETERS
(-)	: MINUS SIGN CONDITIONS OF ESTIMATED PARAMETERS
(N)	: NEGLECTS "t" STATISTICS OF ESTIMATED PARAMETERS
C	: VARIABLE DERIVED FROM CROSS-COUNTRY DATA (Ex. GDPAGR#C)
MAT	: MATRIX VARIABLE (Ex. E#MAT, ESMAT)
LOG	: NATURAL LOGARITHM
DOT	: PERCENTAGE CHANGES OF A VARIABLE Ex. DOT (GDP)
DOT2	: PERCENTAGE CHANGES OF DEVIDED VARIABLES (as WSEI / LPI) Ex. DOT2 (WSEI, LPI)
SUMJ	: SUMMATION OF ROW ELEMENTS IN MATRIX
SUMI	: SUMMATION OF COLUMN ELEMENTS IN MATRIX
SUMT5	: SUMMATION OVER FIVE YEARS (Ex. SUMT5 (NHI#) = NHI#+NHI#. 1...+NHI#. 4)
<SUM>	: SUMMATION OF WORLD TOTAL (Ex. NPG = NP<SUM>)
<SUMA >	: SUMMATION OF AME REGION
<SUMD >	: SUMMATION OF DME REGION
AME	: DEVELOPED MARKET ECONOMIES
DGE	: DEVELOPING ECONOMIES
DME	: DGE + PME
EIT	: ECONOMIES IN TRANSITION
ANIES	: ASIAN NEWLY INDUSTRIALIZING ECONOMIES
NIES	: NEWLY INDUSTRIALIZING ECONOMIES
OILEXP	: OIL EXPORTING COUNTRIES
OECD	: OECD MEMBER COUNTRIES
G5	: THE MAJOR FIVE COUNTRIES
G7	: THE MAJOR SEVEN COUNTRIES
EU	: EU MEMBER COUNTRIES
EU11	: EU ELEVEN MEMBER COUNTRIES
EEA	: EUROPEAN ECONOMIC AREA

ASEAN	: ASEAN MEMBER COUNTRIES
EASEA	: EAST AND SOUTHEAST ASIA
NAFTA	: NORTH AMERICAN FREE TRADE AREA
VEC	: VEHICLE EXPORTING COUNTRIES TO CHINA
WRD	: WORLD
G	: GLOBAL AGGREGATE (Ex. , NPG, CO2 G)
D	: DEVIATIONS FROM ACTUAL VALUES (Ex. FERSID)
F ()	: FUZZY FUNCTION WHERE RELATED VARIABLES HAVE "FLUCTUATION"

EXPLANATORY NOTES

- FLAG.1 -

M	: MATRIX
N	: SEMI-MATRIX
V	: VECTOR
S	: SCALAR

- FLAG.2 -

| T | : TIME SERIES DATA |
| N | : NON-TIME SERIES DATA |

- FLAG.3 -

| D | : ENDOGENOUS VARIABLE |
| X | : EXOGENOUS VARIABLE |

- FLAG.4 -

F	: FLOW
R	: RATIO
P	: INDEX
S	: STOCK

UNIT

MD	: MILLIONS OF 1995 US DOLLARS AT CURRENT PRICES (NCU PRICES)
MD95	: MILLIONS OF 1995 US DOLLARS AT 1995 CONSTANT PRICES
MDS	: MILLIONS OF CURRENT US DOLLARS
ME	: MILLIONS OF EURO CURRENCY
ME95	: MILLIONS OF 1995 EURO
MN	: MILLIONS OF NATIONAL CURRENCY
BN95	: BILLIONS OF NATIONAL CURRENCY AT 1995 PRICES

95 =1	: INDEX NUMBER BASED 1995
%	: PERCENTAGE
TP	: THOUSANDS OF PERSONS
TD95/P	: THOUSANDS OF 1995 US DOLLARS PER PERSON
MT	: METRIC TON
MTOE	: METRIC TON OIL EQUIVALENT
TOE	: TON OIL EQUIVALEEENT
MTCE	: METRIC TON CARBON EQUIVALENT
TCE	: TON CARBON EQUIVALENT
TT	: THOUSAND TON
MM/S	: MM PER SQUARE
HA	: HECTARE
SM	: SQUARE METER
POINT	: POINTS BY EXPERT JUDGMENT (Ex. 0-100)
NU	: NO UNIT
NCU	: NATIONAL OR REGIONAL CURRENCY UNIT (Ex US DOLLAR, EURO)
PPM	: CO2 PPM
PH	: ACID RAIN
$/B	: DOLLAR / BARREL

Data Source

A) CD-ROM, Floppy disk and MT

IMF	: DIRECTION OF TRADE
IMF	: INTERNATIONAL FINANCIAL STATISTICS
IMF	: BALANCE OF PAYMENTS STATISTICS
IMF	: GOVERNMENT FINANCE STATISTICS
OECD	: NATIONAL ACCOUNTS STATISTICS OF OECD MEMBER COUNTRIES
OECD	: LABOUR MARKET DATA BASE OF OECD COUNTRIES
OECD	: FLOWS AND STOCKS OF FIXED CAPITAL OF OECD
OECD	COUNTRIES
OECD	: DAC AID PERFORMANCE
	: GEOGRAPHICAL DISTRIBUTION OF FINANCIAL FLOWS TO DEVELOPING COUNTRIES
OECD	: ENERGY STATISTICS OF OECD MEMBER COUNTRIES

OECD	: ENERGY BALANCES AND ENERGY STATISTICS OF NON- OECD COUNTRIES
OECD	: ENERGY PRICES AND TAXESTATISTICS
OECD	: MAIN SCIENCE & TECHNOLOGY INDICATORS
OECD	: HEALTH DATA
OECD	: MAIN ECONOMIC INDICATORS
UN	: POPULATION STATISTICS
UN	: YEARBOOK OF NATIONAL ACCOUNTS STATISTICS
WORLD BANK	: WORLD DEVELOPMENT INDICATORS

B) Publication

ILO	: YEARBOOK OF LABOUR STATISTICS
UN	: MONTHLY BULLETIN OF STATISTICS
UNCTAD	: WORLD DEVELOPMENT AND TRADE REPORT
WHO	: THE WORLD HEALTH REPORT
OTHERS	: OFFICIAL STATISTICS IN EACH COUNTRY

VARIABLE LIST

VARIABLE:	FLAG:	UNIT:	NOTES:
ACCH	VTDR	%	ACCESS TO LOCAL HEALTH CARE (% OF NP)
ACRAIN	VTDF	PH	ACID RAINFALL MEASURED BY ACID ZONE pH.
AETR	VTDR	CE/OE	ALTERNATIVE ENERGY TECHNOLOGY RATE IN TERMS OF CO2 EFFICIENCY
ALTEGY	VTDF	MTOE	ALTERNATIVE ENERGY SUPPLY (METRIC TON)
ALTEGYR	VTDR	NU	ALTERNATIVE ENERGY RATIO TO TOTAL ENERGY
ALTHTEC	VTDF	MTOE	ALTERNATIVE HI-TECHNOLOGY ON ENERGY USE

Table. Continued

			(COSMIC ENERGY USE ON SUPER CONDUCTOR & NUCLEAR FUSION AT NORMAL TEMPERATURE)
AHLCR	VTDF	POINT	ADHERENCE TO HUMAN LIFE & CULTURAL RIGHTS
AIRPOL	VTDS	POINT	AIR POLLUTION (SO2, NOX, ETC.)
APNHI#	VTDF	MD90	ANTIPOLLUTION INVESTMENT
AOROL	VTDF	POINT	ABSENCE OF RULE OF LAW
ARABLE	VTDS	HA	ARABLE LAND
ARABLER	VTDR	%	ARABLE LAND; ANNUAL INCREASE RATE
BATT	VTDF	MTOE	BATTERY
BEDS	VTDF	NO	HOSPITAL BEDS
BBP	VTDF	MDS	BASIC BALANCE OF PAYMENTS AT CURRENT US DOLLARS
BHENEED	VTDF	POINT	BASIC HUMAN EXISTENCE NEEDS
BIOMASS	VTVF	MT	BIOMASS UTILIZATION
BIOTEC@	VTXF	MTCE	BIOTECHNOLOGY FOR REDUCING CO_2
BIRTHR	VTDR	/TH	BIRTH RATE (PER THOUSAND POPULATION)
BRTC	VTDR	%	BIRTHS ATTENDED BY HEALTH PERSONNEL
BRTW	VTDR	%	BABIES WITH BIRTHWEIGHT BELOW 2500 GRAMS
CAE	VTDF	MD	GOVERNMENT CAPITAL EXPENDITURE
CAE#	VTDF	MD95	GOVERNMENT CAPITAL EXPENDITURE (AT CONST.)
CALTIVA	VTDF	HA	CULTIVATED LAND
CAPM#	VTDF	MD90	CAPACITY TO IMPORT AT CONSTANT PRICES
CBP	VTDF	MDS	CURRENT BALANCE OF PAYMENTS AT CURRENT US DOLLARS
CBPGDP	VTDR	%	CURRENT BALANCE OF PAYMENTS TO GDP

Table. Continued

CBT	VTDF	MDS	CURRENT BALANCE OF TRADE AT CURRENT US DOLLARS
CCG	VTDF	MD	CLAIMS ON GOVERNMENT SECTOR, NET
CEMP	VTDS	TP	CIVILIAN EMPLOYMENT
CEMPF	VTDS	TP	CIVILIAN EMPLOYMENT: FEMALE
CEMPM	VTDS	TP	CIVILIAN EMPLOYMENT: MALE
CEMPR	VTDF	%	CIVILIAN EMPLOYMENT RATE
CFC@	VTXF	MT	CFC EMISSION
CG	VTDF	MD	GOVERNMENT FINAL CONSUMPTION EXPENDITURE AT CURRENT PRICES
CG#	VTDF	MD95	GOVERNMENT FINAL CONSUMPTION EXPENDITURE AT CONSTANT PRICES
CLDP	VTDS	TP	CURRENT LEVEL OF DISPLACED PERSONS
COAL	VTDF	MTOE	COAL REQUIREMENT
COMPE	VTDF	MD	COMPENSATION OF EMPLOYEES AT CURRENT PRICES
COMPE#	VTDF	MD95	COMPENSATION OF EMPLOYEES AT CONSTANT PRICES
CO2	VTDF	MTCE	CO2 EMISSION IN TERMS OMTCE
CO2EMN	VTDF	MTCE	CO2 EMISSION FROM FOSSIL ENERGY USE
CO2ETF	VTDF	RATIO	CO2 EMISSION TECHNOLOGY FACTOR
CO2ESR	VTDF	%	CO2 EMISSION STABILIZATION RATE
CO2G	STDF	MTCE	GLOBAL CO2 EMISSION IN TERMS OF MTCE
CO2PC	VTDF	TCE	CO2 EMISSION PER CAPITA
CO2PPMG	STDF	PPM	GLOBAL CO2 IN TERMS OF PPM (MAUNA LOA)
CP	VTDF	MD	PRIVATE FINAL CONSUMPTION EXPENDITURE AT CURRENT PRICES

Table. Continued

CP#	VTDF	MD95	PRIVATE FINAL CONSUMPTION EXPENDITURE AT CONSTANT PRICES
CP#PC	VTDF	TD95/P	PRIVATE FINAL CONSUMPTION EXPENDITURE AT CONSTANT PRICES (PER CAPITA)
CPI	VTDP	95=1	CONSUMER PRICE INDEX
CPIAME	STDP	95=1	AVERAGE CONSUMER PRICE INDEX OF AMES
CPIEU	STDP	95=1	AVERAGE CONSUMER PRICE INDEX OF EU
CPIDOT	VTDR	%	INCREASING RATE OF DOMESTIC PRICE
CPS	VTDF	MD	CLAIMS ON PRIVATE SECTOR, NET
CQE	VTDF	MD	CORPORATE AND QUASI-CORPORATE ENTERPRISES' OPERATING SURPLUS
CQE#	VTDF	MD95	CORPORATE AND QUASI-CORPORATE ENTERPRISES' OPERATING SURPLUS (AT CONST.)
CUT	VTDF	MD	CURRENT TRANSFERS
CTAXRO@	VTXF	%	CARBON TAX RATE ON OIL
CTAXRC@	VTXF	%	CARBON TAX RATE ON COAL
CTAXRG@	VTXF	%	CARBON TAX RATE ON GAS
CTC	VTDF	MD	CURRENT TRANFERS: CREDIT
CTCGG@	VTXF	MD	CREDIT: GENERAL GOVERNMENT
CTCOS@	VTXF	MD	CREDIT: OTHER SECTORS
CTD	VTXF	MD	CURRENT TRANFERS: DEBIT
CTDGG@	VTXF	MD	DEBIT: GENERAL GOVERNMENT
CTDOS@	VTXF	MD	DEBIT: OTHER SECTORS
CTR@	VTXR	NU	CUSTOMS TARIFF RATE
CTRV@	VTXR	NU	CUSTOMS TARIFF RATE FOR VEHICLE EXPORTING COUNTRIES TO CHINA
CUE	VTDF	MD	GOVERNMENT CURRENT EXPENDITURE
CULTIVAT	VTDS	HA	CULTIVATED LAND

Table. Continued

CUR	VTDR	NU	CAPACITY UTILIZATION RATE
DDP	VTDF	TP	NUMBER OF DISGUISED DISPLACED PERSONS
DEATHR	VTDR	/TH	DEATH RATE (PER THOUSAND POPULATION)
DEFORES	VTDF	SM	DEFORESTATION, NET
DEFORTR	VTDR	%	DEFORESTATION RATE, NET
DER	VTDR	NU	PUBLIC EXTERNAL DEBT / EXPORT RATIO
DERT	VTDR	NU	TOTAL EXTERNAL DEBT / EXPORT RATIO
DESERT	VTDR	NU	DESERTIFICATION
DEVDP	VTDS	TP	ECONOMICALLY DISPLACED PERSONS
DEVI	VTDF	POINT	INTEGRATED DEVELOPMENT INDICATORS
DFAWC@	VTXF	NU	DEGREE AND FREQUENCY IN ABNORMAL WEATHER CONDITION
DFC	VTDF	MD	CONSUMPTION OF FIXED CAPITAL AT CURRENT PRICES
DFOODP	VTDF	MT	DOMESTIC FOODS PRODUCTION
DFI	VTDF	MD	DOMESTIC FACTOR INCOMES AT CURRENT PRICES
DFI#	VTDF	MD95	DOMESTIC FACTOR INCOMES AT CONSTANT PRICES
DGR	VTDR	NU	PUBLIC TOTAL DEBT / GDPS RATIO
DGRT	VTDR	NU	TOTAL EXTERNAL DEBT / GDPS RATIO
DIA	VTDF	MDS	PRIVATE DIRECT INVESTMENT ABROAD AT CURRENT US DOLLARS
DIAO	VTDS	MDS	PRIVATE DIRECT INVESTMENT ABROAD: OUTSTANDING
DIB	VTDF	MDS	PRIVATE DIRECT INVESTMENT, BALANCE AT CURRENT US DOLLARS

Table. Continued

DIL	VTDF	MDS	PRIVATE DIRECT INVESTMENT IN COUNTRY AT CURRENT DOLLARS
DILGDP	VTDR	%	CAPITA INFLOW TO GDP
DILO	VTDS	MDS	PRIVATE DIRECT INVESTMENT IN COUNTRY: OUTSTANDING
DISB	VTDF	MDS	DISBURSEMENTS (LONG-TERM DEBT) TOTAL ALL CREDITORS
DISBOC	VTDF	MDS	DISBURSEMENTS (LONG-TERM DEBT) TOTAL OFFICIAL CREDITORS
DISBPC	VTDF	MDS	DISBURSEMENTS (LONG-TERM DEBT) TOTAL PRIVATE CREDITORS
DISBPNG	VTDF	MDS	DISBURSEMENTS (LONG-TERM DEBT) TOTAL PRIVATE CREDITORS PRIVATE NONGUARANTEED DEBT
DNHC	VTDF	MD	DEPRECIATION OF NON-HOUSING CAPITAL AT CURRENT PRICES
DNHC#	VTDF	MD95	DEPRECIATION OF NON-HOUSING CAPITAL AT CONSTANT PRICES
DOD	VTDS	MDS	PUBLIC DEBT OUTSTANDING (LONG-TERM) TOTAL ALL CREDITORS
DODOC	VTDS	MDS	PUBLIC DEBT OUTSTANDING (LONG-TERM) OFFICIAL CREDITORS
DODPC	VTDS	MDS	PUBLIC DEBT OUTSTANDING (LONG-TERM) PRIVATE CREDITORS
DODPNG	VTDS	MDS	PRIVATE DEBT OUTSTANDING (LONG-TERM)
			NON-GURANTEED

Table. Continued

DP	VTDS	TP	DISPLACED PERSONS
DPNPR	VTDF	%	RATIO OF DP TO TOTAL POPULATION
DPR	DTDF	TP	DISPLACED PERSONS, RECEIVED
DPRNPR	VTDF	%	RATIO OF DPR TO TOTAL POPULATION
DROUGHT	VTDF	POINT	FREQUENCY OF DROUGHT
DSR	VTDR	NU	PUBLIC TOTAL DEBT SERVICE RATIO
DSRLT	VTDR	NU	EXTERNAL DEBT TOTAL (LONG-TERM) DEBT SERVICE RATIO
E	VTDF	MD	EXPORTS OF GOODS AND SERVICES AT CURRENT PRICES
E#	VTDF	MD95	EXPORTS OF GOODS AND SERVICES AT CONSTANT PRICES
E#AGR	VTDF	MD95	EXPORTS OF AGRICULTURAL COMMODITIES
ECUR	VTDR	NCU/ECU	EXCHANGE RATE OF NATIONAL CURRENCY UNIT PER ECU
ECURI	VTDP	95=1	INDEX OF ECUR
E#MAT	MTDF	MD95	EXPORTS (MERCHANDISE, FOB) FROM REGION (I) TO REGION (J) AT CONSTANT PRICES
ECODP	VTDF	TP	ECOLOGICAL DISPLACED PERSONS
EDED@	VTXF	POINT	ETHNIC DIFFERENTIATION AND EXTERNAL DISMISSION
EDUA#	VTDS	MD95	EDUCATIONAL ASSETS AT CONSTANT PRICES
EDUA#PC	VTDF	TD95/P	EDUCATIONAL ASSETS (PER CAPITA)
EGS	VTDF	MD	GOVERNMENT CURRENT EXPENDITURE ON GOODS AND SERVICES

Table. Continued

EMFOB	VTDF	MDS	MERCHANDISE EXPORTS AT CURRENT US DOLLARS (BOP BASE)
EMIGRAN @	VTXF	TP	NUMBER OF EMIGRANTS
EMTFOB#	VTDF	MD95	MERCHANDISE EXPORTS AND IMPORTS TOTAL
ENGYR	VTDF	MTOE	ENERGY REQUIREMENTS (METRIC TON OIL EQUIVALENT)
ENGYRG	VTDF	MTOE	WORLD ENERGY REQUIREMENTS (METRIC TON OIL EQUIVALENT)
ENGYS	VTDF	MTOE	TOTAL ENERGY SUPPLY (METRIC TON OIL EQUIVALENT)
ENVI	VTDF	POINT	INTEGRATED ENVIRONMENT INDICATOR
EPC	VTDF	TOE	ENERGY REQUIREMENTS PER CAPITA
EROSION	VTDF	SM	EROSION
ESMAT	MTDF	MDS	EXPORTS (MERCHANDISE, FOB) FROM REGION (I) TO REGION (J) AT CURRENT US DOLLARS
ESMATAE	VTDR	MDS	EXPORTS FROM USA TO EU
ESMATEA	VTDR	MDS	EXPORTS FROM EU TO USA
ESR	VTDR	%	ENERGY SAVINGS RATE TO GDP# IN TERMS OF ENERGY INTENSITY
ESWARM	VTDF	GEGREE	AVERAGE EARTH SURFACE TEMPERATURE IN EACH REGION
ESWARMG	STDF	DEGREE	AVERAGE EARTH SURFACE TEMPERATURE AT THE GLOBAL LEVEL
ETFOB	VTDF	MDS	MERCHANDISE EXPORTS (FOB) AT CURRENT US DOLLARS
ETFOB#	VTDF	MDS	MERCHANDISE EXPORTS (FOB) AT CONSTANT US DOLLARS

Table. Continued

EUROCR@	VCXR	NCU/EU RO	EURO CURRENCY COVERSION RATES AMONG EU11 COUNTRIES
EXFOOD#	VTVF	MD95	EXPORTS OF FOODS
EXTIM@	VTXF	MT	EXPORT OF TIMBER
FADEDIA@	VTXF	MDS	FADEOUT OF DIA
FADEDIL@	VTXF	MDS	FADEOUT OF DIL
FADEPIA@	VTXF	MDS	FADEOUT OF PRIVATE FOREIGN DIRECT INVESTMENT
FADEPIL@	VTXF	MT	FADEOUT OF PFDI IN HOST COUNTRIES
FCI	VTDF	MDS	FOREIGN CAPITAL INFLOW TO DGE AT CURRENT US DOLLARS
FERE	VTDR	NCU/EU RO	EXCHANGE RATE PER EURO
FEREURO	STDF	ECU/US$	EURO CURRENCY'S EXCHANGE RATE PER US DOLLAR
FEERSI	VTDP	95 =1	EFFECTIVE FOREIGN EXCHANGE RATE INDEX OF US DOLLAR
FERIAME	STDP	95 =1	AME'S WEIGHTED AVERAGE FOREIGN EXCHANGE RATE INDEX PER US DOLLAR
FERISDR	STDP	95 =1	SDR RATE INDEX
FERIEUR	STDP	95 =1	EURO CURRENCY'S EXCHANGE RATE INDEX PER US DOLLAR
FERS	VTDR	NCU / US$	FOREIGN EXCHANGE RATE PER US DOLLAR
FERSI	VTDP	95 =1	FOREIGN EXCHANGE RATE INDEX PER US DOLLAR
FERSIDOT	VTDF	%	PERCENTAGE CHANGES IN US DOLLAR EXCHANGE RATE INDEX

Table. Continued

FERSPPP	VTDF	PPP / FERS	FOREIGN EXCHANGE RATE PER US DOLLAR ADJUSTMENT RATE BY PPP
FLOOD	VTXF	NCU	FREQUENCY OF FLOODS
FOODAID	VTXF	MT	FOOD AID (METRIC TONS)
FOODPOP	VTDF	MT/TP	FOOD-POPULATION IMBALANCE
FOODSS	VTDR	%	RATIO OF FOOD SELF-SUPPLY
FOSSIL	VTDF	MTOE	FOSSIL ENERGY IN METRIC TONS (OIL EQUIVALENT)
FOREST	VTDS	SM	FOREST ZONE
FRESTTC	VTDF	MDS	TECHNICAL COOPERATION FOR FORESTATION
FPROPCI	VTDP	95 =1	INDEX OF FOOD PRODUCTION PER CAPITA AT MT
GAS	VTDF	MTOE	NATURAL GAS REQUIREMENT
GBPREP	VTDF	MD	GOVERNMENT BONDS PRINCIPAL REPAYMENT
GBR	VTDF	MD	NEW ISSUES OF GOVERNMENT BONDS
GBRGE	VTDR	%	GOVERNMENT PRIMARY BALANCE PER GDP
GCE	VTDF	MD	GOVERNMENT CURRENT EXPENDITURE
GCE#	VTDF	MD95	GOVERNMENT CURRENT EXPENDITURE (AT CONST>)
GDF	VTDF	MD	GOVERNMENT DEFENSE EXPENDITURE
GDF#	VTDF	MD95	GOVERNMENT DEFENSE EXPENDITURE (AT CONST>
GDFGDP	VTDR	%	MILITARY EXPENDITURES TO GDP#
GDOS	VTDF	MD	CURRENT GOVERNMENT DEFICIT (-) OR SURPLUS (+)
GDOS#	VTDF	MD95	CURRENT GOVERNMENT DEFICIT (-) OR SURPLUS (+)
GDO	VTDS	MD	CENTRAL GOVERNMENT DEBT OUTSTANDING
GDOGDP	VTDR	%	GDO/GDP RATIO

Table. Continued

GDP	VTDF	MD	GROSS DOMESTIC PRODUCT AT CURRENT MARKET PRICES
GDPDOT	VTDF	%	ANNUAL PERCENTAGE CHANGES IN GDP
GDPE	VTDF	ME	GROSS DOMESTIC PRODUCT AT CURRENT MARKET PRICES (EURO CURRENCY UNIT)
GDPN	VTDF	MN	GROSS DOMESTIC PRODUCT AT CURRENT MARKET PRICES (NATIONAL CURRENCY UNIT)
GDPS	VTDF	MDS	GROSS DOMESTIC PRODUCTS AT CURRENT US DOLLARS
GDPSPPP	VTDF	MDS/PPP	GROSS DOMESTIC PRODUCTS AT CURRENT US DOLLARS ADJUSTED BY PPP (PARCHASING PWER PARITY)
GDPSG	VTDF	MDS	GROSS DOMESTIC PRODUCTS OF THE WORLD AT CURRENT US DOLLARS
GDP#	VTDF	MD95	GROSS DOMESTIC PRODUCT AT CONSTANT PRICES
GDP#DOT	VTDF	%	ECONOMIC GROWTH RATES (ANNUAL PERCENTAGE CHANGES IN GDP#)
GDP#AME	STDF	MD95	TOTAL GROSS DOMESTIC PRODUCTS OF AME REGION
GDP#E	VTDF	ME95	GROSS DOMESTIC PRODUCT AT CONSTANT PRICES (EURO CURRENCY UNIT)
GDP#EU	STDF	MD95	TOTAL GROSS DOMESTIC PRODUCTS OF EU
GDP#DGE	STDF	MD95	TOTAL GROSS DOMESTIC PRODUCTS OF DGE REGION

Table. Continued

GDP#G	STSF	MD95	TOTAL GROSS DOMESTIC PRODUCTS OF THE WORLD
GDP#N	VTDF	MN95	GROSS DOMESTIC PRODUCT AT CONSTANT MARKET PRICES (NATIONAL CURRENCY UNIT)
GDP#PPP	VTDF	MD95/ PPP95	GROSS DOMESTIC PRODUCT AT CONSTANT MARKET PRICES ADJUSTED BY PPP
GDP#PPC	VTDF	TD95/P	GROSS DOMESTIC PRODUCT AT CONSTANT MARKET PRICES ADJUSTED BY PPP (PER CAPITA)
GDPAGR#	VTDF	MD95	GROSS DOMESTIC PRODUCT BY AGRICULTURE
GDPAG#C	SCDF	MD95	RATIO OF AGRICULTURE TO GDP#
GDPIND#	VTDF	MD95	GROSS DOMESTIC PRODUCT BY INDUSTRIAL ACTIVITY
GDPIN#C	SCDF	MD95	RATIO OF INDUSTRY TO GDP#
GDPMF#	VTDF	MD95	GROSS DOMESTIC PRODUCT BY MANUFACTURING INDUSTRIES
GDPMF#C	SCDF	MD95	RATIO OF MANUFACTURING INDUSTRY TO GDP#
GDPSER#	VTDF	MD95	GROSS DOMESTIC PRODUCT BY SERVICE AND OTHERS
GDPP#	VTDF	MD95	PRODUCTION-ORIENTED GROSS DOMESTIC PRODUCT AT CONSTANT PRICES (POTENTIAL GDP#)
GDS	VTDF	MD	DISCOUNT AND INTEREST ON GOVERNMENT BONDS AT CURRENT PRICES
GDS#	VTDF	MD95	DISCOUNT AND INTEREST ON GOVERNMENT BONDS AT CONSTANT PRICES

Table. Continued

GE	VTDF	MD	GOVERNMENT EXPENDITURE & LENDING MINUS REPAYMENT AT CURRENT PRICES
GE#	VTDF	MD95	GOVERNMENT EXPENDITURE & LENDING MINUS REPAYMENT AT CONSTANT PRICES
GEDU	VTDF	MD	GOVERNMENT EDUCATION EXPENDITURE AT CURRENT PRICES
GEDU#	VTDF	MD95	GOVERNMENT EDUCATION EXPENDITURE AT CONSTANT PRICES
GEDUGDP	VTDR	%	EDUCATIONAL EXPENDITURES TO GDP#
GEITI@	VTXF	MD	GOVERNMENT EXPENDITURE ON INFORMATION TECHNOLOGY INVESTMENT
GEOP	VTDF	MD	GOVERNMENT EXPENDITURE ON OTHER PURPOSES
GEOP#	VTDF	MD95	GOVERNMENT EXPENDITURE ON OTHER PURPOSES (CONST.)
GES	VTDF	MD	GOVERNMENT EXPENDITURE ON ECONOMIC SERVICES
GES#	VTDF	MD95	GOVERNMENT EXPENDITURE ON ECONOMIC SERVICES (CONST.)
GEST	VTDF	MD	GOVERNMENT EXPENDITURE ON SCIENCE AND TECHNOLOGY
GEVS	VTDF	MD	GOVERNMENT EXPENDITURE ON VETERANS SERVICES
GFCF	VTDF	MD	GROSS FIXED CAPITAL FORMATION AT CURRENT PRICES
GFCF#	VTDF	MD95	GROSS FIXED CAPITAL FORMATION AT CONSTANT PRICES
GFR	VTDF	Per 1000w	GENERAL FERTILITY RATE
GGO	VTDF	MD	GENERAL GOVERNMENT OPERATING SURPLUS AT CURRENT PRICES

Table. Continued

GGO#	VTDF	MD95	GENERAL GOVERNMENT OPERATING SURPLUS AT CONSTANT PRICES
GH	VTDF	MD	GOVERNMENT HEALTH EXPENDITURE
GH#	VTDF	MD95	GOVERNMENT HEALTH EXPENDITURE AT CONSTANT PRICES
GH#PC	VTDF	TD /P	GOVERNMENT HEALTH EXPENDITURE AT CONSTANT PRICES (PER CAPITA)
GHC	VTDF	MD	GOVERNMENT EXPENDITURE ON HOUSING AND COMMUNITY
GHC#	VTDF	MD95	GOVERNMENT EXPENDITURE ON HOUSING AND COMMUNITY (CONST.)
GITI	VTDF	MD	GOVERNMENT EXPENDITURE ON INFORMATION TECHNOLOGY INVESTMENT
GITI#	VTDF	MD95	GOVERNMENT EXPENDITURE ON INFORMATION TECHNOLOGY INVESTMENT (COST.)
GIP	VTDF	MD	GOVERNMENT CURRENT EXPENDITURE ON INTEREST PAYMENTS
GIP#	VTDF	MD95	GOVERNMENT CURRENT EXPENDITURE ON INTEREST PAYMENTS (CONST.)
GLMR@	VTXF	MD	GOVERNMENT LENDING MINUS REPAYMENT
GLMR#@	VTXF	MD95	GOVERNMENT LENDING MINUS REPAYMENT (CONST.)
GLPF	VTDF	MD	GOVERNMENT EXPENDITURE ON LOCAL PUBLIC FINANCES
GPS	VTDF	MD	GOVERNMENT EXPENDITURE ON GENERAL PUBLIC SERVICES

Table. Continued

GPS#	VTDF	MD95	GOVERNMENT EXPENDITURE ON GENERAL PUBLIC SERVICES (CONST.)
GPW	VTDF	MD	GOVERNMENT EXPENDITURE ON PUBLIC WORKS
GR	VTDF	MD	GOVERNMENT REVENUE AND GRANT AT CURRENT PRICES
GR#	VTDF	MD95	GOVERNMENT REVENUE AND GRANT AT CONSTANT PRICES
GRANT@	VTXF	MD	GRANT REVENUE OF GOVERNMENT
GRANT#@	VTXF	MD95	GRANT REVENUE OF GOVERNMENT (CONST.)
GRR	VTDF	Per woman	GROSS REPRODUCTION RATE
GSS	VTDF	MD	GOVERNMENT EXPENDITURE ON OTHER COMMUNITY SERVICES
GSS#	VTDF	MD95	GOVERNMENT EXPENDITURE ON OTHER COMMUNITY SERVICES (CONST.)
GSW	VTDF	MD	GOVERNMENT EXPENDITURE ON SOCIAL SECURITY & WELFARE
GSW#	VTDF	MD95	GOVERNMENT EXPENDITURE ON SOCIAL SECURITY & WELFARE AT CONSTANT PRICES
GSW#PC	VTDF	TD95/P	GOVERNMENT EXPENDITURE ON SOCIAL SECURITY & WELFARE AT CONSTANT PRICES (PER CAPITA)
GSWGDP	VTDR	%	SOCIAL SECURITY EXPENDITURES TO GDP#
GTE	VTDF	MD	GOVERNMENT TOTAL EXPENDITURE
GTE#	VTDF	MD95	GOVERNMENT TOTAL EXPENDITURE (AT CONST.)
H2OSAFE	VTDR	%	ACCESS TO SAFE WATER, TOTAL, % OF NP
HPI	VTDF	MD	HOUSEHOLD'S PROPERTY INCOME

Table. Continued

HI	VTDF	MD	HOUSING INVESTMENT AT CURRENT PRICES
HI#	VTDF	MD95	HOUSING INVESTMENT AT CONSTANT PRICES
HLTH	VTDR	%	HEALTH EXPENDITURES AS % OF GDP#
HOW	VTDR	HOURS	HOURS OF WORK (ANNUAL AVERAGE)
HRDP	VTDS	TP	HUMAN RIGHT DISPLACED PERSONS
HRI	VTDF	POINT	INTEGRATED HUMAN RIGHT INDICATORS
HYDRO	VTDF	MTOE	HYDRO ELECTRIC GENERATION
IB	VTDR	%	GOVERNMENT LONG TERM BOND YIELD
IBEU	STDR	%	WEIGHTED AVERAGE OF EU GOVERNMENT LONG- TERM BOND YIELD
IC	VTDR	%	CALL MONEY RATE OR FEDERAL FUND RATE
ICC	VTDR	%	INTEREST RATE OF CONSUMERS CREDIT
ICEU	STDR	%	WEIGHTED AVERAGE OF CALL MONEY RATE OF EU
ICII	VTDF	MDS	INVESTMENT INCOME, CREDIT AT CURRENT US DOLLARS
ICIIDIA	VTDF	MDS	DIRECT INVESTMENT INCOME: CREDIT:
ICIIPI	VTDF	MDS	PORTFOLIO INCOME: CREDIT
IDII	VTDF	MDS	INVESTMENT INCOME, DEBIT AT CURRENT US DOLLARS
IDIIDIA	VTDF	MDS	DIRECT INVESTMENT INCOME: CREDIT:
IDIIPI	VTDF	MDS	PORTFOLIO INCOME: DEBIT
IDEBTOC	VTDR	%	RATE OF INTEREST PAID (LONG-TERM DEBT) OFFICIAL CREDITORS

Table. Continued

IDEBTPC	VTDR	%	RATE OF INTEREST PAID (LONG-TERM DEBT) PRIVATE CREDITORS
IDEBTPN	VTDR	%	AVERAGE RATE OF INTEREST PAID (PRIVATE NONGUARANTEED)
IH	VTDR	%	HOUSING LOAN RATE
IIS	VTDF	MD	INCREASE IN STOCKS AT CURRENT PRICES
IIS#	VTDF	MD95	INCREASE IN STOCKS AT CONSTANT PRICES
IMFOOD#	VTDF	MD95	IMPORTS OF FOODS
IMMIDPT	VTDR	%	IMMUNIZED AGAINST DIPHTHERIA (% UNDER 1)
IMMMEAS	VTDR	%	IMMUNIZED AGAINST MEASLES (% UNDER 1)
IMPCERL	VTDF	MT	IMPORTS, CEREALS
IN	VTDR	%	CENTRAL BANK'S OFFICIAL DISCOUNT RATE
INCOMEC	VTDR	MD	INCOME IN CURRENT ACCOUNT: CREDIT
INCOMED	VTDR	MD	INCOME IN CURRENT ACCOUNT: DEBIT
INEU	VTDR	%	EU'S COMMON OFFICIAL DISCOUNT RATE
INCDISTR	VTDR	MD/TP	UNEQUAL INCOME DISTRIBUTION
INFRA#@	VTXS	MD95	INFRASTRUCTURE
INSURGE	VTDF	TP	INSURGENCY
INT	VTDF	MDS	INTEREST PAYMENT (LONG-TERM DEBT, PUBLIC) ALL CREDITORS
INTLWAR	VTDF	POINT	INTERNATIONAL WAR
INTWAR	VTDF	POINT	INTERNAL WAR
INTOC	VTDF	MDS	INTEREST PAYMENTS (LONG-TERM DEBT) OFFICIAL CREDITORS
INTPC	VTDF	MDS	INTEREST PAYMENTS (LONG-TERM DEBT) PRIVATE CREDITORS

Table. Continued

INTPNG	VTDF	MDS	INTEREST PAYMENT (PRIVATE NONGUARANTEED)
INTSPTP	VTDR	NO/ TP	INTERNET SUBSCRIBERS PER THOUSAND PERSONS
INTHPTP	VTDR	NO/TP	INTERNET HOSTS PER THOUSAND PERSONS
IOED	VTDF	POINT	IDEOLOGY OPPRESSION AND EXTERNAL DISMISSION
IP	VTDR	%	PRIME RATE
IPCIDG	VTDR	INDEX.	INTERNATIONAL PER CAPITA INCOME DISPARITIES (COMPARED WITH THE GLOBAL AVERAGE) IN TERMS OF REAL GDP AT 1995 CONSTANT PRICES
IPCIDA	VTDR	INDEX.	INTERNATIONAL PER CAPITA INCOME DISPARITIES (COMPARED WITH THE AME AVERAGE) IN TERMS OF REAL GDP AT 1995 CONSTANT PRICES
IPCIDD	VTDR	INDEX.	INTERNATIONAL PER CAPITA INCOME DISPARITIES (COMPARED WITH THE DGE AVERAGE) IN TERMS OF REAL GDP AT 1995 CONSTANT PRICES
IPCIDP	VTDR	INDEX WORD= 100	INTERNATIONAL PER CAPITA INCOME DISPARITIES (COMPARED WITH THE GLOBAL AVERAGE) IN TERMS OF REAL GDP AT 1995 PPP
IPI	VTDP	95=1	INDUSTRIAL PRODUCTION INDEX
IS	VTDS	MD	INVENTORY STOCK AT CURRENT PRICES
IS#	VTDS	MD95	INVENTORY STOCK AT CONSTANT PRICES

Table. Continued

ISEURO	STDR	%	EURO-DOLLAR RATE
ITD	VTDR	%	TIME DEPOSIT RATE
ITI#	VTDF	MD95	INFORMATION TECHNOLOGY INVESTMENT AT CONSTANT MARKET PRICES
ITKPROT	VTDF	GRAM	DAILY PROTEIN INTAKE OF FISH PER CAPITA
IV#	VTDR	95=1	MONEY SUPPLY (M2) / REAL INCOME INDEX
LANDMIN	VTDF	HA/TP	AGRICULTURAL LAND MINCING
LANDCON	VTDF	HA/TP	AGRICULTURAL LAND CONCENTRATION
LB	VTDS	MD	CLAIMS ON PRIVATE SECTOR, OUTSTANDING
LCLF	VTDS	TP	CIVILIAN LABOUR FORCE
LCLFF	VTDS	TP	CIVILIAN LABOUR FORCE: FEMALE
LCLFM	VTDS	TP	CIVILIAN LABOUR FORCE: MALE
LCLFMIN@	VTXS	TP	INFLOWED CIVILIAN LABOUR FORCE: MALE (NET)
LIBOR	STDR	%	LONDON INTERBANK OFFERED RATE
LIFEEXP	VTDR	YEAR	LIFE EXPECTANCY AT BIRTH
LIFEXPM LIFEXPF	VTDF VTDF	YEAR YEAR	LIFE EXPECTANCY AT BIRTH (MALE) LIFE EXPECTANCY AT BIRTH (FEMALE)
LPI	VTDP	95 =1	LABOUR PRODUCTIVITY INDEX
LLPTP	VTDR	NO/TP	LEASED LINES PER THOUSAND PERSONS
LTCB	VTDF	MDS	LONG-TERM CAPITAL BALANCE AT CURRENT US DOLLARS
LW	VTDS	TP	WAGE EARNER AND SALARIED EMPLOYEES IN ALL ACTIVITY
M	VTDF	MD	IMPORTS OF GOODS AND SERVICES AT CURRENT PRICES
M#	VTDF	MD95	IMPORTS OF GOODS AND SERVICES AT CONSTANT PRICES

Table. Continued

MALNUT	VTDR	%	CHILD MALNUTRITION (% UNDER 5)
MILIAID	VTXF	MDS	MILITARY AIDS
MMFOB	VTDF	MDS	MERCHANDISE IMPORTS AT CURRENT US DOLLARS (BOP BASE)
MMRT	VTDR	RATE	MATERNA MORTALITY RATE (P/1000,000 LIVE BABIES)
MORTY	VTDF	TP	MORTALITY
MPSED	VTDF	%	MASS POVERTY AND SOCIO-ECONOMIC DISPARITIES (SHARE OF INCOME HELD BY POOREST 40% OF HOUSHOLDS)
M1	VTDS	MD	MONEY SUPPLY (M1), OUTSTANDING
M2	VTDS	MD	MONEY AND QUASI-MONEY (M1+MTD), OUTSTANDING
M2EU	VTDS	MTD	M2 OF EU AS A GROUP
MTD	VTDS	MD	QUASI-MONEY (TIME AND SAVING DEPOSITS), OUTSTANDING
MTELPTP	VTDR	NO / TP	MOBILE TELEPHONE NUMBERS PER THOUSAND PERSONS
MTFOB	VTDF	MDS	MERCHANDISE, IMPORTS (FOB) AT CURRENT US DOLLARS
MTFOB#	VTDF	MD95	MERCHANDISE, IMPORTS (FOB) AT CONSTANT PRICES
NATY	VTDF	TP	NATALITY
NCUCR@	VTXF	Millions=1	NATIONAL CURRENCY UNIT CONVERSION RATE (MILLIONS = 1, BILLIONS =1000)
NDISAST@	VTXF	POINT	NATURAL DISASTERS
NETMGT	VTDF	TP	NUMBER OF NET MIGRANTS
NETMGTR	VTDF	/TP	NET MIGRANTS TO POPULATION (PER1000)

Table. Continued

NENGYTB @	VTXF	MTOE	NET ENERGY TRADE IN METRIC TON (COAL EQUIV)
NFCR	VTDF	MDS	NEWLY FOREIGN CAPITAL REQUIREMENTS
NFLOW	VTDF	MDS	NET FLOWS (LONG-TERM DEBT) TOTAL ALL CREDITORS
NFLOWOF	VTDF	MDS	NET FLOWS (LONG-TERM DEBT) TOTAL OFFICIAL CREDITORS
NFLOWP	VTDF	MDS	NET FLOWS (LONG-TERM DEBT) TOTAL PRIVATE CREDITORS
NHFCS#	VTDS	MD95	NON-HOUSING FIXED CAPITAL STOCKS AT CONSTANT PRICES
NHI	VTDF	MD	NON-HOUSING INVESTMENT AT CURRENT PRICES
NHI#	VTDF	MD95	NON-HOUSING INVESTMENT AT CONSTANT PRICES
NHING	VTDF	MD	NON-HOUSING INVESTMENT (NON GOVERNMENT) AT CURRENT PRICES
NHING#	VTDF	MD95	NON-HOUSING INVESTMENT (NON GOVERNMENT) AT CONSTANT PRICES
NMFOOD	VTDF	MD	NET FOODS IMPORTS (AT CURRENT US$)
NOX	VTDF	TT	NOX EMISSION
NP	VTDS	TP	NUMBER OF POPULATION
NPG	STDS	TP	NUMBER OF WORLD POPULATION
NPDGE	STDS	TP	NUMBER OF POPULATION OF DGE REGION
NPF	VTDS	TP	NUMBER OF POPULATION: FEMALE
NPFEA	VTDS	TP	NUMBER OF POPULATION FROM 15 TO 64 YEARS: FEMALE
NPFO65	VTDS	TP	NUMBER OF POPULATION OVER 65 YEARS: FEMALE
NPFU15	VTDS	TP	NUMBER OF POPULATION UNDER 15 YEARS: FEMALE

Table. Continued

NPM	VTDS	TP	NUMBER OF POPULATION: MALE
NPMEA	VTDS	TP	NUMBER OF POPULATION FROM 15 TO 64 YEARS: MALE
NPMO65	VTDS	TP	NUMBER OF POPULATION OVER 65 YEARS: MALE
NPMU15	VTDS	TP	NUMBER OF POPULATION UNDER 15: MALE
NPO65	VTDS	TP	NUMBER OF POPULATION OVER 65 YEARS: TOTAL
NPRURAL	VTDS	TP	NUMBER OF RURAL POPULATION
NPSLUM	VTDF	TP	NUMBER OF URBAN SLUM POPULATION
NPURBAN	VTDS	TP	NUMBER OF URBAN POPULATION
NRR	VTDS	Per woman	NET REPRODUCTON RATE
NTB@	VTXR	NU	NON TARIFF BARRIER
NTR	VTDF	MD	NON-TAX REVENUE OF GOVERNMENT
NTR#	VTDF	MD95	NON-TAX REVENUE OF GOVERNMENT (CONST.)
NUCL	VTDF	MTOE	NUCLEAR ENERGY REQUIREMENT
NUCLPOL	VTDS	POINT	NUCLEAR POLLUTION
NURS	VTDF	P	NUMBER OF NURSES
OBEDU#	VTDF	MD95	OBSOLETE EDUCATIONAL ASSETS
OBTECH#	VTDF	MD95	OBSOLETE TECHNOLOGY ASSETS
ODA	VTDF	MDS	EACH AME'S ODA (NET) AT CURRENT US DOLLARS
ODAB	VTDF	MDS	BILATERAL ODA (NET) AT CURRENT US DOLLARS
ODAM	VTDF	MDS	CONTRIBUTIONS TO MULTI. INSTITUTIONS (NET) AT CURRENT US DOLLARS
ODAMAT	NTDF	MDS	ODA (NET) FROM AME (I) TO DGE (J) AT CURRENT US DOLLARS
ODAR	VTDF	MDS	OFFICIAL DEVELOPMENT ASSISTANCE RECEIVED, TOTAL

Table. Continued

ODABR	VTDF	MDS	OFFICIAL DEVELOPMENT ASSISTANCE RECEIVED, BILATERAL
ODAMR	VTDF	MDS	OFFICIAL DEVELOPMENT ASSISTANCE RECEIVED, MULTILATERAL
ODATC	VTDF	MDS	ODA TECHNICAL COOPERATION
ODATCR	VTDF	MDS	ODA TECHNICAL COOPERATION RECEIVED
OIL	VTDF	MT	OIL REQUIREMENT
OILWRD	STDF	MT	WORLD OIL REQUIREMENT
OLCB@	VTXF	MDS	OTHER LONG-TERM CAPITAL, BALANCE AT CURRENT US DOLLARS
OOF	VTDF	MDS	OTHER OFFICIAL FLOWS
OOFR	VTDF	MDS	OTHER OFFICIAL FLOWS RECEIVED
OOFBR	VTDF	MDS	OTHER OFFICIAL FLOWS RECEIVED BILATERAL
OOFMR	VTXF	MDS	OTHER OFFICIAL FLOWS RECEIVED MULTILATERAL
ORTH	VTDR	%	RATE OF ORAL REHYDRATION THERAPY (% UNDER 5)
OS	VTDF	MD	OPERATING SURPLUS AT CURRENT PRICES
OS#	VTDF	MD95	OPERATING SURPLUS AT CONSTANT PRICES
OSAME	STDF	MD	AME TOTAL OF OPERATING SURPLUS AT CURRENT PRICES
O3G@	VTXF	MT	GLOBAL OZONE EMISSION
PAGR	VTDP	95 =1	DOMESTIC PRICES IN AGRICULTURAL RAW MATERIALS AND FOODS
PCOAL	VTDP	95 =1	DOMESTIC PRICE INDEX OF COAL
PCFD	VTDF	MT/NP	PER CAPITA FOODS DEMAND

Table. Continued

PCG	VTDP	95 =1	IMPLICIT DEFLATOR OF GOVERNMENT CONSUMPTION EXPENDITURE
PCIDOT	VTDR	%	STAGNANT PER CAPITA INCOME
PCP	VTDP	95 =1	IMPLICIT DEFLATOR OF PRIVATE CONSUMPTION EXPENDITURE
PCPTP	VTDF	NO / TP	PERSONAL COMPUTERS PER THOUSAND PEOPLE
PE	VTDP	95 =1	EXPORT UNIT VALUE INDEX
PEC	STDP	95 =1	WORLD AVERAGE EXPORT PRICE INDEX OF COMMODITIES EXCLUDING OIL
PEGOLD	STDP	95 =1	WORLD AVERAGE EXPORT PRICE INDEX OF GOLD
PENA	VTDP	95 =1	IMPLICIT DEFLATOR OF EXPORTS (GOODS AND SERVICES)
PEO	STDP	95 =1	WORLD AVERAGE CRUDE PETROLEUM EXPORT PRICE INDEX IN US DOLLARS
PEOB	STDR	$/B	AVERAGE CRUDE PETROLEUM EXPORT PRICE IN US DOLLAR PER BARREL
PECOAL	STDP	95 =1	WORLD AVERAGE COAL EXPORT UNIT VALUE INDEX IN US DOLLARS
PEGAS	STDP	95 =1	AVERAGE GAS EXPORT UNIT VALUE INDEX IN US DOLLARS
PELC	VTDP	95 =1	DOMESTIC ELECTRICITY PRICE INDEX
PEOHR	VTDR	%	PUBLIC HEALTH EXPENDITURES AS % OF GDP
PEOH	VTDR	MD	PUBLIC HEALTH EXPENDITURE S
PEOH#	VTDR	MD95	PUBLIC HEALTH EXPENDITURES (CONST.)
PEOHPC	VTDF	MD90/PC	PUBLIC HEALTH EXPENDITURES PER CAPITA

Table. Continued

PES	VTDP	95 =1	EXPORT UNIT VALUE INDEX IN TERMS OF US DOLLAR
PESAME	STDP	95 =1	AME EXPORT UNIT VALUE INDEX IN TERMS OF US DOLLAR
PEW	STDP	95 =1	WORLD EXPORT UNIT VALUE INDEX IN TERMS OF US DOLLARS
PFDI	VTDF	MDS	PRIVATE FOREIGN DIRECT INVESTMENT AT CURRENT US DOLLARS
PFDIMAT	NTDF	MDS	PRIVATE FOREIGN DIRECT INVESTMENT FROM AME (I) TO DME (J)
PFDIR	VTDF	MDS	PRIVATE FOREIGN DIRECT INVESTMENT, RECEIVED
PFDIO	VTDF	MDS	OUTSTANDING PFDI FROM COUNTRY<I> TO COUNTRY<J>
PFDIL	VTDF	MDS	LIABILITIES OF PFDI IN HOST COUNTRIES
PGAS	VTDP	95 =1	DOMESTIC GAS PRICE INDEX
PGDP	VTDP	95 =1	IMPLICIT DEFLATOR OF GROSS DOMESTIC PRODUCT
PGDPDOT	VTDP	%	ANNUAL PERCENTAGE CHANGES IN PGDP
PGDPEU	VTDP	95 =1	EU' S WEIGHTED AVERAGE IMPLICIT DEFLATOR OF GROSS DOMESTIC PRODUCT
PGFCF	VTDP	95 =1	IMPLICIT DEFLATOR OF GRO'S FIXED CAPITAL FORMATION
PHI	VTDP	95 =1	IMPLICIT DEFLATOR OF HOUSING INVESTMENT
PHYS	VTDF	P	NUMBER OF PHYSICIANS
PLAND	VTDP	95=1	COMMERCIAL LAND PRICE INDEX OF MAJOR CITIES
PM	VTDP	95 =1	IMPORT UNIT VALUE INDEX

Table. Continued

PMNA	VTDP	95 =1	IMPLICIT DEFLATOR OF IMPORTS (GOODS AND SERVICES)
PMS	VTDP	95 =1	IMPORT UNIT VALUE INDEX IN TERMS OF US DOLLAR
PMW	STDP	95 =1	WORLD IMPORT UNIT VALUE INDEX
PNHI	VTDP	95 =1	IMPLICIT DEFLATOR OF NON-HOUSING INVESTMENT
PNHING	VTDP	95 =1	IMPLICIT DEFLATOR OF NON-HOUSING INVESTMENT (NON GOVERNMENT)
PNUCL	VTDP	95 =1	ELECTRICITY PRICE DERIVED FROM NUCLEAR
POIL	VTDP	95 =1	DOMESTIC PETROLEUM PRICE INDEX
POINA	VTDF	MDS	PORTFOLIO INVESTMENT, ASSETS AT CURRENT US DOLLARS
POINB	VTDF	MDS	PORTFOLIO INVESTMENT, BALANCE AT CURRENT US DOLLARS
POINL	VTDF	MDS	PORTFOLIO INVESTMENT, LIABILITIES AT CURRENT US DOLLARS
POLCNFL	VTXF	POINT	POLITICAL CONFLICTS
POOR20	VTDF	%	SHARE OF INCOME HELD BY POOREST 20% OF HOUSHOLDS
POPBEDS	VTDF	P	POPULATION PER HOSPITAL BEDS
PPFCF	VTDP	95=1	IMPLICIT DEFLATOR OF PUBLIC FIXED CAPITAL FORMATION
POS#	VTDF	MD95	GOVERNMENT EXPENDITURE ON PUBLIC ORDER AND SAFETY (AT CONSTANT PRICES)
POPPHY	VTDF	P	POPULATION PER PHYSICIAN
POVLHC	VTDF	%	HEADCOUNT INDEX: LOWER POVERTY LINE
POVUPHC	VTDF	%	(% OF HOUSHOLDS) HEADCOUNT INDEX: UPPER POVERTY LINE (% OF HOUSHOLDS)

Table. Continued

PREP	VTDF	MDS	PRINCIPAL REPAYMENTS (LONG-TERM PUBLIC DEBT) ALL CREDITORS
PREPOC	VTDF	MDS	PRINCIPAL REPAYMENTS (LONG-TERM, PUBLIC DEBT) OFFICIAL CREDITORS
PREPPC	VTDF	MDS	PRINCIPAL REPAYMENTS (LONG-TERM PUBLIC DEBT) PRIVATE CREDITORS
PREPPNG	VTDF	MDS	PRINCIPAL REPAYMENT (PRIVATE NON-GURANTEED)
PSES	VTDS	MD	PERSONAL SECURITIES EXCLUDING STOCKS
PSDP	VTDS	TP	DISPLACED PERSONS FROM LACK OF PEACE AND SECURITY
PSI	VTDF	POINT	INTEGRATED PEACE AND SECURITY INDICATORS
PUE	VTDF	MD	PRIVATE UNINCORPORATED ENTERPRISES OPERATING SURPLUS
RC	VTDF	MD	CAPITAL REVENUE OF GOVERNMENT
RC#	VTDF	MD95	CAPITAL REVENUE OF GOVERNMENT (CONST.)
RD	VTDF	MD	RESEARCH AND DEVELOPMENT EXPENDITURES AT CURRENT PRICES
RD#	VTDF	MD95	RESEARCH AND DEVELOPMENT EXPENDITURES AT CONSTANT PRICES
RDBE	VTDF	MD	RESEARCH AND DEVELOPMENT EXPENDITURES BY BUSINESS ENTERPRISES
RDBE#	VTDF	MD95	RESEARCH AND DEVELOPMENT EXPENDITURES BY BUSINESS ENTERPRISES (CONST.)

Table. Continued

RDGOV	VTDF	MD	RESEARCH AND DEVELOPMENT EXPENDITURES BY GOVERNMENT
RDGOV#	VTDF	MD95	RESEARCH AND DEVELOPMENT EXPENDITURES BY GOVERNMENT (CONST)
RDOTH	VTDF	MD	RESEARCH AND DEVELOPMENT EXPENDITURES BY OTHERS. (NGO AND NON-BUSINESS)
RDOTH#	VTDF	MD95	RESEARCH AND DEVELOPMENT EXPENDITURES BY OTHERS (COST)
RG	VTDF	MD	TOTAL REVENUE INCLUDING CENTRAL GOVERNMENT BOND REVENUE AT CURRENT PRICES
RICH20	VTDF	%	SHARE OF INCOME HELD BY RICHEST 20% OF HOUSHOLDS
ROED@	VTXF	POINT	RELIGIOUS OPPRESSION AND EXTERNAL DISMISSION
SAFERU	VTDR	%	ACCESS TO SAFE WATER (% OF NP)
SC	VTDF	MDS	EXPORTS OF SERVICES AT CURRENT US DOLLARS
SCOTH	VTDF	MDS	OTHER SERVICES: CREDIT AT CURRENT US DOLLARS
SCTPN	VTDF	MDS	TRANSPORTATION, CREDIT AT CURRENT DOLLARS
SCTR	VTDF	MDS	TRAVEL IN SC, CREDIT AT CURRENT US DOLLARS
SD	VTDF	MDS	IMPORTS OF SERVICES AT CURRENT US DOLLARS
SDOTH	VTDF	MDS	OTHER SERVICES: DEBIT AT CURRENT US DOLLARS

Table. Continued

SDTPN	VTDF	MDS	TRANSPORTATION, DEBIT AT CURRENT DOLLARS
SDTR	VTDF	MDS	TRAVEL IN SD, DEBIT AT CURRENT US DOLLARS
SMV	VTDS	MD	STOCK MARKET VALUE AT CURRENT PRICES
SOILPOL	VTDS	POINT	SOIL POLLUTION
SOLAR	VTVF	MTOE	SOLAR ENERGY USE
SOLARTE@	VTXF	MTOE	SOLAR ENERGY TECHNOLOGY
SOX	VTDF	TT	SOX EMISSION
SPI	VTDF	95=1	SHARE PRICE INDEX (REPRESENTATIVE INDEX)
SSC	VTDF	MD	SOCIAL SECURITY CONTRIBUTIONS
SSC#	VTDF	MD95	SOCIAL SECURITY CONTRIBUTIONS (CONST.)
SSCEE@	VTXF	MD	SOCIAL SECURITY CONTRIBUTIONS FOR EMPLOYEES
SSCEE#@	VTXF	MD95	SOCIAL SECURITY CONTRIBUTIONS FOR EMPLOYEES
SSCER@	VTXF	MD	SOCIAL SECURITY CONTRIBUTIONS FOR EMPLOYERS (CONST.)
SSCER#@	VTXF	MD95	SOCIAL SECURITY CONTRIBUTIONS FOR EMPLOYERS (CONST.)
STDC	VTDF	MD	STATISTICAL DISCREPANCY IN COST-STRUCTURE OF GDP
STDC#	VTDF	MD95	STATISTICAL DISCREPANCY IN COST-STRUCTURE OF GDP#
STDCE@	VTXF	MD	STATISTICAL DISCREPANCY IN EXPENDITURES OF GDP
STDCE#@	VTXF	MD95	STATISTICAL DISCREPANCY IN EXPENDITURES OF GDP#
SUB	VTDF	MD	GOVERNMENT CURRENT EXPENDITURE ON SUBSIDIES (SNA BASE)
SUB#	VTDF	MD95	GOVERNMENT CURRENT EXPENDITURE ON SUBSIDIES (SNA BASE) (CONST.)

Table. Continued

SUBG	VTDF	MD	GOVERNMENT CURRENT EXPENDITURE ON SUBSIDIES (GFS BASE)
SUBG#	VTDF	MD95	GOVERNMENT CURRENT EXPENDITURE ON SUBSIDIES (GFS BASE) (CONST.)
TB	VTDF	MDS	MERCHANDISE TRADE BALANCE (DOT) AT CURRENT US DOLLARS
TBB	VTDF	MDS	MERCHANDISE TRADE BALANCE (BOP) AT CURRENT US DOLLARS
TC	VTDF	MD	CONSUMPTION TAX
TCR@	VTXF	%	CONSUMPTION TAX RATE
TD	VTDF	MD	DIRECT TAXES
TD#	VTDF	MD95	DIRECT TAXES (CONST.)
TDGS	VTDF	MD	DOMESTIC TAXES ON GOODS AND SERVICES
TDGS#	VTDF	MD95	DOMESTIC TAXES ON GOODS AND SERVICES (CONST.)
TDOD	VTDS	MDS	DOMESTIC DEBT OUTSTANDING (SHORT AND LONG-TERM)
TDS	VTDF	MDS	PUBLIC DEBT SERVICE (LONG-TERM DEBT) TOTAL ALL CREDITORS
TDSOC	VTDF	MDS	PUBLIC DEBT SERVICE (LONG-TERM DEBT) OFFICIAL CREDITORS
TDSPC	VTDF	MDS	PUBLIC DEBT SERVICE (LONG-TERM DEBT) PRIVATE CREDITORS
TDSPNG	VTDF	MDS	PRIVATE DEBT SERVICE (PRIVATE NON-GUARANTEED)
TECA#PC	VTDR	MD95/TP	TECHNOLOGY ASSETES AT CONSTANT PRICES PER THOUSAND PERSONS

Table. Continued

TECHA#	VTDS	MD95	TECHNOLOGY ASSETS AT CONSTANT PRICES
TECHE	VTDF	MD	EXPORT OF TECHNOLOGY AT CURRENT PRICES
TECHE#	VTDF	MD95	EXPORT OF TECHNOLOGY AT CONSTANT PRICES
TECHM	VTDF	MD	IMPORT OF TECHNOLOGY AT CURRENT PRICES
TECHM#	VTDF	MD95	IMPORT OF TECHNOLOGY AT CONSTANT PRICES
TEOH	VTDF	MD	TOTAL HEALTH EXPENDITURES
TEOH#	VTDF	MD95	TOTAL HEALTH EXPENDITURES (CONST.)
TECHPC	VTDF	MD95/PC	TOTAL HEALTH EXPENDITURES PER CAPITA
TECHR	VTDF	%	TOTAL HEALTH EXPENDITURES AS % OF GDP
TELMPTP	VTDR	NO / TP	TELEPHONE MAINLINES PER THOSAND PERSONS
TEPM@	VTXF	MD	EMPLOYERS PAYROLL OR MANPOWER TAXES
TERRA	STDF	Terra	TERRA CURRENCY UNIT
TERRAS	STDF	Terra/$	TERRA EXCHANGE RATE PER DOLLAR
TERRASI	STDF	95=1	TERRA EXCHANGE RATE INDEX PER DOLLAR
TFOODR	VTDF	MT	TOTAL FOODS REQUIREMENT
TFOODS	VTDF	MT	TOTAL FOODS SUPPLY
TFCE	VTDF	MTOE	TOTAL FINAL CONSUMPTION OF ENERGY
TFCALT@	VTXF	MTOE	TFC ON ALTERNATIVE ENERGY
TFCOAL	VTDF	MTOE	TFC ON COAL.
TFCOALI	VTDF	MTOE	TFC ON COAL IN INDUSTRY
TFCOALT	VTDF	MTOE	TFC ON COAL IN TRANSPORT
TFCOALO	VTDF	MTOE	TFC ON COAL IN OTHER SECTORS
TFCELC	VTDF	MTOE	TFC ON ELECTRICITY
TFCELCI	VTDF	MTOE	TFC ON ELECTRICITY IN INDUSTRY

Table. Continued

TFCELCT	VTDF	MTOE	TFC ON ELECTRICITY IN TRANSPORT
TFCELCO	VTDF	MTOE	TFC ON ELECTRICITY IN OTHER SECTORS
TFCGAS	VTDF	MTOE	TFC ON GAS
TFCGASI	VTDF	MTOE	TFC ON GAS IN INDUSTRY
TFCGAST	VTDF	MTOE	TFC ON GAS IN TRANSPORT.
TFCGASO	VTDF	MTOE	TFC ON GAS IN OTHER SECTORS.
TFCOIL	VTDF	MTOE	TFC ON OIL
TFCOILI	VTDF	MTOE	TFC ON OIL IN INDUSTRY
TFCOILT	VTDF	MTOE	TFC ON OIL IN TRANSPORT
TI#	VTDF	MD95	INDIRECT TAXES (SNA BASE) (CONST.)
TID	VTDF	MD	INDIRECT TAXES (GFS BASE)
TID#	VTDF	MD95	INDIRECT TAXES (GFS BASE) (CONST.)
TIN	VTDF	MD	INDIRECT TAXES (SNA BASE)
TIPC	VTDF	MD	TAXES ON INCOME AND PROFIT, AND CAPITAL GAIN
TIPC#	VTDF	MD95	TAXES ON INCOME AND PROFIT, AND CAPITAL GAIN (CONST.)
TIR	VTDF	MD	OTHER INDIRECT TAXES
TIR#	VTDF	MD95	OTHER INDIRECT TAXES (CONST.)
TITT	VTDF	MD	TAXES ON INTERNATIONAL TRADE AND TRANSACTIONS
TITT#	VTDF	MD95	TAXES ON INTERNATIONAL TRADE AND TRANSACTIONS (CONST.)
TLAND@	VTXS	HA	TOTAL LAND IN EACH COUNTRY
TOU	VTDF	MD	OTHER UNALLOCABLE TAXES ON INCOME
TOU#	VTDF	MD95	OTHER UNALLOCABLE TAXES ON INCOME (CONST.
TP	VTDF	MD	TAXES ON PROPERTY
TP#	VTDF	MD95	TAXES ON PROPERTY (CONST.)

Table. Continued

TPI	VTDF	MD	TAXES ON INCOME OF PROPERTY AND COMPENSATION OF EMPLOYEES
TPI#	VTDF	MD95	TAXES ON INCOME OF PROPERTY AND COMPENSATION OF EMPLOYEES (CONST.)
TR	VTDF	MD	TAX REVENUE (CENTRAL GOVERNMENT) AT CURRENT PRICES
TR#	VTDF	MD95	TAX REVENUE (CENTRAL GOVERNMENT) AT CONSTANT PRICES
TVSPTP	VTDR	NO / PT	TELEVISION SETS PER THOUSAND PERSONS
TYC	VTDF	MD	TAXES ON INCOME OF PRIVATE CORPORATE
TYC#	VTDF	MD95	TAXES ON INCOME OF PRIVATE CORPORATE (CONST.)
UNEMP	VTDS	TP	UNEMPLOYMENT
UNEMPR	VTDR	NU	UNEMPLOYMENT RATE
UNEMPRF	VTDR	NU	UNEMPLOYMENT RATE: FEMALE
UNEMPRM	VTDR	NU	UNEMPLOYMENT RATE: MALE
UTGB@	VTXF	MDS	UNREQUITED TRANSFERS OF GOVERNMENT, BALANCE
UTPB@	VTXF	MDS	UNREQUITED TRANSFERS OF PRIVATE, BALANCE
VHRI@	VTXF	POINT	VIOLATION OF HUMAN RIGHTS INDICATORS
WATPOL	VTDS	POINT	WATER POLLUTION (BOD, ETC.)
WPI	VTDP	95 =1	WHOLESALE PRICE INDEX OR PRODUCERS PRICE INDEX. DOMESTIC CORPORATE GOODS PRICE INDEX (DCGPI)

Table. Continued

WSEI	VTDP	95 =1	INDEX OF AVERAGE WAGE AND SALARY PER EMPLOYEE
WSEIAME	STDP	95 =1	AME'S INDEX OF AVERAGE WAGE AND SALARY PER EMPLOYEE
XPDFOOD	VTDR	%	EXPENDITURE AS % OF GDP#, ALL FOODS
XPDSTPL	VTDR	%	EXPENDITURE AS % OF GDP#, STAPLES
XPDPROT	VTDR	%	EXPENDITURE AS % OF GDP#, PROTEINS

APPENDIX B:

WORLD TRADE MATRIX: A - SUMMARY TABLE
(MILLIONS OF CURRENT US DOLLARS)

1995 YEAR -1											
1	2	3	4	5	6	7	8	9	10		
1	World	5051777	3335310	362755	296345	54154	944674	166414	778260	2027891	1906902
2	Developed Economies	3416727	2416285	181376	134475	37124	573508	148792	424716	1661400	1556382
3	Developed Asia-Pacific	510345	246373	30757	14410	10888	133687	6934	126753	81930	78168
4	Japan	445449	211302	9729	0	8104	127862	5828	122034	73711	70367
5	Australia	51730	26489	16017	12185	0	4240	882	3358	6231	5865
6	North America	800691	508771	86213	72829	11564	278920	126024	152896	143638	134897
7	Canada	189970	174632	9434	8531	776	152896	0	152896	12302	11282
8	United States	610721	334139	76779	64298	10788	126024	126024	0	131336	123615
9	Western Europe	2105691	1661140	64406	47236	14671	160902	15834	145067	1435832	1343316
10	EU15	1981642	1559285	59195	43040	13807	148799	13586	135214	1351290	1259699
11	Euro Area	1625394	1273532	43287	32793	9063	107144	9615	97529	1123101	1051059
12	France	282751	218018	7109	5583	1276	18593	1877	16716	192316	180067
13	Germany	506957	381131	17334	13157	3674	41046	2870	38176	322752	290323
14	Italy	231802	170247	7149	5347	1543	19051	2151	16899	144047	134280
15	United Kingdom	229634	178782	9971	5972	3312	32038	2857	29182	136773	129095
16	Developing Countries	1448749	824875	177514	158139	16905	363200	17251	345949	284161	273907
17	Asia-Pacific	939923	473633	136691	119995	14592	194199	11180	183019	142743	137096
18	East Asia	577150	281499	78077	69633	7351	122236	8229	114006	81186	77400
19	China	147099	76501	30325	28466	1626	26277	1533	24744	19899	19258

Table. Continued

20	Southeast Asia	313998	161626	52713	46269	5625	62223	2377	59846	46690	45278
21	Indonesia	43489	26602	13237	12201	908	6703	363	6341	6661	6571
22	South Asia	44536	26980	3560	2979	493	9517	551	8966	13903	13456
23	India	29260	16699	2539	2130	351	5597	292	5305	8563	8233
24	Pacific Islands	4241	3527	2340	1113	1123	223	22	201	964	963
25	Middle East	124376	71225	27068	25492	1382	16451	589	15862	27707	27127
26	Saudi Arabia	49915	27619	8802	8103	591	8836	360	8476	9981	9977
27	Africa	94084	68742	3523	3113	351	14743	1045	13698	50476	49413
28	North Africa	32617	26562	527	505	11	2686	293	2393	23348	22882
29	Sub-Saharan Africa	61467	42180	2996	2608	340	12056	752	11304	27128	26531
30	South Africa	20387	11650	1731	1409	282	1479	137	1341	8440	8273
31	Latin America and the Caribbean	251629	186529	9930	9318	511	135555	4286	131269	41043	38595
32	Brazil	46524	26122	3446	3102	299	9260	461	8799	13416	12912
33	Mexico	79056	73457	988	928	56	68455	1979	66475	4014	3389
34	Mediterranean	32882	21362	294	220	63	2117	143	1974	18951	18526
35	Turkey	21525	13221	234	180	44	1610	96	1514	11378	11084
36	Economies in Transition	186439	94165	3865	3731	125	7966	371	7595	82334	76617
37	South-Eastern Europe	19155	10580	77	58	17	562	62	500	9941	9733
38	CIS	109585	45757	3477	3441	34	5869	155	5714	36412	31861
39	Russian Federation	75889	38473	3203	3173	29	5213	121	5092	30057	26051

1995 Year - 2											
11	12	13	14	15	16	17	18	19	20		
1	World	1528588	271124	448481	186375	262473	1527293	953053	543471	160026	346324
2	Developed Economies	1239150	233453	356486	141968	213222	897951	492028	278680	58751	180470
3	Developed Asia-Pacific	57856	6768	21500	5217	16734	261478	221942	126263	24573	87415
4	Japan	53040	6067	20328	4065	14073	232054	196282	113169	21934	77912
5	Australia	3808	556	843	957	1829	24963	22212	11285	2293	8452
6	North America	96986	15534	24652	10142	31494	285631	125264	78184	14041	41531
7	Canada	8257	1284	2276	1274	2667	14967	8822	6529	2293	1816
8	United States	88730	14250	22376	8868	28827	270663	116442	71655	11749	39715
9	Western Europe	1084308	211151	310333	126609	164994	350841	144822	74232	20136	51525

Table. Continued

1995 Year - 2										
10	EU15	1023214	199999	286046	119240	151329	331557	134903	68803	19237	47964
11	Euro Area	847320	170854	234907	102042	139363	268616	105928	55793	16518	36587
12	France	145709	0	50092	27373	26262	58483	20260	9936	2637	7847
13	Germany	226208	59024	0	38194	40650	87457	41282	22307	7465	14425
14	Italy	111425	30580	44158	0	14579	50094	16525	10166	2695	4552
15	United Kingdom	118826	21980	29053	11403	0	45537	20995	8797	1299	8518
16	Developing Countries	218748	33250	62740	34736	43364	602479	449021	258119	96651	162765
17	Asia-Pacific	104116	14176	37000	10421	26997	455097	395378	230849	91457	146753
18	East Asia	59784	8114	23206	6089	13804	288953	252084	180054	82102	64257
19	China	15602	1844	5672	2067	2791	67392	58434	45346	0	10475
20	Southeast Asia	33955	4656	10372	2847	9823	149516	133193	46023	8838	79342
21	Indonesia	5212	529	1410	762	1131	16722	14136	6931	1832	6517
22	South Asia	9735	1234	3081	1479	3068	15921	9408	4396	438	2932
23	India	5974	683	1841	974	1881	11275	6727	2791	283	2372
24	Pacific Islands	642	173	341	7	301	707	694	376	78	223
25	Middle East	20828	4231	2347	5187	4000	51112	31178	14509	1464	9711
26	Saudi Arabia	8523	1962	256	1976	734	22293	14163	7061	278	4828
27	Africa	43144	8938	7094	10054	5276	24252	7831	3430	981	2230
28	North Africa	21451	4676	3510	7429	988	5590	1189	332	161	248
29	Sub-Saharan Africa	21693	4261	3585	2626	4289	18662	6641	3098	820	1982
30	South Africa	5813	342	1255	664	2285	8570	3349	2170	289	861
31	Latin America and the Caribbean	31384	3803	7254	4545	5332	63228	13245	8743	2625	3469
32	Brazil	10994	1038	2158	1713	1326	19417	5499	3292	1204	1607
33	Mexico	2838	483	515	197	504	5591	943	660	37	254
34	Mediterrane an	16243	1966	7880	3266	1680	7158	1319	533	97	595
35	Turkey	9516	1033	5036	1457	1136	5134	1046	468	67	418
36	Economies in Transition	70693	4421	29255	9670	5887	26884	12005	6673	4624	3089
37	South-EasternEuro pe	8532	753	3079	3054	485	5783	909	356	226	336
38	CIS	28215	1850	7569	4536	3503	17735	9694	5787	4263	2232
39	Russian Federation	22895	1516	6079	3292	3103	13053	7797	4505	3377	1982

Table. Continued

	1995 YEAR - 3										
		21	22	23	24	25	26	27	28	29	30
1	World	36113	58420	35726	4838	123384	29996	117045	45367	71679	24822
2	Developed Economies	23836	29205	19996	3672	81498	21837	81048	34553	46494	17938
3	Developed Asia-Pacific	11905	6079	3436	2185	10055	3087	8278	1634	6644	3008
4	Japan	9969	4746	2543	455	8606	2704	7330	1408	5922	2483
5	Australia	1737	1130	813	1346	1190	276	751	108	642	483
6	North America	3833	5331	3598	218	18191	6413	11000	5224	5776	2909
7	Canada	438	469	303	8	1023	328	1094	726	368	158
8	United States	3395	4862	3296	211	17168	6085	9906	4497	5409	2751
9	Western Europe	8098	17795	12961	1269	53252	12337	61770	27696	34074	12022
10	EU15	7688	16876	12358	1260	49829	11069	60024	27100	32923	11405
11	Euro Area	6431	12384	9075	1164	37778	7688	50196	24448	25747	8038
12	France	1036	1662	1054	814	6896	1328	17749	8879	8870	1006
13	Germany	2748	4359	3195	192	10603	2472	11062	4359	6703	4003
14	Italy	749	1759	1095	48	8451	1524	8078	4772	3305	1134
15	United Kingdom	828	3614	2655	67	9398	2594	7483	1624	5859	893
16	Developing Countries	12058	26975	14133	1163	38291	7973	33426	8858	24568	6715
17	Asia-Pacific	10227	16742	6758	1033	20585	5178	14301	3328	10973	3915
18	East Asia	7542	7663	3071	109	9843	2819	8495	1944	6551	2794
19	China	1438	2574	765	40	2852	734	2463	679	1784	634
20	Southeast Asia	2052	7007	3541	821	7094	1680	3911	1061	2850	827
21	Indonesia	0	662	375	25	1190	394	530	290	239	77
22	South Asia	627	2043	138	37	3648	678	1887	323	1565	291
23	India	501	1548	0	16	2509	425	1482	178	1304	269
24	Pacific Islands	6	29	8	66	1	0	8	1	7	3
25	Middle East	638	6864	4969	94	10860	1142	3957	1334	2623	1278
26	Saudi Arabia	500	2270	1560	3	4012	0	1432	749	683	167
27	Africa	415	2159	1728	11	1985	613	10790	1786	9005	698
28	North Africa	67	609	517	1	767	190	1792	1349	443	11
29	Sub-Saharan Africa	347	1550	1211	11	1219	422	8998	437	8561	687
30	South Africa	153	315	193	3	656	90	3845	44	3802	0
31	Latin America and the Caribbean	741	1011	615	21	2468	526	2957	1317	1640	748
32	Brazil	366	594	320	6	1288	360	1586	712	873	261
33	Mexico	16	29	25	0	75	37	25	21	3	0
34	Mediterranean	37	188	55	3	2330	506	1255	1050	206	72
35	Turkey	32	159	42	1	2050	470	1066	900	165	67
36	Economies in Transition	218	2240	1597	3	3595	186	2573	1956	617	169
37	South-Eastern Europe	64	216	115	0	823	64	928	566	362	80

Table. Continued

1995 YEAR - 3

38	CIS	83	1675	1243	0	2086	33	1116	925	190	32
39	Russian Federation	81	1310	998	0	1287	28	755	640	116	16

1995 YEAR - 4

	31	32	33	34	35	36	37	38	39
1 World	273163	49757	61674	50252	32745	189307	25301	89178	52738
2 Developed Economies	201146	31128	56891	35403	22452	102497	15976	34692	26121
3 Developed Asia-Pacific	19564	2882	3702	1610	1218	2494	187	1583	1392
4 Japan	18555	2599	3572	1267	905	2093	74	1344	1170
5 Australia	566	241	57	234	210	279	109	125	109
6 North America	127545	12351	47097	3427	2913	6290	622	3971	3194
7 Canada	3795	908	786	220	186	371	31	171	128
8 United States	123750	11444	46312	3208	2727	5919	591	3800	3066
9 Western Europe	54037	15895	6092	30365	18321	93713	15168	29137	21535
10 EU15	51284	14956	5749	29126	17441	90803	14670	28367	21034
11 Euro Area	44129	13114	5101	24785	14821	83249	12579	24954	18438
12 France	10363	1409	897	2975	1832	6251	915	2211	1673
13 Germany	13098	5053	2377	9325	6356	38369	4852	10721	7217
14 Italy	8162	3170	616	6756	3233	11462	4143	3563	2869
15 United Kingdom	4291	1067	434	2954	1827	5315	871	1776	1371
16 Developing Countries	69881	18062	4705	9655	6845	21420	5096	12523	9579
17 Asia-Pacific	21261	5580	3027	3554	2663	11196	873	6686	5684
18 East Asia	16409	4214	2251	2119	1766	6699	295	4048	3410
19 China	3131	759	195	507	431	3206	214	2019	1674
20 Southeast Asia	4289	1195	703	1024	554	2856	511	1247	1100
21 Indonesia	727	202	92	138	120	165	41	6	6
22 South Asia	560	170	73	409	342	1635	66	1390	1174
23 India	360	98	50	189	156	1286	43	1119	1031
24 Pacific Islands	3	0	0	1	1	7	1	0	0
25 Middle East	2055	1575	34	2990	2591	2039	503	1293	564
26 Saudi Arabia	1133	1094	0	1550	1330	3	4	2	0
27 Africa	2004	1115	83	1377	1081	1091	499	395	278
28 North Africa	455	309	44	1153	896	465	376	120	102
29 Sub-Saharan Africa	1548	806	39	224	185	626	122	276	176
30 South Africa	609	290	31	104	98	167	42	68	64
31 Latin America and the Caribbean	43882	9749	1547	630	444	1872	351	1152	1061
32 Brazil	10719	0	496	307	198	985	159	629	569
33 Mexico	4541	800	0	7	7	9	5	0	0

Table. Continued

34	Mediterranean	629	40	14	312	23	4363	2067	2652	1714
35	Turkey	583	28	8	280	0	3170	652	2094	1238
36	Economies in Transition	2136	566	78	5194	3449	65390	4229	41964	17039
37	South-Eastern Europe	326	83	5	1678	777	2792	1661	1714	972
38	CIS	1223	294	32	3295	2468	46092	2229	34144	12675
39	Russian Federation	928	108	28	2047	1632	24362	1536	15389	0

Source: FUGI Global Nodeling System (FGMS200).

APPENDIX C: WORLD POPULATION

NP - NUMBER OF POPULATION (AVERAGE PERCENTAGE CHANGES)						
UNIT: %						
- LONG TERM -	2001-2005	2006-2010	2001-2010	2011-2015	2016-2020	2011-2020
World	1.2	1.1	1.1	1.1	1.1	1.1
Developed Market Economies	0.1	0.1	0.1	0.1	0.1	0.1
Developed Asia-Pacific	0	-0.1	0	0	-0.1	0
Japan	0.1	-0.1	-0.1	-0.1	-0.1	-0.1
North America	0.4	0.3	0.3	0.2	0.2	0.2
Canada	0	-0.1	-0.1	-0.1	-0.1	-0.1
United States	0.4	0.3	0.4	0.3	0.2	0.2
Western Europe	0	0	0	0.1	0	0.1
EU15	0	0	0	0.1	0	0.1
France	0.2	0.2	0.2	0.2	0.2	0.2
Germany	0	0	0	0	0	0
Italy	-0.2	-0.1	-0.1	0.1	0	0
United Kingdom	0.1	0.1	0.1	0.1	0.1	0.1
Developing Economies	1.4	1.4	1.4	1.3	1.2	1.3
Asia-Pacific	1.2	1.1	1.1	1	0.9	1
East Asia	0.7	0.7	0.7	0.7	0.6	0.6
China:Mainland	0.7	0.7	0.7	0.6	0.6	0.6
Southeast Asia(ASEAN)	1.3	1.2	1.2	1.1	1	1
Indonesia	1.3	1.3	1.3	1.3	1.2	1.2
Malaysia	1.7	1.6	1.6	1.5	1.4	1.5
Philippines	1.7	1.4	1.5	1	0.7	0.9
Singapore	0.8	0.8	0.8	0.8	0.8	0.8
Thailand	0.6	0.5	0.6	0.4	0.3	0.4

Table. Continued

NP - NUMBER OF POPULATION (AVERAGE PERCENTAGE CHANGES)						
UNIT: %						
- LONG TERM -	2001-2005	2006-2010	2001-2010	2011-2015	2016-2020	2011-2020
South Asia	1.6	1.4	1.5	1.3	1.2	1.2
India	1.4	1.2	1.3	1	0.9	0.9
Middle East	2.2	2.1	2.1	2	1.9	2
Africa	2.3	2.2	2.2	2.2	2.2	2.2
North Africa	1.8	1.7	1.8	1.6	1.5	1.6
Sub-Saharan Africa	2.4	2.3	2.4	2.3	2.3	2.3
Latin America and the Caribbean	1.4	1.3	1.4	1.2	1.2	1.2
Brazil	1.2	1.1	1.2	1	0.9	0.9
Mediterranean	1.2	1.1	1.1	1	0.9	0.9
Economies in Transition	0	0.1	0.1	0.5	0.6	0.6
Eastern Europe	-0.1	0	-0.1	0.4	0.4	0.4
CIS	0.1	0.2	0.1	0.5	0.7	0.6
Russian Federation	-0.3	-0.3	-0.3	0.1	0.2	0.1
1 Japan	-0.1	-0.2	-0.1	0	-0.1	-0.1
2 Australia	0.4	0.3	0.3	0.2	0.1	0.1
3 New Zealand	0.6	0.6	0.6	0.6	0.6	0.6
4 Canada	0	-0.1	-0.1	-0.1	-0.1	-0.1
5 United States	0.4	0.3	0.4	0.3	0.2	0.2
6 Belgium	0	0.1	0.1	0.1	0.1	0.1
7 Denmark	0	0	0	0	0	0
8 France	0.2	0.2	0.2	0.2	0.2	0.2
9 Germany	0	0	0	0	0	0
10 Greece	-0.1	-0.1	-0.1	0	-0.1	-0.1
11 Ireland	0.3	0.2	0.3	0.2	0.1	0.1
12 Italy	-0.2	-0.1	-0.1	0.1	0	0
13 Luxembourg	0.2	0.2	0.2	0.2	0.3	0.3
14 Netherlands	0.1	0.1	0.1	0	0	0
15 Portugal	-0.2	-0.2	-0.2	0	-0.1	0
16 Spain	-0.1	0	0	0	-0.1	0
17 United Kingdom	0.1	0.1	0.1	0.1	0.1	0.1
18 Austria	0.1	0.1	0.1	0.1	0.1	0.1
19 Finland	0	0	0	0	-0.1	0
20 Iceland	0.8	0.8	0.8	0.8	0.8	0.8
21 Norway	0.2	0.2	0.2	0.2	0.2	0.2
22 Sweden	-0.1	0	0	0	-0.1	0
23 Switzerland	0.1	0.1	0.1	0	0	0

Table. Continued

NP - NUMBER OF POPULATION (AVERAGE PERCENTAGE CHANGES)						
UNIT: %						
- LONG TERM -	2001-2005	2006-2010	2001-2010	2011-2015	2016-2020	2011-2020
24 China: Mainland	0.7	0.7	0.7	0.6	0.6	0.6
25 China: Hong Kong	0.3	0.3	0.3	0.2	0.2	0.2
26 China: Macau	0.8	0.8	0.8	0.7	0.7	0.7
27 Taiwan(Province of china)	1.1	1.2	1.2	1.5	1.7	1.6
28 Korea: Republic of	0.8	0.7	0.7	0.7	0.7	0.7
29 Korea: North	1.4	1.6	1.5	2.1	3	2.6
30 Brunei	1.6	1.6	1.6	1.7	1.8	1.7
31 Indonesia	1.3	1.3	1.3	1.3	1.2	1.2
32 Malaysia	1.7	1.6	1.6	1.5	1.4	1.5
33 Philippines	1.7	1.4	1.5	1	0.7	0.9
34 Singapore	0.8	0.8	0.8	0.8	0.8	0.8
35 Thailand	0.6	0.5	0.6	0.4	0.3	0.4
36 Cambodia	2.1	2.3	2.2	2.3	2.4	2.4
37 Lao P. D. Rep	2.4	2.3	2.4	2.3	2.3	2.3
38 Myanmar (Burma)	1	0.8	0.9	0.6	0.5	0.5
39 Viet Nam	1.3	1.1	1.2	1	0.9	0.9
40 Afghanistan	2.7	2.8	2.7	2.9	2.9	2.9
41 Bangladesh	1.7	1.5	1.6	1.2	1	1.1
42 Bhutan	2.6	2.7	2.7	2.7	2.6	2.6
43 India	1.4	1.2	1.3	1	0.9	0.9
44 Mongolia	1.4	1.2	1.3	1	0.8	0.9
45 Nepal	2.2	2.1	2.1	1.9	1.8	1.9
46 Pakistan	2.6	2.6	2.6	2.6	2.6	2.6
47 Sri Lanka	1.1	1	1	0.8	0.6	0.7
48 Fiji	1.4	1.4	1.4	1.3	1.2	1.2
49 French Polynesia	1.7	1.6	1.6	1.6	1.5	1.6
50 Guam	1.7	1.7	1.7	1.6	1.6	1.6
51 Kiribati: Rep. of	1.8	1.8	1.8	2	2.1	2
52 Maldives	2.6	2.5	2.6	2.5	2.4	2.4
53 Nauru	1.7	1.7	1.7	1.8	1.9	1.8
54 New Caledonia	1.5	1.5	1.5	1.5	1.5	1.5
55 Papua New Guinea	2.1	2.1	2.1	2.1	2.1	2.1
56 Solomon Islands	3	3.1	3	3.1	3.1	3.1
57 Tonga	1.6	1.5	1.5	1.2	1	1.1
58 Tuvalu	1.7	1.8	1.8	1.9	2	1.9
59 Western Samoa	1.5	1.4	1.5	1.4	1.4	1.4

Table. Continued

NP - NUMBER OF POPULATION (AVERAGE PERCENTAGE CHANGES)						
UNIT: %						
- LONG TERM -	2001-2005	2006-2010	2001-2010	2011-2015	2016-2020	2011-2020
60 Vanuatu	2.3	2.2	2.3	2.1	2	2
61 Bahrain	1	0.8	0.9	0.6	0.4	0.5
62 Iran: I.R. of	1.2	1	1.1	0.7	0.4	0.6
63 Iraq	2.8	2.9	2.9	2.9	3	3
64 Israel	1.2	1.2	1.2	1.2	1.1	1.2
65 Jordan	2.9	2.8	2.8	2.7	2.6	2.6
66 Kuwait	2.6	2.6	2.6	2.6	2.7	2.6
67 Lebanon	1.4	1.3	1.4	1.1	1	1
68 Oman	3.2	3.2	3.2	3.2	3.1	3.1
69 Qatar	1.6	1.7	1.6	1.7	1.8	1.8
70 Saudi Arabia	3.1	2.9	3	2.8	2.7	2.7
71 Syrian Arab Rep	2.4	2.3	2.3	2.2	2.2	2.2
72 United Arab Emirates	1.5	1.2	1.3	0.7	0.4	0.5
73 Yemen Rep	3.6	3.6	3.6	3.5	3.4	3.5
74 Algeria	2.1	2.1	2.1	2	2	2
75 Egypt	1.7	1.6	1.7	1.4	1.2	1.3
76 Libya	2.5	2.6	2.5	2.9	3.3	3.1
77 Morocco	1.7	1.6	1.6	1.5	1.5	1.5
78 Tunisia	1.3	1.2	1.3	1.2	1.1	1.1
79 Angola	3	3	3	3	3	3
80 Benin	2.9	3.1	3	3.3	3.4	3.3
81 Botswana	1.2	1.3	1.2	1.3	1.4	1.4
82 Burkina Faso	2.4	2.2	2.3	2.1	2.1	2.1
83 Burundi	2.1	2	2.1	1.8	1.6	1.7
84 Cameroon	2.6	2.5	2.5	2.5	2.4	2.5
85 Cape Verde	2.4	2.5	2.5	2.5	2.6	2.6
86 Central African Rep.	1.8	1.7	1.8	1.6	1.5	1.6
87 Chad	2.7	2.7	2.7	2.7	2.7	2.7
88 Comoros	2.6	2.4	2.5	2.2	1.8	2
89 Congo	2.6	2.4	2.5	2	1.8	1.9
90 Djibouti	1.7	1.2	1.4	0.2	0.1	0.2
91 Eritrea	2.4	2.3	2.4	2.4	2.4	2.4
92 Equatorial Guinea	2.5	2.5	2.5	2.6	2.6	2.6
93 Ethiopia	2.3	2.2	2.2	2.2	2.1	2.2
94 Gabon	2.2	2.2	2.2	2.2	2.2	2.2
95 Gambia: The	2.5	2.4	2.4	2.2	2	2.1
96 Ghana	2.6	2.5	2.6	2.4	2.3	2.3

Table. Continued

NP - NUMBER OF POPULATION (AVERAGE PERCENTAGE CHANGES)						
UNIT: %						
- LONG TERM -	2001-2005	2006-2010	2001-2010	2011-2015	2016-2020	2011-2020
97 Guinea	2.3	2.2	2.3	2	1.7	1.9
98 Guinea Bissau	2.1	2	2.1	2	2	2
99 Ivory Coast	2.1	2.2	2.1	2.2	2.2	2.2
100 Kenya	1.9	2.1	2	2.2	2.4	2.3
101 Lesotho	2.1	2.1	2.1	2.1	2.1	2.1
102 Liberia	3.3	3.1	3.2	3	2.6	2.8
103 Madagascar	2.6	2.3	2.4	1.9	1.4	1.6
104 Malawi	1.6	1.5	1.6	1.4	1.4	1.4
105 Mali	3.1	3.1	3.1	3.2	3.2	3.2
106 Mauritania	2.8	2.9	2.8	2.9	2.9	2.9
107 Mauritius	0.8	0.8	0.8	0.7	0.7	0.7
108 Mozambique	2.8	2.8	2.8	2.7	2.7	2.7
109 Namibia	0.9	1	0.9	1	1.1	1.1
110 Niger	3.1	2	2.5	1.2	0.7	0.9
111 Nigeria	2.3	2.2	2.2	2.1	2	2.1
112 Reunion	1.1	1.1	1.1	1.1	1	1.1
113 Rwanda	1.9	2.2	2.1	2.7	3.2	3
114 St. Helena	2.3	1.9	2.1	1.6	1.2	1.4
115 Sao Tome & Principe	2.3	2	2.2	1.8	1.6	1.7
116 Senegal	2.6	2.5	2.6	2.5	2.4	2.4
117 Seychelles	2.6	2.5	2.6	2.5	2.5	2.5
118 Sierra Leone	2.4	2.6	2.5	2.9	2.9	2.9
119 Somalia	2.8	2.5	2.7	2.3	2.2	2.3
120 South Africa	0.9	1.1	1	1.2	1.2	1.2
121 Sudan	2	1.9	1.9	1.8	1.7	1.7
122 Swaziland	2.7	2.6	2.6	2.5	2.4	2.4
123 Tanzania	2.3	2.3	2.3	2.4	2.5	2.5
124 Togo	2.6	2.5	2.6	2.5	2.5	2.5
125 Uganda	3.5	3.7	3.6	3.8	3.8	3.8
126 Zaire	3.4	3.2	3.3	3.2	3.2	3.2
127 Zambia	2.2	2.2	2.2	2.1	2.2	2.1
128 Zimbabwe	1.2	1.4	1.3	1.5	1.6	1.6
129 Argentina	1.1	1.1	1.1	1	1	1
130 Antigua and Barbuda	1.2	1.1	1.1	1.1	1.1	1.1
131 Bahamas The	1.5	1.5	1.5	1.5	1.4	1.4
132 Barbados	0.3	0.2	0.2	0.1	0.1	0.1
133 Belize	2.2	2	2.1	1.9	1.8	1.8

Table. Continued

NP - NUMBER OF POPULATION (AVERAGE PERCENTAGE CHANGES)						
UNIT: %						
- LONG TERM -	2001-2005	2006-2010	2001-2010	2011-2015	2016-2020	2011-2020
134 Bermuda	1	1	1	1	0.9	1
135 Bolivia	2.1	1.9	2	1.7	1.5	1.6
136 Brazil	1.2	1.1	1.2	1	0.9	0.9
137 Chile	1.3	1.3	1.3	1.3	1.3	1.3
138 Colombia	1.6	1.6	1.6	1.5	1.5	1.5
139 Costa Rica	1.7	1.5	1.6	1.4	1.3	1.3
140 Cuba	0.3	0.2	0.3	0.1	0.1	0.1
141 Dominica	1.6	1.6	1.6	1.5	1.5	1.5
142 Dominican Republic	1.6	1.7	1.6	2.7	7.6	5.1
143 Ecuador	1.8	1.7	1.7	1.6	1.4	1.5
144 El Salvador	1.7	1.7	1.7	1.7	1.7	1.7
145 Greenland	0.7	0.6	0.6	0.5	0.4	0.5
146 Grenada	1.5	1.4	1.4	1.3	1.3	1.3
147 Guadeloupe	1.1	1.2	1.2	1.3	1.3	1.3
148 Guatemala	2.6	2.4	2.5	1.8	1.1	1.4
149 Guiana: French	1.9	1.9	1.9	1.9	1.9	1.9
150 Guyana	1	0.9	0.9	1	1.1	1
151 Haiti	1.5	1.5	1.5	1.4	1.4	1.4
152 Honduras	2.5	2.1	2.3	1	1.4	1.2
153 Jamaica	1.1	1.1	1.1	1	1	1
154 Martinique	0.7	0.7	0.7	0.7	0.8	0.8
155 Mexico	1.5	1.4	1.4	1.2	0.9	1.1
156 Montserrat	1.7	1.8	1.7	1.9	2.2	2
157 Netherlands Antilles	0.7	0.5	0.6	0.4	0.3	0.3
158 Nicaragua	2.7	2.6	2.6	2.5	2.5	2.5
159 Panama	1.4	1.4	1.4	1.4	1.4	1.4
160 Paraguay	2.4	2.3	2.3	2.2	2.1	2.1
161 Peru	1.6	1.5	1.5	1.4	1.3	1.3
162 Puerto Rico	0.1	0.3	0.2	0.7	1.5	1.1
163 St. Kitts Nevis	1.6	1.6	1.6	1.7	1.7	1.7
164 St. Lucia	1.6	1.6	1.6	1.6	1.7	1.7
165 St. Pierre Miquelon	1.7	1.8	1.7	1.8	2	1.9
166 St. Vincent	1.8	2.1	1.9	2.7	3.7	3.2
167 Suriname	0.5	0	0.3	0	0	0
168 Trinidad and Tobago	0.7	0.8	0.8	1	1.3	1.2
169 Uruguay	0.7	0.7	0.7	0.7	0.7	0.7
170 Venezuela	1.7	1.6	1.7	1.7	1.8	1.7

Table. Continued

NP - NUMBER OF POPULATION (AVERAGE PERCENTAGE CHANGES)						
UNIT: %						
- LONG TERM -	2001-2005	2006-2010	2001-2010	2011-2015	2016-2020	2011-2020
171 Cyprus	0.7	0.7	0.7	0.6	0.6	0.6
172 Malta	0.5	0.4	0.4	0.4	0.3	0.4
173 Turkey	1.4	1.3	1.4	1.1	1	1.1
174 Bosnia and Herzegovina	2.1	2.1	2.1	2.1	2.1	2.1
175 Croatia	-0.2	-0.2	-0.2	0	0	0
176 Slovenia	-0.1	0	0	0.1	-0.2	0
177 TFYR Macedonia	0.7	0.4	0.5	0.1	-0.1	0
178 Yugoslavia:FR (Serbia/Montenegro	0	0	0	0	0	0
179 Albania	0.9	0.8	0.8	0.8	0.7	0.7
180 Bulgaria	-0.5	-0.4	-0.5	0.2	1.2	0.7
181 Czech Republic	-0.2	-0.1	-0.2	0	0	0
182 Hungary	-0.5	-0.4	-0.4	-0.3	-2	-1.1
183 Poland	0.1	0.5	0.3	1	1	1
184 Romania	-0.4	-0.4	-0.4	0	0	0
185 Slovakia	0	-0.2	-0.1	-0.4	-0.4	-0.4
186 Armenia	0.8	1	0.9	1.1	1.3	1.2
187 Azerbaijan	0.6	1	0.8	1.6	2.3	1.9
188 Belarus	-0.3	-0.3	-0.3	0.1	0.5	0.3
189 Estonia	-0.4	-0.4	-0.4	0	0.1	0
190 Georgia	0.2	0.2	0.2	0.2	0.3	0.3
191 Kazakhstan	1.8	1.9	1.8	1.9	2.1	2
192 Kyrgyzstan	1.6	1.7	1.6	2	2.3	2.1
193 Latvia	-0.7	-0.6	-0.7	0.3	0.4	0.3
194 Lithuania	0.1	1.2	0.7	3.1	6.3	4.7
195 Republic of Moldova	0.2	0.1	0.2	0.1	0.1	0.1
196 Russian Federation	-0.3	-0.3	-0.3	0.1	0.2	0.1
197 Tajikistan	2.2	2.2	2.2	2.3	2.4	2.4
198 Turkmenistan	1.7	1.5	1.6	1.3	1	1.2
199 Ukraine	-0.6	-0.8	-0.7	-0.4	-0.4	-0.4
200 Uzbekistan	1.7	1.6	1.6	1.6	1.7	1.7

Source: FUGI global modeling system.

ACKNOWLEDGMENTS

The author, Akira Onishi, is grateful to supports from UNCTAD (United Nations Conference on Trade and Development) Secretariat in Geneva, United Nations Secretariat in New York, UNESCO-EOLSS Secretariat in Paris, WHO Secretariat in Geneva, the World Bank Secretariat in Washington D.C., the United Nations ESCAP Secretariat in Bangkok and FOST(Foundation for Fusion of Science and Technology in Japan). Special thanks is also extended to a number of scholars around the world for their helpful suggestions in regard to the global modeling work, in particular, Prof. L.Klein, Prof. W. Leontief, Prof. J. Tobin, Prof. R.Courbis, Dr. H. Chestnut, Prof. H. Guetzkow, Prof. B. Hickman, Prof. W. Krelle, Dr.T.Oren, Dr. A. Costa, Prof. M. Scobie, Dr. A. Kolodziejak, H. Flassbeck, H. Sarkar, Prof. H. Fromlet, Prof. T. Utsumi and Prof. R. Shiratori.

BIBLIOGRAPHY

Onishi, A. (1965). Projections of economic growth and intra-regional trade for the developing ECAFE Region, 1960-1970, *Developing Economies*, Vol. 3(2), (pp.158-172).

Onishi, A. (1977). Report on Project FUGI: future of global interdependence, *Fifth IIASA Global Modeling g Conference*, (pp.1-183), Ref., Tables, Maps, Graphs, Figures, IIASA, Laxenburg, Austria, September 1977.

Onishi, A. (1980). FUGI-futures of global interdependence in input-output approaches in global modelling, *Proceedings of the fifth IIASA symposium on global modelling*, IIASA proceedings series 9, (pp. 91-357), Oxford: Pergamon.

Onishi, A. (1981). Projections of the world economy, 1980-1990, using FUGI global macroeconomics model, Type IV 011-62 - Scenario forecasts of the OPEC strategy for oil pricing, *Seminar on Comparative Simulations of Global International Economic Models*, Stanford University; (pp.1-34), IAER, June 1981.

Onishi, A. (1983a). Project FUGI and the Futures of ESCAP Developing Countries, (Co-authors; Y.Kaya and Y.Suzuki), *Global International Economic Models,* (Eds.) B. Hickman, North-Holland Amsterdam, New York, Oxford.

Onishi, A. (1983b). FUGI Macroeconomic model. FUTURES, the journal of forecasting and planning, Voul.13, No.2, April, 1963. (99-110).

Onishi, A. (1984). Long-term projection of economic growth in ESCAP member countries (Co-authors: Y.Kaya and H.Smit), (pp.47-92), *Proceedings of the Seventh International Conference on Input-Output Techniques,* United Nations New York, 1984.

Onishi, A. (1986a). Alternative futures of the world economy, 1986-2000, – policy simulations by the FUGI model, *Dynamic modelling and control of national economies* 1986,In: B. Martus, E.Pau and M. Ziermana, (Eds.) Fifth IFAC/IFORS Conference, Budapest, Hungary, June 17-20, (pp.125-130). Amsterdam: Pergamon.

Onishi, A. (1986b). A new generation of the FUGI model – a global early warning system for national and international conflicts, Proceedings of the second workshop and conference of the IFAC working group on supplemental ways for improving international stability (SWIIS), in June 3-5, 1986, (H. Chestnut and Y. Haimes, Eds.), *Contributions of technology to international conflict resolution*, Cleveland, OH: Case Western Reserve University.

Onishi, A. (1986c). North-South Interdependence: Projections of the World Economy, 1085-2000, *Journal of Policy Modeling, Special Science Forum of World Issues*, Vol. 8, No, 2, Summer 1986, (pp.181-198).

Onishi, A. (1986d). Economics of global interdependence – projections of the world economy using the FUGI global macroeconomic model – a report to the United Nations – Institute of Applied Economic Research, Soka University, (pp.1-411), September.

Onishi, A. (1986e). A new generation FUGI model– a global early warning system for national and international conflicts, *Contributions of technology to international conflict resolution, in H. Chestnut,* (Ed.), IFAC, Pergamon Press, (pp. 39-55) 1986 IFAC, Amsterdam: Pergamon.

Onishi, A. (1987). Global early warning system for displaced persons: Interlink ages of environment, development, peace and human rights, *Technological Forecasting and Social Change*, Vol.31 (3), May.

Onishi, A. (1988). Projections of the OECD economies in the global perspective, 1986-2000: policy simulations by FUGI global macroeconomic model, (pp.11-30), H. Motamen Ed. *Economic Modeling in the OECD Countries,* Chapman and Hall, London.

Onishi, A. (1989). Prospects for the World Economy and Asian-Pacific Region, *Global Adjustment and the Future of Asian-Pacific Economy,* (Ed., M. Shinohara and Fu-chen Lo) IDE and APDC, PMC Publications, Japan.

Onishi, A. (1990). Uses of global models: a new generation FUGI model for projections and policy simulations of the world economy", *International Political Science Review*, vol., No.2, Butterworths, April, 1990, (pp.280-293).

Onishi, A. (1991). Global model simulations of energy requirements and CO_2 emissions, International Conference on Coal, Environment and Development, Coal, The Environment and Development: Technologies to reduce

Greenhouse Gas Emissions, Proceedings, Sydney, Australia, 18-21 November, 1991 (pp. 215-224), OECD 1992.

Onishi, A. (1991b). Growth and Environment: Simulations of CO_2 Cutbacks against Global Warming, Simulation & Gaming Vol.2, No.1, Sep. 1991 (pp.1-8), *JASAG (Japan Association of Simulation &Gaming)*.

Onishi, A. (1992). Outlook of the Asia-Pacific Economy in the 1990s, using the FUGI Global Model, The Futures of Asia-Pacific Economies, Emerging Role of Asian NIES & ASEAN (Edited by FU-Chen Lo & Narongchai Akrasanee), Asian and Pacific Development Centre, Allied Publishers Limited, New Delhi etc. 1992 (pp.32-46).

Onishi, A. (1993). FUGI global model 7.0 – a new frontier science of global economic modelling, *Economic & Financial Computing*, Vol.3 Number 1 Spring 1993, A Journal of the European Economics and Financial Centre, May 1993 (pp.3-67).

Onishi, A. (1994). A new frontier of global model simulation: Global linkages of biology, ecology, economic development and human health, *CISS-First Joint Conference of International Simulation Societies Proceedings*, J. Halin, W. Karplus and R. Rimane (Eds.), August 22-25, 1994, ETH Zurich, Switzerland, August 1994. (pp.558-561).

Onishi, A. (1994). Global *Model Simulation: A New Frontier of Economics and Systems* Science, Soka University Institute for Systems Science, September 1994 (pp.1-252).

Onishi, A (1995a) FUGI global model: Simulations of global CO_2 cut-back and arms reduction on the world economy, In: Lawrence R, Klein and Fu-chen Lo (Eds.), *Modelling Global Change*, United Nations University Press, (pp.363-390).

Onishi A. (1995b). FUGI global model as GEWS (Global early warning system model). In O. Tuncer and L. G. Birta, Eds. The Proceedings of the 1995 Summer Computer Simulation Conference, Ottawa, Canada, SCS. July 1995. (pp.1070–1077).

Onishi A. (1996a). Projections of the world economy and population growth using the FUGI global model, 1995-2015, *The Soka Economic Studies Quarterly*, XXVI (1–2). (pp.1–99).

Onishi A. (1997a). Impacts of global disarmament on the sustainable development of the world economy, 1996–2015, FUGI global model simulation, Paper prepared for *the ECAAR Session* at Waseda University, Tokyo, 14 September. (pp.1-17).

Onishi A. (1997b). FUGI global model as global early warning system (GEWS). Paper prepared for the United Nations ISPAC International Conference on

Violent Crime and Conflicts. Towards Early Warning and Prevention Mechanism. Courmayeur, Mont Blanc, Italy, 4–6 October. (pp.1-7).

Onishi A. (1998a). FUGI global model simulation: Integrated global model for sustainable development, Soka University Institute for Systems Science, 1998. (pp.1-347).

Onishi A. (1998b). The FUGI model as a Global Early Warning System for Refugees, (pp. 159-173) Preventive Measures: Building Risk Assessment and Crisis Wary Warning Systems, (Edited by J. Davies and T. Robert Gurr), Rowman & Littlefield Publishers, New York, Oxford.

Onishi A. (1999). FUGI global model 9.0 M 200 / 80—Integrated global model for sustainable development, Soka University Institute for Systems Science, (1-pp423).

Onishi A. (2000). *FUGI global model 9.0 M200: Integrated global model for sustainable development,* Soka University Institute for Systems Science, 2000. (pp.1-415).

Onishi, A. (2001a). The world economy to 2015, Policy simulations on sustainable development, *Journal of Policy Modeling*, Volume 23, Number 2, February 2001, (pp.217-234).

Onishi A. (2001b). FUGI global model 9.0 M200PC: a new frontier of economic science in 21st century, *Economic & Financial Computing*, Spring Issue, 2001, London, (pp.1-74).

Onishi A. (2001c) Integrated global models of sustainable development, *Our Fragile World, Challenges and Opportunities for Sustainable Development,* Vol. II (Ed. M.K. Tolba), UNESCO, Eolss Publishers Co. Ltd. Oxford, UK, (pp.1293-1311).

Onishi A. (2002a). Prospect for Globalization, Employment and Quality of Life in the 21st Century, Ed. Donald Lamberton, *Managing the Global; Globalization, Employment and Quality of Life*, L.B.Tauris Publishers, London, New York, 2002, (pp.195-208.)

Onishi A. (2002b). FUGI Global Modeling System (FGMS200)—Integrated global model for sustainable development, *Journal of Policy Modeling*, Vol.24, 2002, (pp561-590)

Onishi A. (2003a). FUGI global model 9.0 M200, *Integrated Global Models for Sustainable Development*, UNESCO Encyclopaedia of Life Support System, EOLSS Publisher, Oxford, UK, 2003 (http://www.eolss.net)

Onishi A. (2003b) FUGI global model for early warning of forced migration (http://www.forcedmigration.org) Forced Migration Online, Refugee Studies Centre, University of Oxford

Onishi A. (2005), Futures of global interdependence(FUGI) global modelling system—Integrated global model for sustainable development, *Journal of Policy Modeling*, Vol.27 2006, (pp101-135

Onishi A. (2006), *Integrated Global Models for Sustainable Development*, UNESCO Encyclopaedia of Life Support System, EOLSS Publisher, Oxford, UK, 2003-2006 [Available on line at (http://www.eolss.net)].

Onishi A. (2007), The impact of CO_2 emissions on the world economy—Policy simulations of FUGI global model, *Journal of Policy Modeling*, Vol.29 2007, (pp797-819). [Available on line at www.sciencedirct.com].

AUTHOR BIOGRAPHY

Akira Onishi, born in January 5, 1929, is Director, Centre for Global Modeling, professor emeritus, former vice president, Soka University, economics and global modeling educator. His academic background is both economics and systems engineering. He got Ph.D. in Economics from Keio University, Tokyo and Ph.D. in Engineering from Tokyo Institute of Technology. He had an opportunity to work at the United Nations ESCAP and the ILO, 1966-70. Then he has served at Soka University, Tokyo. Dean, Department of Economics, 1976-91. Dean, Graduate School of Economics, 1976-1991. Director, Soka University Institute for Systems Science (SUISS), 1990- 2001. Dean, Faculty of Engineering, 1991-95. Dean, Graduate School of Engineering, 1995-99. Vice President, 1989-2001.Visiting professor, Westminster Business School, 2002. He served as President of Japan Association of Simulation and Gaming, 1993-97. He received many academic awards. The International Biographical Roll of Honor to the Global Modeling Profession from American Biographical Institute, USA, 1989. The first Supreme Article Award from the Japanese Association of Administration and planning, 1991. The 20th Century Award for Achievement from the International Bibliographic Centre, Cambridge, England to Global Modeling, 1993. The Excellent Article Award from ECAAR, 1997. The Japan Assn. Simulation and Gaming Award, 1998. 2000 Outstanding Intellectuals of the 20th Grand from the IBC, 1999. He was selected as First Five Hundred in 2000 for the service to Economics by the IBC. He has made a great contribution to global modeling through numerous articles and conferences. He is well known as an original designer of FUGI (*Futures of Global Interdependence)* global model. The United Nations Secretariat, Department of International Economic and Social Affairs adopted this model for the long-term projections and policy simulations of the world economy from 1981-1991. During the period, 1985-86, he designed the

Global Early Warning Systems for Displaced Persons (GEWS) under the auspices by the United Nations Independent Committee of Human Rights. See Onishi A. (2003b) *FUGI global model for early warning of forced migration* (http://www.forcedmigration.org) Forced Migration Online, Refugee Studies Centre, and University of Oxford

INDEX

T